Electronic Document Management Systems

Electronic Document Management Systems

*A User Centered Approach
for Creating, Distributing, and
Managing Online Publications*

Larry Bielawski
Goucher College

Jim Boyle
RWD Technologies, Inc.

*To join a Prentice Hall PTR Internet mailing list,
point to http://www.prenhall.com/register.*

Prentice Hall PTR, Upper Saddle River, New Jersey 07458

© 1997 Prentice Hall PTR
Prentice-Hall, Inc.
A Simon & Shuster Company
Upper Saddle River, New Jersey 07458

Editorial/production supervision: *Joe Czerwinski*
Acquisitions editor: *Mike Meehan*
Manufacturing manager: *Alexis Heydt*
Cover design director: *Jerry Votta*
Cover design: *Design Source*
Composition: *Lisa Jahred*

The publisher offers discounts on this book when ordered in bulk quantities.
For more information contact:

Corporate Sales Department
Prentice Hall PTR
One Lake Street
Upper Saddle River, NJ 07458
Phone: 800-382-3419
Fax: 201-236-7141
e-mail:corpsales@prenhall.com

Printed in the United States of America

10 9 8 7 6 5 4 3 2 1

ISBN 0-13-591520-1

Prentice-Hall International (UK) Limited, *London*
Prentice-Hall of Australia Pty. Limited, *Sydney*
Prentice-Hall Canada Inc., *Toronto*
Prentice-Hall Hispanoamericana, S.A., *Mexico*
Prentice-Hall of India Private Limited, *New Delhi*
Prentice-Hall of Japan, Inc., *Tokyo*
Simon & Schuster Asia Pte. Ltd., *Singapore*
Editora Prentice-Hall do Brasil, Ltda., *Rio de Janeiro*

Dedicated to

Malyce

and

Janice, Jimmy, & Jordan

Contents

Preface   **xi**

    About This Book   xi
    Acknowledgments   xiii

Part I – EDMS Concepts

1 A New Paradigm for Managing Online Documents   **1**

    Adding Value with an EDMS   2
    Is This Really A New Approach?   5
    Organization of the Book   8

2 Electronic Document Management: Needs, Benefits, and Risks   **13**

    The Need for Document Management   13
    Focusing the Need   17
    Benefits of Document Management   19
    Risks of Document Management   21
    INTRAnets: An Emerging Need   23
    Problem Solving Through EDMS Technology   25
    Industry Examples   28

3   The Document Management Space   **31**

A Brief History of Document Management   32
The Four Elements of Document Management   36
Summary   51

Part II – EDMS Technology

4   Repository   **55**

Repository Architecture   55
Object Oriented Model for Document Management   62
Server Functionality   63
Standards   88
Summary   90

5   Conversion   **91**

Electronic Conversion   93
Paper Conversion   97
Summary   103

6   Indexing and Searching   **105**

Speeding Information Retrieval   105
Accomplishing Automated Indexing   106
Searching   110
Summary   113

7   Creation   **115**

Planning and Design   115
Designing for Online Use vs. Printed Use   116
Authoring Requirements and Standards   119
Creating Documents   121
Tools for Creation   122
Creation and Document Management   126
Summary   130

8   Workflow   **131**

Document Management and Workflow   132
Integration With Repository   133
Process   136

Actions	138
People	138
Features and Functions	139
Summary	145

9 Distribution — **147**

Paper Distribution	148
Benefits of Electronic Document Delivery	150
Distribution and Document Management Issues	164
Summary	167

Part III – EDMS Methodology

10 Methodology — **171**

Philosophy	172
Business Approach	177
Technical Approach	180

11 Analysis — **193**

Planning	194
Analysis	203

12 Prototyping — **217**

The Prototyping Process	218
Defining Scope	219
Storyboarding	221
Tool Evaluation and Selection	222
Building a Prototype	223
User Reviews	226
Gap Analysis	228

13 Infrastructure — **231**

Same but Different	232
Architecture Design	233
Installation	234
Standards	235
Migration Plan	238

14   Design and Development   **239**
             Issues in Design and Development   240
             Design   241
             Development   246

15   Implementation and Support   **249**
             Planning   250
             Support   257

Part IV – EDMS Marketplace

16   Select Vendor Profiles   **261**

             Documentum   263
             Interleaf   278
             Open Text   294
             PC DOCS   308

17   EDMS Vendor Listing   **321**
             Featured Vendors   322
             EDMS Vendors (Alphabetical)   322

Index   **325**

Preface

About This Book

The recent explosion of electronic documents produced through online publishing systems has created a complementary need for robust Electronic Document Management Systems (EDMS) that can be easily integrated with existing client-server architectures and Web-based publishing efforts. For this reason, there are now literally dozens of EDMS development tools and approaches in the marketplace that address this need. The purpose of this book, therefore, is to offer an in-depth investigation of EDMS technology in four diverse areas: Concepts, Base Technologies, a Development Methodology, and Profiles of four distinctive tool vendors and their various EDMS approaches. We believe that this broad-based treatment of EDMS technology will enable enterprise managers, document designers, online publishing personnel, and information system professionals to meet the demand of an ever-expanding electronic publishing workplace that will be largely dependent on EDMS technology.

As a relatively new class of information system, EDMS addresses the creation, management, distribution, and updating of document-based information. EDMS technology also provides information publishers, such as enterprise-wide documentation producers and distributors, with the ability to offer *accurate, up-to-date* and *on-demand* document delivery systems that can conditionally assemble documents on-the-fly from different repositories into virtual documents that can be presented in real-time through common text display systems, such as those based on HTML. Clearly, over time EDMS technology will become fully integrated with general file and data-level management, as well as data-compression technologies, within most organizations once it is fully understood. What makes this book even more practical is that it contains a detailed EDMS methodology as distilled from RWD Technologies, Inc. business practices (and those of its clients), which show *real problems* being solved through *commercially available* EDMS technologies.

Founded by Robert W. Deutsch and John Beakes in 1988, RWD Technologies, Inc. focuses on improving human performance in the workplace. By emphasizing *people* and their *performance* in complex operational environments over technology for its own sake, the company has offered its Fortune 100 clients measurable productivity gains as a primary service within its consulting, training, documentation, software development, and systems integration services. Moreover, RWD's pioneering work in EDMS technology has yielded a user-centered approach that is embedded within the core of this text. Thus, our EDMS methodology is, in large part, derived from numerous RWD initiatives to find improved ways for handling document management tasks more effectively. We therefore believe that this methodology is as much about improving human performance in the workplace as it is about creating a new generation of EDMS technology. For this reason we are grateful to RWD for having undertaken this pioneering work and for allowing us to share it here.

Yet this book also demonstrates how EDMS technology can add value while cutting costs and improving productivity. This is why we have included four select vendor profiles that reveal contrasting, though sometimes complementary, approaches to EDMS development. In this sense, this book is at once a reference work on EDMS technology, a repository of text-based consulting through its RWD-tested methodology, and an opportunity to have an in-depth look at four EDMS products in today's marketplace. To keep it up-to-date, the book also has a permanent Web site, located at the following URL:

http://www.goucher.edu/~docman

Here our readers will find current information on EDMS issues as well as additional vendor-related information and case study materials.

Acknowledgments

The development, authoring, and production of this book requires an acknowledgment to many people. First, we would like to thank the administration of Goucher College for their support and for hosting this book's Website. We are also greatly indebted to RWD Technologies, Inc., to its innovative clients, and in particular to the Electronic Document Solutions group, whose hard work and dedication to improving human performance in the workplace have given us a remarkably rich topic to write about. We also extend our appreciation to the vendors--Documentum, Interleaf, Open Text and PC DOCS--not only for their contributions to this book, but for their vision as EDMS pioneers who have helped to define the document management marketplace. We would like to offer our sincere gratitude to Mike Meehan of Prentice Hall for his foresight in the value of this work and his efforts to make it a reality. To Dean Robert Welch, Robert Deutsch, John Beakes, and Butler Newman we owe a debt of many thanks for their support and guidance over the years, and especially through the development of this text. Finally, we would like to acknowledge the terrific work of our book designer, Lisa Jahred.

A New Paradigm for Managing Online Documents

The current document management market has developed to meet an increasing need to manage a corporation's most valuable asset: knowledge. Industry estimates place over 80% of corporate knowledge assets in documents. The need for speeding business processes which are driven by documents to gain an edge on the competition has fueled the rapid development of document management systems over the last five years. With most documents today being created electronically, the focus of document management systems has shifted from managing paper documents through Imaging Systems, to Electronic Document Management Systems (EDMS), where the electronic versions of the documents are stored and managed.

EDMS applications focus on the control of electronic documents, document images, graphics, spreadsheets, word processing files, and complex-compound documents throughout their entire life cycle, from creation to eventual archiving. Document management allows organizations to exert greater control over the creation, management, distribution and revision of corporate information that lies outside of databases, thereby controlling valuable corporate assets. Document management systems can also provide the ability to reuse information, to control documents through business processes, and to reduce document life-cycle times. The full range of functions that a document management system may perform includes document creation, storage and retrieval, management, versioning control, workflow, and document delivery in multiple formats.

To date, these systems have focused on the documents themselves. But when these various processes focus exclusively on documents, an EDMS becomes an end unto itself. The EDMS exists only to control and manage the document collection, creating an electronic library of sorts. When viewed from this perspective, these systems are seen as just an overhead expense, not a mission critical application. The EDMS application must be seen as an enabling technology, one where the system is a means to an end, not the end itself. This view shifts the focal point from the document to the end user. In this context, the system can become one that adds value to the organization, not costs. In other words, the EDMS helps generate revenue, or reduce costs, and therefore its use should be expanded, not minimized. This paradigm shift toward a more user-centered EDMS is the focal point of this book and requires an in-depth understanding of the concepts involved in systems that add value to an organization and what is required in terms of people, technology, and methods.

Adding Value with an EDMS

In any effort or project undertaken today that involves new technology, there had better be bottomline results or benefits that usually take the form of increasing revenue or a reduction in costs, measured by either a cost-benefit-analysis or return-on-investment. However this result is measured, the way to get there is to improve the productivity of the organization overall.

Oftentimes, improving productivity means putting in new technology to solve a perceived problem or fulfill an organizational need. Technology permeates the workplace today as seen in Email, voice-mail, laptop computers, cellular faxes, and of course, Internet connectivity. Over the last generation, the growth and penetration of technology has been unparalleled and is only accelerating. Over the last 15 years, the personal computer has dominated this technological revolution, culminating with some form of computer now residing in virtually every office, factory floor workstation, or retail point of sale.

Still, we must ask: Has this revolution in technology improved our overall productivity? Have we gotten the benefits we had hoped for? Usually not. This is not to say there haven't been significant benefits, just that they haven't lived up to our expectations. Why is this? The answer is actually quite simple: We have only addressed part of the problem.

Improving productivity in our complex business environments through technology means improving *human* performance--enabling *people* to do more with less, and to do it better, faster, cheaper. Technology can be an enabler, but not the panacea predicted with each new wave. Each technology must be targeted at the correct problem, and people must become the masters of the technology in order for benefits to be realized. The formula for improving productivity is about striking a balance between people and technology, but the people must take center stage in this production enhancement process.

When we set out to develop a new information system for an organization, it must add value by improving human performance. The concept of using an electronic system to support users in the performance of their jobs was presented and explored by Gloria Gery in her book *Electronic Performance Support Systems (Gery Performance Press, 1991).* Her premise was that a system should be built to support users by providing them with the information, processes, tools, and training they need to accomplish their jobs. This has led to a new class of information system called EPSS for short.

An EPSS is much more a concept or philosophy than a specific system that can be bought off the shelf. However, these concepts can be used to drive the development process. In order to use this concept to construct or shape a system, a more workable definition of EPSS technology is necessary. A more useful definition of a system that really adds value to an organization might be:

A system which delivers the correct information to the right person, at the proper place and time.

This system definition can be very narrowly or broadly interpreted, but we will keep this definition fairly narrow in scope for the immediate discussion. An expanded definition along with further explanation is provided later in this text.

For a system to meet the definition above, it must have several key characteristics or functions. First, in order to deliver the correct information, the system must be capable of collecting, storing and managing this information. The definition of correct must also mean accurate and up to date. Second, the system must be able to pass all the information through some type of filter so that only the needed information is presented. In order to present the information needed, the system must either know what the user wants, or what information is designed for a particular user. Third, the system must be available in the place the user needs it, whether that's in an office, on the factory floor, or in a remote location. And finally, the system must deliver the information only when the user requires it. Otherwise users are encumbered by having to wade through volumes of information that are not pertinent in order to get what they need.

The most crucial element of this system is, of course, the information itself. But information is a very elusive concept to understand in the abstract. It is easy to understand in a practical sense, in large corporations there are often two broad classes of information: data and documents. Current industry estimates indicate that only 10-20% of all corporate knowledge is stored in data. The remaining knowledge, 80% or more, is therefore stored in documents. So when we talk about being able to deliver the right information, we usually mean that information, or knowledge, which is contained within documents.

It is also important to note that while only a small percentage of corporate information assets are in data, most of it is very well controlled and managed. It resides in databases throughout our organizations where nearly everyone has access to this important corporate resource. Databases are a primary concern for the company's information systems groups. However, documents are not usually controlled the same way.

Over the last five years, the term document has undergone a radical change in definition. Previously, a document was simply considered to be a set of words set down on a page. This definition evolved into documents that included graphics, which were typically cut-and-pasted into the final document to get the desired layout. This task gave rise to desktop publishing systems, where graphics could be combined with text to more effectively communicate the points being made. And as computing power grew, graphics embedded within electronic documents became the norm.

So with the advent of suites of tools from vendors such as Microsoft and Interleaf the definition of a document expanded again to the point where they can now house graphics, text, and multimedia objects, such as audio or video clips. The document is no longer the place where words are put on a page, but rather where a collection of elements or objects related to a particular topic are brought together. Therefore, a more accurate and up-to-date definition of a document might be:

> *A document is a container which brings together information from a variety of sources, in a number of formats, around a specific topic to meet the needs of a particular individual.*

If we look back at our definition for a system, we find that the user is the most central part of the system. It was the user who defined the filter criteria for the information. The user defined the proper location for the information delivery. And, of course, the user determined when the information was to be delivered. So we find that a current definition of an effective system now matches this new definition of documents. In both cases it is the user who is the focal point of the system.

To summarize, we have identified the need for the following high-level information system requirements:

- User focused
- Collect, Store, and Manage Documents
- Filter and Deliver Documents to a User

This system description has many general characteristics of a robust and practical Electronic Document Management System (EDMS) in that it reflects our expanded definition: It is user-centered and not document-centered and the document container of related objects is geared toward the user, not the author. Figure 1-1 shows the model for this new definition of an electronic document management system:

Figure 1-1
The New
EDMS
Paradigm

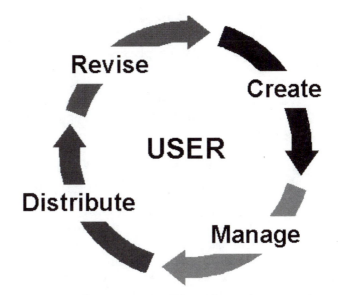

Is This Really A New Approach?

As with any reconceptualization of a problem, its related solution also requires a new definition. So before we explore our new EDMS approach to match the new paradigm outlined above, let's look at why the old approaches will not fit existing needs. There are four primary reasons why traditional approaches to document management will not address the problem:

- The focus is on systems not solutions.
- The systems are moving from proprietary to open systems.
- The documents are not user-centered.
- The organization is ill-equipped to re-use existing information.

We will first briefly review these reasons and then present our new EDMS approach.

The first item to consider is the maturity of the technology. Most corporations have spent much available computing power and information systems research over the last thirty years addressing the data management problem. But systems focused on document management have only been around for the last ten years or so. And whenever technology is new, the market is often driven by vendors and not their customers. This generally results in projects focusing on how to get the system from a vendor up-and-running, rather than on crafting a solution to fit users, which runs contrary to the idea of building a user-driven system.

The second reason for needing a new approach is the change in EDMS technology itself. For the first few years, the market was dominated by a few key players who had proprietary solutions to the document management problem. Often, the vendor provided most, if not all, of the tools needed to address the problem. Therefore, once EDMS developers selected a vendor, they would use its proprietary solution and follow its recommended approach to electronic document management.

Today, the market is moving rapidly towards open EDMS systems, which are supported by industry standards. Also, the power now available in most desktop PCs has made document management practical in most organizations. Finally, these two elements have converged to the point where there is no longer a handful of companies offering solutions, but rather dozens if not hundreds. Along with this trend has been the move for some vendors to concentrate on just one piece of the document management problem, while others continue to try to address it from start to finish.

Organizations are now able to define what parts of the overall document management problem they have and therefore need to solve. This enables them to select only tools that meet their specific need. While this gives the organization more choices in vendors, features, and pricing schemes, it leaves them without a process to follow in order to implement the system. Following the scheme from one vendor may not work well when using tools and technology from a collection of vendors. Hence the need for a common understanding and a vendor-independent approach to follow for putting a robust EDMS solution in place.

The third major obstacle is the old view of the document management problem itself, one that is document driven and not user centered. The earliest document management systems were paper clips, staples, folders and filing cabinets. These systems were totally focused on the documents. As we moved into the electronic age, we built systems that mimicked these existing manual processes. These systems were built around the documents. The model for this paradigm is shown in Figure 1-2 below.

Figure 1-2
The Document-
Centered
Paradigm

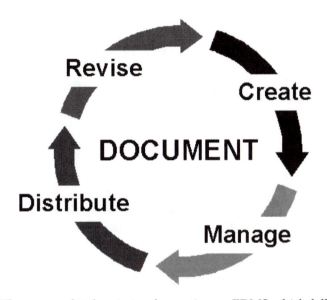

The approach taken in implementing an EDMS which follows the document centered model uses the document to drive the system. The approach generally begins by identifying the documents being used in the organization. Then each document is traced through its life. The system focuses on how the authors create, manage, and distribute these documents. It is effective because the people who understand the documents the best are those who create them: the authors. It is usually clear who owns each document, and all the necessary information required to design and develop the system can be gathered quickly and easily. These systems become the domain of the authoring community.

But the value of a document is realized when it is consumed or used, not when it is created. Thus, the old paradigm did not allow the EDMS to be user-centric, while the new approach will maximize the value of user-driven documents by matching them with users who support the business objectives of the organization. We must have an approach that seeks to maximize this value, not simply install a system that controls documents.

The last and final hurdle is change in the organization. If a system is implemented around a document, it will mimic current processes, good or bad. But with a user-centered view, the resulting EDMS is likely to begin to change the way the organization works. The idea is to ask users what they need and want, then figure out how to deliver it to them through the EDMS. Developers should not, therefore, be quite as concerned whether or not the EDMS fits current processes, but rather look for ways in which the EDMS will change the business processes and user responsibilities within the organization's support structure to maximize value. In doing so, there are much larger issues of human change, organizational structure, and job-task redefinition. These are all part of re-engineering the organization to go hand-in-hand with the new EDMS solution, where the breadth and depth of this change will require a different approach to solving the document management problem

For an EDMS to be truly effective, it must support the business goals and objectives of the organization. The EDMS can accomplish this goal by focusing on the user, the human performer in the business process. In the past, most EDMS systems were focused on the documents, or perhaps the authors, not the users. Therefore a new approach, a user centered one, is required. Figure 1-3 shows that this approach must start where the documents are consumed, not created.

Figure 1-3
The New
EDMS
Approach

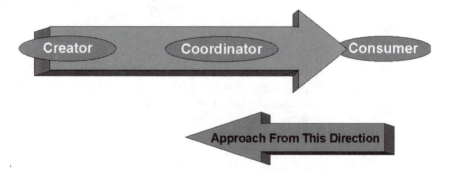

Organization of the Book

The goal of this book is to acquaint the reader with a detailed methodology for implementing a user-centered electronic document management system. This methodology requires several stages. First, developers must understand why document management systems are important, the benefits they offer, and the concepts behind them. Second, they must understand the philosophy of the user-centered or performance-based approach. Third, they must have an awareness of the many technologies involved with EDMS. And finally, they must have a thorough understanding of the EDMS methodology itself. This book is therefore organized into four major parts to meet these objectives, as shown in Figure 1-4, where each part builds on the previous one.

Figure 1-4
Organization of
the book

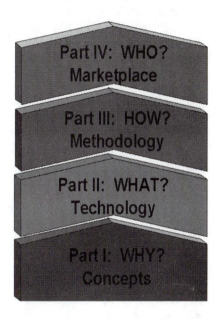

Part IV: WHO? Marketplace

Part III: HOW? Methodology

Part II: WHAT? Technology

Part I: WHY? Concepts

Part I: Concepts

Including this chapter, the goal of this part of the book is to introduce and educate the reader in electronic document management systems. It includes an overview of the concepts, theories, and ideas that are central to an EDMS. It also includes a brief history of document management systems, and how they have evolved. It will also discuss the basic notion of performance based systems and solutions to solidify the paradigm shift to a user centered approach to document management.

Part one includes of two additional chapters:

Chapter 2.   Electronic Document Management: Needs, Benefits, and Risks

Chapter 3.   The Document Management Space

Part II. EDMS Technology

This section gives the reader an overview of the six major technologies that comprise the electronic document management system architecture. This section is designed to provide sufficient detail so that the reader can ask the correct questions of users and vendors and then evaluate the need for these technologies. Two items preclude presenting an in-depth technical discussion on each of the technologies. First, every vendor takes a different approach to using these technologies. Second, the technology, at the lowest level, is constantly changing. The detailed information about how or why some technology is utilized is best left to the various vendors at the time of tool selection.

Part two is divided into six chapters:

Chapter 4.   Repository

Chapter 5.   Conversion

Chapter 6.   Indexing and Searching

Chapter 7.   Creation

Chapter 8.   Workflow

Chapter 9.   Distribution

Part III. EDMS Methodology

This section is the heart and soul of the book. It presents a detailed and step-by-step methodology for taking the idea for an EDMS and turning it into a mission critical system. The methodology is, however, presented as a guideline, not a mandate. It is hoped that after reading the entire book, the reader can then take this methodology, and the general knowledge gained from this text, and modify the approach to fit the needs of the project or situation at hand.

While the entire methodology is important, the two chapters, Analysis and Prototyping, are given more weight and detail than the rest. This is in recognition that no amount of effort in development and implementation can overcome a design that was built on incorrect requirements or assumptions gathered in the first two stages.

Part Three consists of six chapters:

Chapter 10.   Methodology

Chapter 11.   Analysis

Chapter 12.   Prototyping

Chapter 13.   Infrastructure

Chapter 14.   Design and Development

Chapter 15.   Implementation and Support

Part IV. The EDMS Marketplace

This part of the book provides a mechanism for the reader to get an understanding of the current state of technology in the market, which will be presented from the vendors' point of view. Several of the leading tool providers will present their perspective on the EDMS problem and marketplace and then discuss how their tools and technologies meet user needs. Our intent is to show four different approaches to EDMS solutions. While all are viable and deployed in a number of organizations, they approach the problem, and therefore the solution, from a slightly different perspective. The vendors profiled include:

- Documentum, Inc.
- Interleaf, Inc.
- Open Text Corporation
- PC DOCS, Inc.

Part Four consists of two chapters:

Chapter 16.   Select Vendor Profiles
Chapter 17.   A Listing of EDMS Vendors

In addition to these chapters, this book will have a parallel web page, that will catalog and organize all relevant information regarding document management on the World Wide Web. The URL for this site is:

http://www.goucher.edu/~docman/

2

Electronic Document Management: Needs, Benefits, and Risks

Electronic document management can be a confusing term, since it can mean different things to different people. Some think of it as the process of *delivering* documents electronically, such as on the World Wide Web. Others think of it as a system for controlling how documents are created so that all the documents from a workgroup are organized and look the same. Still others think of it as only controlling files for security purposes and for providing revision control.

But document management is actually all three of these elements. The total spectrum of document management deals with the *creation*, *management*, and *distribution* of document-based information. The impact, and therefore the deployment of related systems and tools to address each of these major elements, will vary with the organization as a whole, as well as within various departments.

The Need for Document Management

Why are corporations so concerned with the document management issue? There are three major reasons:

13

- The need for information sharing
- Better management of information assets
- Support of knowledge workers

Information Sharing

In today's environment of global economies, downsizing, competitive pressures and emphasis on financial performance, companies are looking for creative ways to improve productivity. In examining the way they do business, they are quickly recognizing the need to share information widely throughout the organization. When the pace of business was measured in years and months, paper did the job. It was the lowest common denominator, and everybody could use it at relatively the same level of effectiveness.

But as the pace of business has accelerated, so has the need to share information. Paper is too slow a medium for such purposes. Consider this question: When was the last time you actually received anything important in the "regular" mail. Most have come to expect a faxed document or a courier service for such purposes. More and more businesses need information *now*. With more than half the information in an organization created electronically, there is a mandate to share it electronically. However, the growth of these electronic systems has led to veritable "stovepipes" of information within each business group. The organization ends up with the situation where engineering can't share with manufacturing, and the sales group can't share with accounting, etc.

This results in working without all of the information that's available, which of course leads to negative outcomes. One possible result is that actions are taken or decisions made with less than optimal information. This leads to poor or even disastrous consequences or performance. Take, for example, production runs scheduled in the context of inaccurate sales forecasts. Products needed are not produced leading to lost opportunity; products that can't be sold are produced anyway and put into inventory. The result: lower revenues from lost sales and higher costs from inventory-carrying costs, a double hit on profits.

A second possible negative outcome is that people recognize the first problem and set out to find the "right" information. In a typical professional's workday, from 20 to 40% of their time is spent looking for information. This is not a productive task for someone who's annual cost, with benefits, can run into six-figures. Companies are battling for one and two percent differences in profits, and here there can be an enormous productivity gap. Imagine running a manufacturing facility, and finding that your production rates were off by 30% because the workers couldn't find the right parts. It wouldn't take very long before a process was put in place to get the right parts to the right person or place.

The issue is that in non-tangible product environments these problems are often hidden. A hard look at the business, commonly in a reengineering project, often brings these situations to light. This forces organizations to open up these stovepipes of information and share them with the rest of the organization. It also demands that each organization develop a process to manage the creation and distribution of this information. This has lead to a vast increase in the awareness of and need for electronic document management systems.

Managing Information Assets

An in-depth look at business processes and the use of documents has also uncovered another equally difficult problem, that of effectively managing assets. Again, to use the manufacturing analogy, well-run plants manage their valuable assets, be they equipment, raw materials, or the finished goods themselves. They are all very carefully controlled and this control usually takes the form of some type of Manufacturing Resource Planning (MRP) and/or Inventory Control System. And it is not considered good practice to leave these resources uncontrolled. Yet this is exactly the situation most organizations find themselves in when it comes to the management of documents.

In many organizations the majority of electronic documents are scattered across floppies, local hard drives and LAN file servers. They are not organized, structured, or even cataloged. Often they cannot be found by anyone except authors, and only if they have good memories for file names. There is rarely any security for changes, backups, or disaster recovery, leaving these valuable resources uncontrolled.

To understand the magnitude of this problem it is important to consider what these documents represent, or what they contain. For example, at a global level, what is the difference between Chrysler, General Motors, and Ford? They all produce cars, and if you look closely at their business processes, they all have a lot in common. They even use the same robots and equipment in the plant, and they buy their steel from the same producers. They use the same computer systems for design, and they have the same labor agreements for the most part. So what is it that sets them apart? It is the skills, experience, and processes that lead to slight product quality or buyer preference differences, and these human assets are contained within their employees.

In fact, these human assets are often referred to as "corporate knowledge," or "intellectual capital" in the latest industry vernacular. In many organizations, much of this information is preserved by writing it down into documents. They represent the sum total of knowledge within the organization. In the US, with an aging work-force, many companies are working on major projects to capture this knowledge base before it retires. They often couple subject-matter experts (SME's) with teams of knowledge engineers and writers to cap-ture and record the knowledge embedded in the experience of these SMEs. The resulting documents often embody the corporation's "best practices."

These documents become the foundation for training, proce-dures, guidelines and many other activities involved in improving business processes, and the documents become invaluable because they contain the skills, processes, data, information, and collective knowledge that would take considerable effort to relearn from scratch. It is difficult to quantify the value of these documents explicitly, and therefore difficult to justify the cost of a document management system for these documents. However, when one looks at the cost of simply capturing this knowledge base, it is easy to justify. These projects are often in the hundreds of thousands if not millions of dollars and it is not uncommon in Fortune 100 companies to have several of these projects in progress at once.

If an organization is willing to spend millions of dollars to cap-ture and record this knowledge, it is an easy parallel to assume it is a valuable enough asset that it should at least be managed electronically. Secure and controlled storage, cataloging and indexing, and keeping the contents current are all worthwhile and justifiable tasks from a con-trol perspective. Recall that industry estimates put corporate knowl-edge as only 10 to 20% data (i.e. information that can be fit into columns and rows). The remainder resides in the unstructured format known as documents. This remaining 80% is relatively unmanaged, out of control and underutilized. In an environment as competitive as today's this can be an opportunity for developing a competitive advantage through EDMS technologies.

Knowledge Workers

The changing of organizations to meet the demands of the more globally competitive environment has led to developing knowledge workers - individuals with the skills, capabilities and the information necessary to complete tasks with little supervision. The days of auto-cratic, highly supervised, low-decision jobs are, in large part, gone. As this global competition has heated up, the middle layers of manage-ment and supervision have been eliminated. Workers are left to their own devices.

Because of these cutbacks and reductions in the workforce, today's businesses demand more of the people who remain. They are often handed far more responsibility, and along with this increased responsibility have come more demands from customers for better service, higher quality goods, all with little or no increase in price. How can these objectives be met?

By properly enabling workers with the right information (usually in documents) and by adding some greater level of training, these knowledge workers can become experienced enough to make their own decisions. Even in the manufacturing world, especially on the production line, the work environment has changed dramatically. Production workers are now responsible for inspecting and testing their own work and are empowered to stop the production process if a problem arises, without contacting a supervisor. In many instances the workers decide what needs to be fixed, how to fix it, and when to resume production. This is the epitome of a knowledge worker.

In order to effect this level of change, workers in every job are expected to have easy access to accurate and up-to-date information. With the majority of information on billing, product specifications, operating procedures, decision guidelines, etc. residing in documents, the need for a document management system is clear.

Focusing the Need

There is a dominant theme in each of the needs for EDMS applications that augment human performance. It is the intent of improving productivity in the workplace by assisting the employees to better execute their tasks. In other words, supporting the performance of workers in their jobs. This class of system is often called an Electronic Performance Support Systems (EPSS).

An EPSS is a system, that is designed from the ground up, to improve and enhance the performance of the knowledge worker in the organization. It embodies the organizations goals, the processes, accomplishments, jobs and tasks, along with clear performance measures for each user. It combines a mix of training, documentation and decision support.It can include just-in-time learning, coaching and tutoring along with policies and process document. Also included are systems that can use available data to guide the decision process. These systems also track and provide feedback on performance against critical objectives.

In order for an EPSS to be effective it must have some key elements. First and foremost, it must be focused on the user. Second, it must have a representation of the users job and task functions. Third it must have the work processes and the business rules which guide the users.And , finally, it must have access to all the information required to make intelligent and informed decisions - both data and documents.

Then the system can be truly effective in improving human performance in the workplace.

Simplifying this concept and restricting it's domain to that of the EDMS, the goal of an EPSS becomes:

Deliver the correct information to the right person at the proper place and time.

This information can be document based or data driven.

These EPSS systems must be driven by determining what information is needed by the person conducting the task, in order to be able to perform that task at the level of an SME. If the information is all document driven then a user focused EDMS may be a complete solution in and of itself. If it is all data driven, then a Graphical User Interface (GUI) tied to a database may be the solution. If the solution is mixed, then an EDMS will likely play some role. This role may be as a sub-system that can communicate with a database system, or one where a custom front end may be developed with data being served by a database, while documents are being served by a repository and other parts of an EDMS.

Regardless of the technology of the solution, it must remain focused squarely at improving the performance of the worker. One of the recognized experts in looking at job-based performance, and what can be done to improve it, is Joe Harless. He has developed several texts, processes and methods by which performance can analyzed, measured, monitored and ultimately improved. Synthesizing some of his work gives us a performance based processes definition illustrated in Figure 2-1.

Figure 2-1
Performance
Based
Process

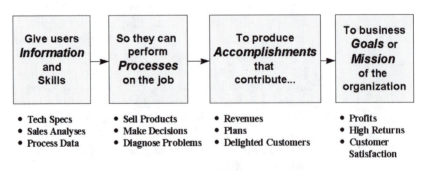

Give users **Information** and **Skills**	So they can perform **Processes** on the job	To produce **Accomplishments** that contribute...	**To business Goals or Mission** of the organization
• Tech Specs • Sales Analyses • Process Data	• Sell Products • Make Decisions • Diagnose Problems	• Revenues • Plans • Delighted Customers	• Profits • High Returns • Customer Satisfaction

In this process, the initial step is to give users the information and skills needed to perform the jobs they are asked to do. And skills are typically developed through a variety of training interventions.

In order to improve the performance and business practices of any organization, those implementing them must understand the Goals, Accomplishments, and Processes so the correct information can be delivered. Therefore, a user centered philosophy demands that the problem be analyzed from right to left, as shown in Figure 2-2. First, determine what is needed, then find out why it is needed, and ultimately concentrate on how best to deliver it.

Figure 2-2
Performance-
Based
Analysis
Process

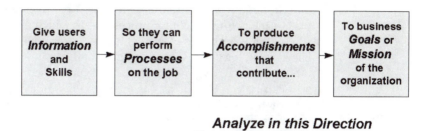

| Give users **Information** and **Skills** | So they can perform **Processes** on the job | To produce **Accomplishments** that contribute... | **To business Goals or Mission** of the organization |

Analyze in this Direction

This concept of performance support is important to ensure that the focus of an EDMS remains on the business problem and the workers, not on the documents themselves. This is the key success criteria; to remain focused on improving performance, and not to fall into the comfortable position of simply looking at documents alone. This user-centric (rather than document-centric) theme is prevalent throughout the text, but will come heavily into play in the methodology section of the book.

Benefits of Document Management

Having looked at the need for document management, we now turn to the benefits that can be expected from electronic document management systems (EDMS):

1. Lower Cost of Document Creation and Distribution
2. Improved, Customized Access to Documents
3. Faster Document Creation and Update Processes
4. Increased Reuse and Leverage of Existing Information
5. Better Employee Collaboration
6. Reduced Cycle Times in Document Centered Processes
7. More Complete Regulatory Compliance
8. Refined Managerial Control and Reporting
9. Enhanced Document Control and Security
10. Improved Productivity/Reduced Headcount
11. Better Customer/Client Satisfaction

When looking for the benefits in an EDMS application, the tendency is to look at the distribution aspects alone. The first major advantage includes lower production costs for information products defined in terms of both dollar savings and reduced time investments for individual staff members. For example, with online publishing, many intermediary steps that are often used in paper-based document production processes are eliminated, such as the need for paste-up, blue lining, etc. Also, online distribution removes the most expensive part of the print publishing process itself, which is the need for expensive paper stocks. For example, it may cost between $3-$5 per paper-based book for the cost of the paper itself, along with the printing and binding process, whereas a single network-based publication of equal size can be created for less than fifty cents today, and the text-based information that it contains may be enough to fill several print-based volumes.

Another advantage of the paperless distribution model is ease of access and maintenance. Electronic documents can be presented in several different forms or listed in custom tables of contents based upon user needs or the context in which the document might be used. Often a major reason for online distribution is to keep documents "evergreen" or always up to date. For example, take a set of customer service guidelines that is distributed to several hundred people in the organization. Each time a new change is issued, it can take weeks to get new paper-based copies to each person, and there is still no guarantee the manuals are updated and in-sync. However, put that same document collection on a single file server and allow everyone to look at that one copy, and it can take as little as five minutes to issue a change and guarantee that everyone will be using it.

A document management system can also become a document production and distribution system, even if the final product remains in paper. This frees the author from the rather mundane tasks of making sure the documents get printed and mailed, and the workflow engine can drive this process. On the authoring side, the workflow engine can also help to reduce the time it takes a document to get from one step in the production process to the next, or will support parallel reviewing, which can cut days or even weeks off the business processes or document cycle. In the pharmaceutical industry, for example, getting a drug to market a couple weeks sooner can mean owning the market and result in additional revenues measured in millions.

When all documents are properly cataloged and indexed, this provides the means to quickly and accurately find the desired information. This not only reduces the time spent searching, but the time spent re-creating it if it was not found. This effort can be enormous when information is recreated, either by simply re-keying or more often by being reworked. More importantly, if information in a usable form can be located quickly and easily, people in cross-functional teams can better share and collaborate, doing the things that add the most value, rather than simply shuffling electronic files back and forth.

The ability to reuse information, either directly or indirectly, allows organizations to begin to leverage corporate knowledge resources. Information provided from an SME can be reworked into guidelines for experienced operators, demonstrating a leveraging effect.

One final benefit which is often difficult to quantify as a positive outcome of an EDMS application is control over corporate knowledge contained within its documents. This is often best viewed as a cost-avoidance measure. For example, what are the consequences if:

- Documents are Lost or Destroyed?
- Outdated Information is Used for a Decision or Action?
- Inaccurate Information is Provided to Customers?

The area of regulatory compliance for companies involved with things such as ISO 9000 or Process Safety Management in the Petrochemical industry are important drivers for such types of document control.

Risks of Document Management

There are, however, several serious risks in implementing document management, such as:

- Online Distribution without Document Control
- Non User-Focused Products
- Poor Information Organization
- Information Overload
- Difficult Document Control
- Poor Technology Infrastructures (such as networks)

But the most serious risk to any EDMS solution is that it will only be partially implemented. With so many benefits from the online distribution of document-based information, and the relatively low cost of related tools and technologies such as the Web, organizations often look at only this one aspect of the overall issue. They rush headlong into putting documents online and providing access to them, while the creation and management aspects are ignored.

In today's market, this can be seen at almost any World Wide Web site, where content is out of date, sometimes seriously out of date. Organizations, in a rush to build a presence on the Web, "throw up" text content and then spend more on producing slick graphics than on a process for controlling and maintaining the Web site itself. Then, when the novelty wears off and the information grows stale, there are few resources left to update and maintain the Web site. There is no simple document management system to keep the online version of a document in synch with its originally authored version.

In some cases, a conversion team or Webmaster is hired to keep all this information current and up-to-date. The organization must develop a process, training the authors and Webmasters on it, and ensure that it is followed. This tends to dampen the Web's rallying cry of "Fast, Cheap and Easy." In sum, document distribution on the Web without some type of control is a serious issue for many organizations.

Despite this issue, there is a much larger issue looming on the user's side. Those who access this information will quickly call into question the validity of the information on the entire site by virtue of finding one piece of out-of-date information. For example, if a training schedule is out of date, what confidence will users have in the rest of the information online? Once confidence is lost in any system, the cost to regain it is several times the cost of implementing it in the first place.

Another risk is that the EDMS is driven by the documents or technology and not by the end users. This can result in a system that will greatly increase training costs and require more support since users will have to be taught how to use it - it won't be intuitive to them. This can lead to further acceptance problems. Many systems have died at the implementation stage from not adequately addressing the users' needs up-front than from a poor implementation plan.

A very common risk with these types of systems is information overload. The number of documents in an organization is already overwhelming, but just making them electronic will not help. Careful organization and presentation of these materials is very important. Putting all the content in the organization online and simply saying "it's all there, just go search for what you want " is not adequate. How many times do you actually find what you want on the Web by searching, and how long does this process take? Focusing on the user, and not forcing them to wade though lots of unimportant information to complete a task, is crucial.

Controlling documents within an EDMS will, therefore, demand more from both authors and users. Documents will have to be checked in and out, and additional information will have to be provided, such as the title, author, subject, document type, etc. for each unit of information. This is all overhead but a necessary evil. And like all evils, if the perceived gain does not outweigh the pain, the system will slowly die because it is simply too hard to construct or use. It must be carefully worked into the normal job tasks and in such a way that the value outweighs the effort. As with most systems, a process that is not correctly done the first time will be much harder to try a second time. Fortunately, careful planning, a solid methodology, a good choice for a pilot within an organization, and a very strong champion are ways to mitigate this risk.

A final risk to online distribution is that interest in EDMS technology or the approach taken might wane over time, not for want of inherent advantages, but simply because, to some, the technology may not be perceived to be as easy to implement or use as books and other paper-based materials are today. This is because print-based media pose few challenges to the end user, whereas software still has a steep learning curve associated with it in most cases, and the portability of online documents still cannot match that of books or hardcopy materials today. For this reason, each organization will need to research whether the many benefits of electronic documents to information consumers are significant enough to outweigh the difficulty of getting access to them through the tools that are available today.

Here a major stumbling block may be that today's text viewing technologies are not always optimal for electronic document delivery, as many were designed, it seems, for excellence in rendering drawings and pictures rather than for displaying and navigating through dense information spaces that contain hypertext. Here visual display systems that can handle two pages of text--while offering scaleable on-screen fonts that can image characters at 600-1200 dots per inch (like paper)-- would go a long way toward getting users to become comfortable reading documents online. However, with graphical environments like Windows, and technologies like HTML and Acrobat, we've come a long way since MS-DOS screens of 80 columns and 25 rows of ASCII-based characters, and we are well into the transition toward better viewing technologies for online text.

INTRAnets: An Emerging Need

INTRAnets, the use of Web technology inside corporate firewalls, is exploding. By the end of 1997 it is expected that nearly two-thirds of all Web servers purchased will be for INTRAnets, not Internet sites. The simple, inexpensive cross-platform technology offers incredible power to an organization. Though in their infancy, these systems are already becoming publishing or information dissemination vehicles. They are growing rapidly beyond that into enterprise-wide client-server based information systems. In this text, however, we will consider only the INTRAnet's publishing aspects. The continuum is shown in Figure 2-3.

Figure 2-3
Continuum of
Web
Technology

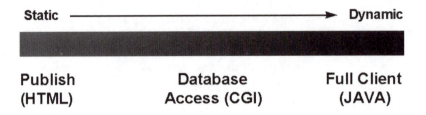

Static ────────────────────────────▶ **Dynamic**

| **Publish** | **Database** | **Full Client** |
| **(HTML)** | **Access (CGI)** | **(JAVA)** |

These systems have caught on like wildfire. People are implementing them throughout corporations, including at the executive, divisional, departmental, and even workgroup level. In many corporations the INTRAnet moves from a "skunkworks" operation to a mission-critical installation nearly overnight. These systems grow from a couple of hundred pages to tens of thousands of documents very rapidly.

But the sheer volume of document-based information on the Web creates its own set of problems. Information is often not clearly categorized, organized, or presented to users. For these reasons, and others that follow, INTRAnets are often touted as the best living example of why an organization needs document management. Unfortunately, the pain of running a Web site without a document management system behind it often takes six to nine months to surface. When it is recognized, however, the problem is already out of control, the Webmaster is overwhelmed with the day-to-day maintenance of the site and trying to handle the required conversion and revisions.

In addition, the processes for getting content up on the Web are often informal and under-estimated. Most organizations use many tools to create documents, and practically none of the documents are created directly in a Web-compatible format such as HTML or GIF. Therefore, most documents placed on the Web are converted to HTML, GIF or PDF. This conversion process introduces several significant problems:

- File Synchronization
- Level of Effort
- Exponential Growth of Files

File synchronization is the issue of keeping the source document, perhaps a Word or WordPerfect file, in step with its HTML counterpart on the Web. There must be a process by which any change to the Word documents triggers someone to update the HTML document. It is very common for the Word document, usually distributed on paper, to stay several versions ahead of its online counterpart. This may be due to delays in the conversion or a breakdown in communication between disparate authors and a single Webmaster.

Conversion efforts can also be enormous. As the Web site grows from a few hundred to several thousand documents, the conversion task can be overwhelming. Formal processes and even automation must be considered just to keep up with the workload. This means careful consideration of native file formats and the accuracy of the conversion process itself. Also, the effort in cleaning up or correcting inaccuracies is often underestimated by an order of magnitude.

Finally, we need to consider the explosive growth of files themselves. But the growth from user interest and a desire to put more information online is not this issue. The problem is that what was originally one file may now be *many* files. HTML stores text in one file, and references the graphics by filenames. Simply put, one word processing document that contains three graphics all embedded into one file will now become four files, one HTM formatted file and three GIF formatted files

Now the HTML or online version of a document is a group of files. In an operating system they must be given specific names that allow them to recognized as related. They are often stored in a directory to "keep them together." These file and directory names are crucial as they are part of the references between the HTML file and the graphic files. For example, keeping the original compound Word document in synch with one HTML text file and three graphic files just became far more difficult.

The issues raised here are major and will be faced by any Webmaster or INTRAnet system manager. These problems make a very compelling case for using a document management system that encompasses all critical EDMS elements, such as document security, control, versioning, workflow, indexing/searching, conversion, authoring, and online viewing. Simply put, the Web creates the real need for an electronic document management system.

Problem Solving Through EDMS Technology

Clearly EDMS technology would not be making the in-roads it is today within organizations if it did not respond effectively to a number of problems relating to document delivery and the control/maintenance of complex documents. In fact, for many common problems relating to document delivery, we discover that there are demonstrable solutions that document management offer, as revealed in the following list:

Problem: Finding/locating and retrieving important textual information in a timely enough manner to be used in a real-time setting, such as in a help-desk application.

Solution: The distribution component of an EDMS allows this problem to be solved through the use of automated indexing, outlining, hypertext features, and Boolean searching techniques, where the major benefit is time savings in finding pertinent information. Because the information is indexed, it can be located and retrieved much more quickly, while hypertext facilitates information accessing that is based on a train-of-thought browsing process.

Problem: Finding a more cost-effective and user-friendly way of online information delivery as an alternative to paper publishing.

Solution: Organizations often save thousands of dollars by adopting an online distribution approach, including delivery options such as, CD-ROM, LANs, and WANs or even the Web where the principal benefits are lower distribution costs, added-value in terms of document usability, and easier maintainability of text-based materials.

Problem: Online reference books or document sets are seen as stand-alone entities or as somehow "distinct" from other software products and, therefore, are not very well integrated into the total software solution or company enterprise.

Solution: The document management or distribution portions of an EDMS can be easily integrated with other computer information systems in real-time settings to deliver complete Electronic Performance Support Systems. These can include database information, graphics, and multi-media materials, and interactive applications along with document access, retrieval and display. The key is to take advantage of inter-process communication capabilities between concurrently running programs and then design the system in such a way that it is context-sensitive and thereby complements other applications.

Problem: Offering adequate copies of up-to-date text-based materials within an organization.

Solution: An EDMS offers several strategies for dealing effectively with this problem by showing how online publishing solutions can be used to overcome the time lag often associated with revising documents that are much in demand, used constantly, and not easily taken out of service for long periods of time. And in a networked environment, the added benefit is that once an up-to-date document is put "online" it is immediately available to everyone attached to that network.

Problem: The document is fragmented, perhaps stored in multiple locations (with multiple copies) with the result that users can unknowingly get the wrong version.

Solution: An EDMS can solve this problem by taking advantage of networking and client/server architectures where documents "live" in only one place, in only one version, but are accessed simultaneously by many users. This strategy also reduces the likelihood that mis-matched versions of documents will be replicated across many individual machines.

Problem: The format of the online document is not consistent with the paper version and is therefore disorienting.

Solution: Many tools for online publishing solutions on the market today go to great lengths to make the look-and-feel of a document as close to its paper counterpart as is possible. The result is that the online versions look identical with the paper versions, which can reduce the training and time to competency for users of these new online systems.

Problem: Valuable time is wasted searching for the electronic copy of a paper document. The subject, the author, and approximately when it was created are known, but filename or location are not.

Solution: Through the use of attributes or information about the documents, which can be stored in a document repository, documents can be cataloged in a variety of ways. Sophisticated search engines for both attributes as well as full text indexing make document retrieval fast and easy.

Problem: A document is copied and edited, independently, by multiple people. How can these multiple versions be reconciled?

Solution: Library services, which oversee the check-in and check-out of documents from the repository are designed to prevent this situation from occurring. Documents are commonly locked from further access when one person has checked out a document for editing.

Problem: Decisions are made based on information contained in an out of date document. This mistake could have safety, operational, financial or legal ramifications.

Solution: An EDMS can provide access to documents based on a system username. Some users, creators perhaps, are granted access to all versions of a document. Other users, consumers, are granted access to only the latest version. Even if the document is published to a Web, a complete EDMS can ensure that only the latest version is posted.

Problem: Documents are now published on both paper and online within the organization. The online version is one revision behind the paper.

Solution: An EDMS that couples the repository and online publishing process can keep both the paper and online versions in synch. The repository along with workflow can drive both the printing and online production processes, but uses the single master copy of the document to do so.

Problem: Documents are stored on a LAN server, and a new version was copied to the wrong directory, overwriting the document with changes made by a co-worker. That work is lost.

Solution: A document repository can track both major and minor changes to a document. It will keep master copies of documents according to a set of predetermined rules. These rules are usually designed to ensure that any new edits are kept as minor changes or sub-versions of a document. This protects the integrity of the document assets.

Problem: Getting a document reviewed and approved is too slow. The process involves a number of people in different physical locations and most of the process is serial to give successive users the comments from the earlier reviewers

Solution: An EDMS can couple workflow, version control, online editing including comments and electronic delivery to streamline the process. The dead time of document transport and "in-boxes" is eliminated. Also, with real time comment tracking many reviews can be executed in parallel instead of serial, cutting the time further.

Problem: Documents created in different groups using different packages are difficult to share other than on paper.

Solution: Automated document conversion to a neutral format or use of multi-format viewers as part of the EDMS can make electronic information sharing a real possibility. Documents can be put into widely accepted formats such as HTML or Acrobat's PDF, or even converted from one proprietary format to another.

Industry Examples

A number of generic industry applications of effective document management systems are outlined in the following sections. While these examples are industry specific, their situations can be easily extrapolated to other industries and problems. They are from a broad range of industries and emphasize different aspects of the document management process. None of these examples are places where one might expect a document-centered problem or concern to exist. Often people assume that document problems exist only in publishing or technical writing departments and organizations.

Pharmaceutical

In order to get new drugs to market, pharmaceutical companies must get them approved by the Food and Drug Administration (FDA) through a process of a new drug application (NDA). This report, which often fills a tractor trailer with paper, must encapsulate all the research and clinical trial information about the drug. This often involves thousands of people around the world and requires that massive volumes of information be gathered, processed, organized, and produced into reports according to the FDA's guidelines.

Many companies have utilized EDMS systems in order to reduce the time to generate these reports. This can speed the processes dramatically, and getting to market first can often means millions of dollars in additional revenue over the life of the drug. These systems often have the side benefit of reducing headcount, as more of the information gathering, processing, review, comment and approval can be done electronically.

ISO 9000

Many organizations are becoming ISO certified for quality to better compete in the global market place. Many of these are manufacturing organizations. In short the ISO 9000 process requires that an organization, "Says what it does, and does what it says". This requires the organization do three things:

1. Define its processes.
2. Follow the processes.
3. Prove they followed them.

This usually requires that the processes be documented and that there is a process which defines the control of these documents. In order to follow the processes, they must be accessible to everyone. Finally, in order to prove the processes were followed, objective quality assurance evidence must be available.

From these simple steps come the requirements to control and distribute documents. In addition, many of these processes themselves require that other documents be created. For example, one process might require that a set of specifications and drawings be created for each part in the design of an assembly, and that they be reviewed and approved by specific individuals. These documents serve as the objective quality evidence that the processes were followed; again an EDMS system can assist in maintaining this ISO certification.

Process Safety Management / Regulatory Compliance

In order to promote safer operations in processing plants such as chemical or petroleum refineries, the Occupational Safety and Health Administration(OSHA) issues regulatory guidelines. They require that each plant generate a set of documented processes for how the plant will be run. OSHA also requires that all operators be trained on these documents and that a method be devised to keep them up to date.

Because of the size of many refineries, sometimes that of small cities, there may be the need for 20, 30 or 40 copies of these operating procedures scattered throughout the site. Keeping the paper copies up to date is a nearly impossible task. Many of these refineries have moved to online distribution to allow all users to look at one electronic copy. Changes now take minutes instead of weeks. Having spent millions of dollars to generate or update the existing procedures to this new standard, many organizations have taken to using a document management system to protect this investment, and support the revision process as well.

Customer Service

The customer service representative at any company is a challenging job. It requires a very broad set of knowledge about the company, its policies, procedures, products, and services. In the past, the latitude a rep had in handling a problem was limited. All non-standard requests were passed to a supervisor. Reengineering and competitive pressures, however, have resulted in the shift of these jobs into far more self-sufficient positions, to be assumed by knowledge workers. The goal was to give the rep far more latitude on handling questions, issues, and problems.

To facilitate this process, the reps had to be given far more information about nearly everything in the company. The handbook that guides these workers ballooned from a few dozen pages to several hundred. But being armed with this information, and being able to search it effectively, customer service reps could quickly find what they needed to answer and resolve key questions. Not only was it important to get this information out to the reps in the form of online documentation, but the consequences of it being incorrect went up dramatically. Thus, document management systems have been used to ensure that only the latest, approved information is available to these front-line workers. The reps are now far more productive, and client satisfaction has been improved as problems are now resolved on the spot.

The Document Management Space

Document management is not a single entity or technology but rather a combination of elements. It is the interaction of information and different users in a business process, combined with the technology that permits this interaction. This is why the term can mean so many different things to so many people. For years, document management systems meant imaging systems--transforming paper documents into digital media. Most recently, though, the term is used in conjunction with Web sites to refer to the process of checking links to verify that all documents are available. This range of definitions, while accurate, make it hard to narrowly define the overall document management space.

In this chapter, each of the four major elements of the document management space will be explored. These are:

- Documents
- People
- Processes
- Technology

Having an understanding of these elements will enable one to see the different applications and focal points for document management systems. However, before exploring what comprises these elements, let's look at the history of document management.

A Brief History of Document Management

Before getting into the history of document management and control, it is valuable to look at several interesting parallels that can be drawn to document management. As with most business events there is a cyclical nature to them, as things tend in one direction, reach an extreme, then tend back toward the original direction.

Information Systems

In the late seventies and early eighties, the information systems departments saw a shift from large central mainframes to distributed PCs on the desktop. This shift moved control of information systems and resources from a highly central organization to a widely distributed one, which created numerous problems for the IS organization as well as the lines of business where these PCs were deployed. IS organizations were forced to modify the way they operated to adapt to this changing environment. The introduction of LANs has changed the balance of central versus distributed systems again. The LAN made desktop computing a greater productivity-enhancing tool.

Networks have grown dramatically because of improvements in networking power, performance, and price. People have learned to exploit the advantages of a network by sharing files and using new technologies such as Email. How are Information Systems organizations coping with this distributed environment? As best as they can by mainly trying to *control* it in some cost-effective way. The two most common ways are by establishing a common operating systems environment so that each machine is configured in a similar fashion with common hardware, software, and networking connectivity. This greatly simplifies support. A second strategy is to move toward the use of application servers, where all typical desktop applications are loaded from a server at execution. In this fashion the IS team is re-centralizing some functions to regain control.

In the period of the late 1980s and early '90s, users had a greater desire to access and share structured data. This led to the next major wave in information technology: client-server. This approach allowed for a division of computing power between the desktop, or client machine, and the server. This was a balance of central and distributed resources. The client or server could be made fatter or slimmer depending upon the environment in which the application had to run.

Finally we reach today, when the hottest trend in information technology is the Internet and World Wide Web. We now have visionaries talking of replacing desktop PCs with $500 Internet-ready boxes that are the equivalent of interactive TVs connected to the Web. While PCs are unlikely to disappear anytime soon, this concept is simply an extension of the client-server model where the client is tiny and the servers are very large. Is this a return to the mainframe approach? Probably not since there are also hundreds of thousands of servers on the Internet right now, offering the ultimate client-server model of computing. In fact, leading edge Web technologies, such as Java, JavaScript, and ActiveX, where applications are stored on a server and then simply downloaded and executed on a client's machine, are trying to leverage the power of the desktop PC even more. So any claim of moving back to the mainframe era is probably overstated. The diagram in Figure 3-1 illustrates the history and cyclical nature of computing and networking technologies over the last twenty years.

Figure 3-1
Cycles in Computing Technology over the Last 20 years

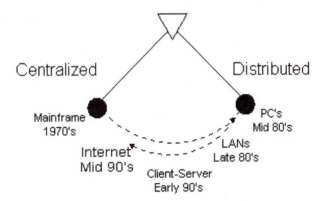

Why is this historical context important to understanding the document management context of today? To begin, there are amazing similarities between the changes in document management systems and the overall changes in information technology itself. However, the changes in information technology are much more apparent to IS individuals and organizations than to those who confront document management issues daily. Finally, and most importantly, the changes in document management have lagged behind those in the information systems arena, so it may be possible to predict where this is all going and how it may be possible to benefit from what the IS organization has already learned.

Document Control

The very first document control technology was very likely the paper clip. This was followed by the staple, then the manila folder, and ultimately the filing cabinet. All of this evolved to meet the need of the time: controlling paper. It should be expected that as documents are less paper-based and more digital, other tools and approaches should be expected to evolve. The last twenty years shows this evolution rather well.

In the mid to late seventies information publication or dissemination was reserved for all but the most important items. Documents were often hand written by the author, reviews and edits were done on the original and then forwarded to the clerical/typing staff. The finished document was then returned to the author for signature and release. Since there was a single point of control within the clerical pool, documents were often managed here. Each document was usually assigned some type of coding number and a copy was filed in the central records. Everyone one knew who to go to for a copy of the document. Revisions or updates were filed with the original, so it was easy to get the latest copy.

As typewriters advanced into word processors, document production became more flexible and documents could be stored electronically. However, not much changed in the area of document control as the responsibility for managing these electronic files remained within the clerical side of the organization. The data files were numbered and stored in a logical fashion, similar to paper documents.

Then, in the early 1980's the PC revolution began. This moved computing power in an organization from the centralized control of the IS department into the hands of users in each department. As computing power became decentralized, so did the capability to harvest and create information, particularly in the form of documents. As PC's really hit the mainstream by the mid 1980's, the roles for clerical/word processing pools and the average employee began to change dramatically. Documents were often created directly by the authors, but to get them printed, formatted, etc. they were often handed to someone else responsible for the administration of the organization.

The administration of the documents in an organization still followed many of the rules established in the clerical pools. Floppy disks containing the electronic copy of the documents were filed with the paper copies in the central records. Given the limited availability of WYSIWYG word processors and printers, documents continued to go through the document administrator, providing a single choke point where control mechanisms were firmly in place.

By the late 1980s, though this model was still in place, the sheer volume of information being generated was straining it severely. Then the introduction of Local Area Networks (LANs) changed the landscape once again. In the early days of LANs, the primary use of the network was for file and print services. Disk space was limited so only the most important files were stored on the server. Shared printing was the primary advantage. As networking performance improved and mass storage prices fell, networking began to change. It was now possible to store and share files on the server.

But the ability to share files electronically created its own set of questions: How do users know what file to get and where to get it? To resolve problems such as these, many administrators established file-naming standards to control and manage electronic documents. If a filenaming standard is sufficiently developed and rigidly enforced, it can be a reasonably effective method for document control in small workgroups with a limited number of document sets.

Networking improvements also brought more capability to the individual users. In many organizations, particularly where the administrator had become a bottle neck, the introduction of the LAN was heralded as a productivity breakthrough. As always, the improvement was a double edged sword. By removing the choke point, the control mechanism was also removed. This was the beginning of the end for controlling documents, and a degree of document chaos followed.

One of the most radical changes that networking brought to the business context was Email. Email fostered the concepts of information sharing and informal communication. This technology began to change the way people worked together. At the same time, applications became more powerful and easier to use as hardware performance improved. These enabled a whole new class of users to create and publish their own documents. Email systems became a mechanism by which to share and distribute this information. While this offered another leap in personal productivity, it was also another step deeper into document chaos.

Users became intimately familiar with LANs, servers, and other networking technologies. This familiarity enabled them to understand how to leverage the resources, such as file servers, to their advantage. They could suddenly store far more information than their individual hard disks might hold, and they could share this information with an entire team of people. Nothing was ever "deleted," only moved to the server. After a while, no one could tell what was important and what was not, what was new and what was superseded.

Now with WANs connecting all of the offices of a corporation to the Internet, or INTRAnets, the document management problem is growing exponentially. Some studies estimate that in 1985 the volume of documents doubled at a rate of once every five years. In 1996, that figure is down to nine months. This has been one of the major reasons why, despite all the technology advances to improve productivity, there has been limited actual improvement. We can create information more easily and quickly than ever, but it takes us longer to wade through it to find what is needed. Organizations are now looking for the answers that EDMS solutions can provide.

Upper management is also recognizing the intrinsic value associated with document control. It helps reduce the information overload situation, where people often find themselves drowning in information, but thirsting for knowledge. Fortunately the technology is now available at the desktop level. Figure 3-2 illustrates the history of the document control problem over the last twenty years. Note the similarity, but with a time lag, between this diagram and the one for computing technology (Figure 3-1).

Figure 3-2
Document
Control over
Last 20 years

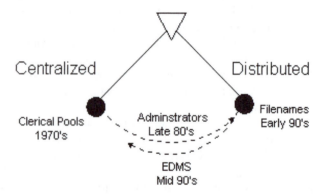

This overview sets the stage for a broader understanding of where document management was, how it has evolved, and ultimately how it arrived at its mainstream place in the business community today.

The Four Elements of Document Management

Documents

In corporate America there are two broad classes of information: data and documents. While current industry estimates indicate that only 10-20% of all corporate knowledge is stored in data, this leaves the remaining information, 80% or more, stored in documents.

Defining and Understanding the Role of Documents

It is important to note that only a small percentage of corporate information assets are in data, and most of it is very well controlled and managed. In fact, most of it resides in IS-controlled databases throughout the organization. And because nearly everyone has access to this corporate resource, databases are a primary concern for the company's information systems groups. However, documents are not usually controlled the same way for two primary reasons. Over the last five years, the term document has undergone a radical change in definition. A document used to be considered a set of words on a page. This definition evolved into including graphics within the document. Graphics were used in documents, but were typically cut-and-pasted into the final document to get the desired layout. This task gave rise to desktop publishing systems, where graphics could be combined with text to more effectively communicate the points being made. As computing power has grown and far more of it is available to the typical user, graphics in a document have become more mainstream.

With the advent of new document integration tools, the definition of a document expanded again. A document can now house graphics, text, and multimedia objects, such as audio or video clips. As pointed out in Chapter 1, a document is no longer the place where words are put onto a page, but rather where a collection of elements or objects related to a particular topic are brought together. Recall the document definition that was offered earlier:

A document is a container which brings together information from a variety of sources, in a number of formats, around a specific topic, to meet the needs of a particular individual.

Documents vs. Data

A second reason documents have not been managed very well is that the focus of the industry has been on managing numbers. Computers were originally built to crunch numbers. This was the underlying value in most systems. For scientists, computers could run complex calculations or even models for simulation. For businesses, they provided automated accounting, billing and payments, reduced headcount, improved accuracy and shortened cycles. All of this dealt with numbers.

This focus has lead to the creation of a variety of databases that run on everything from mainframes to PCs. Managing data in row and column format is very useful if the information can be structured. Corporations have poured billions of dollars into managing their data, all of it with the goal of more effectively managing the business. This has supported, directly and indirectly, the necessary research to improve these tools.

But people are only now beginning to see the extended value of online documents. In trying to manage documents, one quickly discovers that documents do not follow anywhere near the structure required to be effectively managed in a typical database. Another approach is needed, but with the industry focus on data management, document management has been left to a very small number of vendors. With changes in the technology, such as faster hardware and improved networking, as well as better authoring tools, document management is now hitting its stride in the marketplace. Table 3-1 summarizes some of the differences between data management and document management technologies.

Table 3-1: Characteristics: Data vs. Documents

Issue	Data	Documents
Age of Technology	30 Yrs+	<10 Yrs
Relationships	Simple. Structured	Complex, Loose
Workflow	Transaction	Ad-hoc
Datatypes	Numeric	Multimedia
Element Size	Small (Bytes)	Large (Megabytes)
Underlying Model	Relational	Object Oriented

Critical vs. Support

There are many types of data and documents within an organization. It is important to recognize what should and should not be managed, or at least to what degree. This distinction is commonly made in the data world and often overlooked in the document world.

Mission critical data, that set of data or information without which the company cannot function, is usually well defined in every company and organization. Some examples might be payroll, accounting, finance, manufacturing, and sales figures. The corporate IS team usually oversees the development, implementation and support for these mission-critical systems. These systems are designed for around-the-clock operation, have redundant systems, and are routinely backed up and protected.

However, this is not the only type data found in the company. Other organizational data are used in the normal course of business processes to derive the mission critical data or simply support the operation of the organization. Examples might include sales break-downs, project budgets, or revenue "what if" models. As important and useful as these may be, the corporation can run without them. These systems may or may not be backed up, often run only when a specific person is available, and usually have no redundant systems.

Often the distinction between data that is mission critical and that which is support can be determined by where the system resides and who tends to it. Often mission-critical information in the form of data is controlled by IS and runs on larger database applications, such as Oracle, Sybase, DB2, etc., whereas these support systems often run on desktop applications such as Filemaker Pro, Access, Excel, or Lotus 1-2-3. These lower level data-driven systems are usually maintained by each department, with perhaps some support from the central IS team.

When it comes to documents, though, these distinctions are often never made. Nearly everything is routinely considered support, that is until a document is lost or the wrong version of it is used. This is the time when organizations realize just how valuable their documents really are, along with the consequences of not managing them well. In some organizations when this realization is made, the snap judgment becomes "manage everything" but this is not a good decision either. It may be better than doing nothing but not by much. By trying to manage everything, the system becomes too big, too expensive, or too hard to implement.

The right approach is to manage only those documents that are truly mission-critical. Later in the methodology and analysis section of this text, a job task and criticality analysis will be presented to help separate the critical documents from the support class. Critical documents are those which house the information that run the business: how to operate a plant, how to handle payroll, etc. The key is to have a place (i.e., a system) where each document type should be housed.

It should be clear that critical documents belong in an environment where they are rigidly controlled and managed, preferably within an EDMS. Similarly, the documents which are non-critical may be managed in workgroup tools such as CollabraShare or Lotus Notes, while Email may be sufficient for disseminating less formal documents. Of course, Email applications are being used for many other purposes other than passing short documents back and forth. Once again, the goal is to have the right information, in the right system, at the right time.

In looking for a place to house each type of information, one must consider the type of information (data or document?) as well as its classification (mission-critical or support?) as illustrated in Figure 3-3. In this model, each type and classification of information is matched against the best type of system to deal with it. The most important element is to recognize that although this figure is drawn in very clearly defined boxes, the reality is actually a continuum, or shades of gray, where judgments must be made.

Figure 3-3
Data /
Document
Classification
Matrix

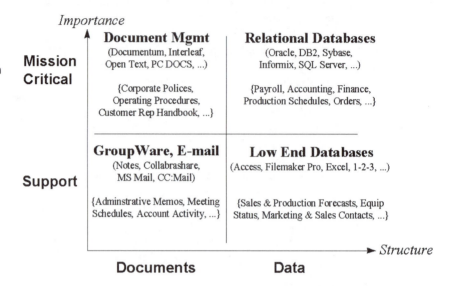

For example, in the gray area between data and documents, where the information is still critical, lies a system that is a mix of both. In a manufacturing environment, there may be documents of many types that need to share data with engineering models built in design. In years past, this information would be physically entered into the documents, leaving the task of updates to a purely manual process. In many companies this need has been filled by a class of systems called Product Data Management (PDM). In some organizations, they have been built using databases and extending them to store documents; in others they have extended an EDMS to handle data. Still others have bought systems from vendors that have developed these hybrid PDM systems into commercial products such as Computervision or MetaPhase. None of these approaches is wrong, just a different way of accomplishing the same objective, but it does show that the lines of distinction are less than clear.

People

A document management system serves a variety of different users. In the context of document management, users fill one of three roles. These roles and their relationships to one another are illustrated in Figure 3-4.

Figure 3-4
Roles in
Document
Management

In most cases any individual will fulfill different roles for different documents. For example, in the case of creating a new document, the creator (author) may have the occasion to locate and use information in another document. This individual is, therefore, fulfilling several roles. However, each of these roles has a different need. As with the distinction between support and critical documents, the responsibility of these varying roles is actually a continuum rather than a distinct set.

Creators

Information creators generate document content. To do this they need access to a variety of information sources such as paper documents, images, electronic documents, Email messages, data and perhaps even the Internet and World Wide Web. They need to be able to search for and locate the desired information quickly. Ideally they need it in a format where it can be reused or re-purposed quickly. In the 1990s, this means in a digital format.

The creators may also get involved with scanning and optical character recognition technology to turn paper into a usable digital form. They may be involved with format conversions to put all the information for one project into a common format or perhaps a limited set of acceptable formats. The creators must also possess tools to allow for writing, editing, laying out and producing this information. These tools can be simple word processors, spreadsheets, or complex page layout systems, even database report writers.

Ultimately the creator must produce a finished document or a set of documents. These documents will always need to be reviewed and approved, a process that may remain in the domain of the creator or be moved into that of the coordinator. Regardless of who is responsible, no mission-critical documents should ever be released without some type of formal release process.

In the past these tools were focused solely at producing paper, now they must be far more flexible. The desired output may be paper *and* online materials in several formats. The job of the creator is changing. Before it was sufficient to be a good technical writer. Today, technical writers must be equally adept at document scanning and conversion, as well as document production for multiple media outputs.

Coordinator

The coordinator, sometimes also called the document "producer," is responsible for a variety of tasks centered around the delivery of a document. They often serve as gatekeepers, ensuring a document is properly reviewed and approved for release. They also function to organize the materials and assemble them into larger document sets, such as chapters into complete manuals. Finally, as coordinators serve as the distributor of documents, they get them to those who need them most: consumers. As coordinators oversee the document production process, they are often involved in the production of paper copies as well, which are still the most widely-used distribution media. The coordinator may also be involved with document conversion, just as the creator was. This person may have to take one input format and produce several outputs, where the creator had the opposite problem.

The title "coordinator" comes from having to bridge the gap between the creator and consumer, taking input from the creator, and to the extent practicable, transforming it to meet the needs of the end user. As the creators' tools have gotten more flexible and capable, and as user demands have changed, so has the role of the coordinator.

Perhaps the largest, most obvious change is the pace of operations. Documents can be generated more quickly, consumers are demanding this new information at their finger tips immediately. This places an enormous burden on the coordinators to streamline the process, but ensure it is correctly executed. For just as the value of getting information out there more quickly has risen, so has the consequence of putting out the wrong information.

Consumer

The consumers are the individuals who take documents, open them, read them, or locate specific content. In some cases, the information is read for training purposes, to understand the theory or concepts behind work processes. However, in most cases, once the consumers find the information they are seeking, they use it to guide their actions.

This process is the point where information is transformed into knowledge or where value is added. It may appear that a creator provides a very valuable service by putting information into a usable form, such as document. But if that document is never used again, then the effort is wasted. The value-adding process around the document exists only if someone uses it to complete a task, to make a decision, or to pursue some form of action.

Consumers often search and navigate through a body of documents, be they paper or electronic media, to find just the specific information they need. Many times the information they seek is there, but they just can't access it in the domain in which they expect. This is why the time spent looking for information by a professional person is widely believed to range between 20 and 40%.

Consumers often rely on the coordinator to get them what they want, and hopefully in a format that matches the way they work or think. This requires consumers to define their needs and clearly articulate them to the coordinator, and this communication is vital if the time spent looking for information is to be minimized.

Processes

After establishing the roles of the individuals involved with documents, the next issue to understand in the document management domain is *process*. Here process refers to a document's lifecycle, the stages that it goes through from conception to consumption. The best place to start looking at this process is at the start of the "knowledge chain." Figure 3-5 illustrates the process of taking data, transforming it into information, and then further transforming information into knowledge.

Figure 3-5
Knowledge
Chain

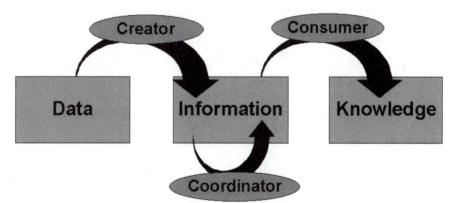

In this simple diagram, the first transformation from data to information occurs in the domain of the creator. The second transformation from information to knowledge occurs in the domain of the consumer. The coordinator is there to make sure that the information gets from the creator to the consumer.

Next, let's look at a typical document lifecycle, Figure 3-6. It begins where the information to be used as source material for a document is first located. The creator then digests this information and

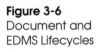

Figure 3-6
Document and
EDMS Lifecycles

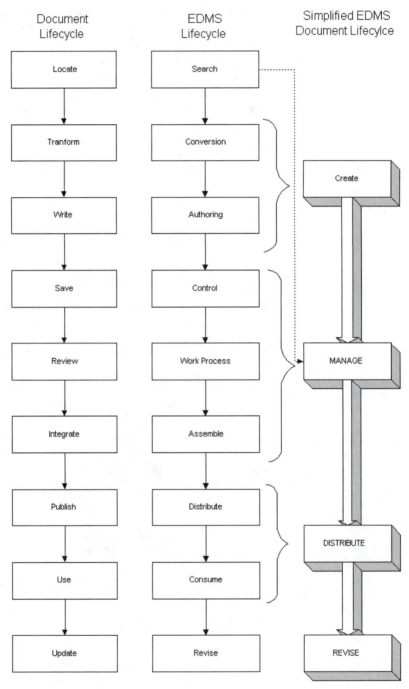

begins to set the thoughts to paper by writing them down. The next step is to "preserve" the document or file it electronically. Such documents are usually sent around for review and then integrated into a larger set of related documentation, such as a complete user's manual. Only then is the document published for wider use. Updates are made after people have used the document for a while and have provided feedback on changes to the author.

Taking this process to the next logical step, the elements in the document lifecycle are mapped into the functions of an EDMS. These include authoring and conversion, followed by document control and workflow processes. Finally, the document is assembled into a larger set of documentation. The overall document is then made available for use by electronic distribution. Revisions are made when change requests have been received from the user community as a whole. The searching process, which is only available for online documents, comes into play in both managing and using a document.

Finally, for discussion purposes only, we have reduced this EDMS process into a simplified diagram, where only the four major phases exist: Create, Manage, Distribute and Revise. This is illustrated in Figure 3-7.

Figure 3-7
Simplified EDMS
Document
Lifecycle

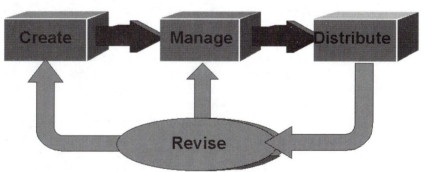

Working Together

In order to achieve any level of effectiveness, it is necessary to understand how the roles of various people and processes involved in the document lifecycle fit together within an EDMS. Overlaying Figures 3-4 and 3-7 shows that the creator comes into play only at the creation phase, the coordinator in the document management phase, and the consumer in the final distribution phase. What is interesting to note here is that, over time, the people who are at the center of this entire process can change roles from time to time. Document management is a fluid process.

For many years document creators drove the process. They determined what was to be created and set about doing it. The final document, always in paper, was provided to the coordinator to get it to those who needed it. It was considered a PUSH model, where the document was pushed from the author out to the consumer, whether they could use it effectively or not.

As this process developed over the years, the coordinator took on a much larger role. Since significant cost was involved in printing and distributing paper, the coordinators slowly took control. They began to dictate standards for layout and presentation. This forced the creators to work more closely with the coordinators. On the other hand, the consumer was still getting what someone else dictated they should get.

This change was supported by cost reductions and advancements in word processing and desktop publishing tools. As this approach grew in popularity, the need for document management tools became apparent. Hence, the document management market for corporate publishing was born and document management systems grew to meet the needs of creators, coordinators, and users. This meant a new focus on storing, editing, and producing documents from the publishing side of the process.

But as the late 1980s and early '90s found corporate America in a more competitive situation, companies reacted. Corporations downsized, rightsized, or generally got "leaner and meaner." They removed layers of middle management, and pushed responsibility down to front-line folks. This meant giving them far more information than ever before. Armed with this information, they could successfully perform without the middle layer of management. Thus, the knowledge worker was born.

From a document management perspective, the problem suddenly changed. No longer was it satisfactory for these workers to receive what ever the authors wanted to send them. They became the power brokers, they would decide what they needed, how, when and where they needed it. The consumer was now driving the process. This is often referred to as a PULL model.

We have seen a similar push in many sectors of our economy. In retail, consumers are now demanding lower prices, increased quality, better services, and greater convenience. These are no longer differentiators; they are merely the price of admission. The document user community is no different. If one IS or management group won't give them the documents they need--where, when and how they need them--they will go to someone else to provide them, inside or outside the company.

The emphasis for documents and document management, then, is clearly on the consumer. This approach, put forth earlier in the this book, is the basis for the entire methodology in Part III, which is built on two related principals:

1. Put the user at the focal point of the create, manage, distribute, revise EDMS process.
2. Start at the downstream side of the process (consumer) and work back towards the origin of the material (creator).

One of the most glaring examples of this is the use of Web technology on both the Internet and INTRAnets. The Web belongs to those who use it, and not necessarily those who created it. If a Web site has content that meets the need of the intended audience, it will be successful. If the site does not have the right content, presentation, and organization for the targeted audience, it will perish.

Technology

In the document management space, the items one can touch, feel, and see are the documents, people and processes. Technology should be invisible to these issues, at least as much as possible. However, it would be remiss not to recognize that technology is an enabler that has, in part, brought about the document management problem at the same time that it now offers a solution.

With the power of the desktop PCs doubling and the cost halving every 18 months, a powerful PC running a Graphical User Interface (e.g., Windows or Mac OS) is common on most business desktops. This has put the technology within reach of almost everyone. The price-to-performance ratio drops making far more power available at a much lower cost. Processes that used to take hours now take seconds.

Putting this type of power on nearly every desk has laid the foundation for a significant convergence of document management technologies which have allowed EDMS, in all its incarnations, to take hold in the mainstream market. The four key technological elements that have converged to give rise to effective document management are illustrated in Figure 3-8.

Imaging

The first technology besides word processing that was known to have a profound effect on document management is imaging. In fact, imaging was synonymous with document management for most of the 1980s. Document management was considered the process of converting paper to digital images, and then indexing those images for search, retrieval and printing processes.

Often the systems used were very proprietary and very expensive. To be able to quickly retrieve and display an image is a very com-

Figure 3-8
Converging
Technologies
for Document
Management

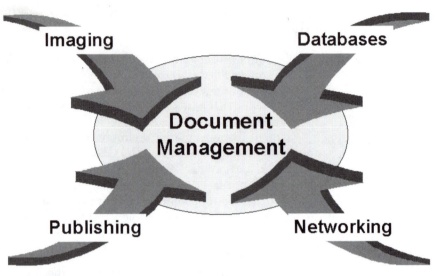

putationally-intensive task. Special add-on boards for graphics acceleration, high resolution monitors, and large storage devices all demanded solutions beyond the mainstream. Today however, the typical PC has enough computational power, while screens and video cards of sufficient resolution are now low enough in cost such that images can be processed readily on a desktop.

This is not to say that custom hardware and software are not a good investment if imaging is the bulk of what's being done, and there is still a place for such specialized solutions. Another breakthrough is the cost of scanners and OCR software. For many years, scanners were in the tens of thousands of dollars; now scanners can be purchased for a few hundred dollars and OCR software can be run on a typical PC rather than on workstations. So the reduction in cost of many imaging components for scanning, document archival, and retrieval make it still a viable part of an EDMS, often as a complete subsystem.

Databases

Similar to imaging technologies, the database market has been able to leverage the lower cost of computing power to work its way down to most desktops. The development and deployment of many successful client-server database systems have helped move many databases from the mainframe platform down to workgroup servers. This has also brought the skills of database administration and use down to many workgroups, rather than in isolation within the corporate IS department.

The improvement in speed and data storage in many databases finally make them practical to consider for document management. These databases can handle gigabytes or terabytes of storage, allowing them to handle hundreds of thousands or even millions of documents. The indexing capability within these database applications can also make searching and access to the documents very quick. This prevents the document management system from adversely affecting a user's productivity.

Finally, the cost of licenses for an enterprise wide RDBMS application is now under $1,000 per seat, and in some cases well under this figure. This makes EDMS systems based on these tools attractively priced. But even at $1,000 or less per seat, many people still see this as an expensive solution, so we need to ask: What is the cost of losing a document or using the wrong information in some job task? Or, how much time and money is wasted each year looking for a piece of information? If a job pays $25,000 a year, it only takes 4% of that employee's time to be wasted to pay for the per-seat license.

Publishing

As an economy we are producing far more information today than we ever have before. There is a word processor on every desktop PC and very likely someone at that desk who knows how to use it effectively. If users believe they possess information which is important, odds are they will write it down, creating in effect a new document. The cost of creating this electronic material is minimal, as document information can be created and edited numerous times without having to re-key it, while production and revision cycles are shortened.

As publishing abilities have grown, so has the cost of printing paper. The demand for paper is up significantly over the past three years and with this new demand, relative costs. Considering that paper is a limited natural resource, it is not unreasonable to assume its price will continue to go up and, as a result, organizations have been turning to electronic publishing in record numbers.

The tools to generate electronically-viewable documents used to be cost prohibitive, cumbersome, and proprietary, even as short as eighteen months ago. But the invasion of the World Wide Web, along with its open standard of HTML, has transformed this market nearly overnight. Some conversion tools for taking word processing documents to HTML have dropped by 50% or more in the last six months, and many are now shareware or free vendor-supported products. And the capability for so many people to easily, cheaply, and quickly generate new or updated HTML content, and put it into many different forms, has provided some of the needed technology for full-scale EDMS deployment.

Networking

Tying computers together began with Local Area Networks (LAN) to connect workgroups, then offices, and finally entire enterprises, as networks enabled the sharing of vital resources, such as printing and file services. In doing so, they truly changed our ability to share information, especially in digital form, and because of their information sharing capabilities, they fostered more informal communications with tools such as Email.

Networking has, unfortunately, also had a pivotal role in creating the document management problem, so hopefully through EDMS technology, it can now partially solve it. The current networking infrastructure allows us to move large documents, those containing graphics, images and multi-media objects quickly and easily across the organization. The capability of this network allows for the effective deployment of client-server based document management systems or repositories.

As computing technology becomes more and more distributed, the continual increases in networking technology will allow document repositories to be built in key locations, yet be accessed from remote locations. This will allow the power and flexibility of desktop computing and networks to be leveraged throughout the organization. It will also support the control mechanisms of a more centralized set of document repositories. Networks are now fast enough so that users won't know, nor care, if the documents they seek are on the server across the hall or accessed from a site half-way around the world.

The second major advantage of an EDMS provided by networks is that it can provide a complete electronic publishing solution. It is actually ironic that most networks originally resulted from the desire to effectively utilize printers, but now these very same networks will greatly reduce the use of such organizational resources. Information can be published almost immediately, and electronic media offers many benefits over paper, as outlined in the previous chapter. For example, a typical LAN, running at 10 Mbits per second, makes client-server applications including document management and electronic publishing practical. What is interesting here is that wide-area networks (WANs) and the Internet are now bringing together company offices from around the world, as in the case of Silicon Graphics, Inc. which maintains an HTML Internet-based solution for conveying most organizational information and related documents. Even though in such environments many users access these networks at slower speeds of, say, 28.8 Kbps, the World Wide Web continues to see phenomenal growth. Our current corporate information systems infrastructure, tied to Web-based resources, has given us a sufficient foundation upon which to build effective document control and delivery systems using EDMS technologies.

Summary

As our global economy continues to put competitive pressures on corporations, they will continue to restructure themselves as jobs are reengineered. And more and more emphasis will be placed on improving productivity. Workers will move from simply being *doers* to *thinkers*, and therefore require more information, more quickly, with greater accuracy than ever before. This will place a higher emphasis on information-container (i.e., document) storage, retrieval, access, control, and security.

Additionally, EDMS processes will be reviewed, revised, and streamlined to squeeze every ounce of productivity out of them. Since most business processes are centered around documents and people, these elements will continue to be the focal point for the successful document management solution providers, those folks who recognize that the document management problem is one of achieving an effective mix of documents, people, processes, and technology.

EDMS Technology

An electronic document management system is not a single entity but rather a collection of different, converging technologies. These technologies can be categorized into six distinct functional groupings as follows:

- Repository (Management includes Security)
- Conversion (Electronic and Imaging)
- Searching and Indexing (includes Retrieval)
- Creation (Authoring)
- Workflow (Routing)
- Distribution (Paper & Online Viewing)

Not every EDMS solution uses all of these components, nor does every document within an EDMS utilize these functions. There is, however, a relationship between these groupings. In some cases, the simple model of Create-Manage-Distribute, works well to show these relationships. However, if the process involves conversion, the question becomes where does the conversion step go? Between the create and manage, or between the manage and distribute stages? Furthermore, the process may vary by individual document, not just document classes.

To understand how these various EDMS technologies interrelate, it is best to consider them from the view of their primary users, or the roles these users play. This is not an absolute, however, since many technologies or functions cut across several job roles, but it does serve as a good framework in which to explore the technology. The layers of this model match the roles or types of users presented earlier: Consumers, Creators, Coordinators. Also included in the Coordinators' layer is the EDMS development and support teams. The pyramid in Figure II-1 shows this framework for mapping EDMS roles and technology. The roles are positioned along the vertical axis. Note that the bottom or foundation layer of the pyramid is the domain of the IS department, and is shown for completeness only.

Figure II-1
EDMS
Technology
Framework

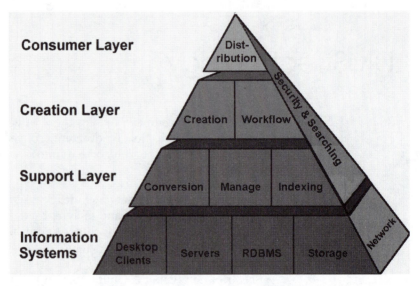

The following six chapters explore and detail the technology involved in the three upper layers. These chapters also provide a host of considerations and issues for using these elements in constructing an EDMS for your own organization.

4

Repository

A repository is a single place where objects are stored and controlled. In the context of this book, the term object is used to refer to a document or element within a document, that can and must be managed on its own. This element is usually a file, but the size, type, and format of the file is unimportant. This object (file) can be a word processing document, graphic, spreadsheet or a compound, complex document. This file may also be an element of a larger document. For example, it may contain only one section of a chapter from a manual. It could just as easily be the entire book.

The repository within an EDMS exists within the support layer and works in conjunction with the conversion, indexing, searching and security functions in the support layer. It is also acted upon by the authoring layer in the creation or workflow functions. Depending upon the actual system architecture employed, it may be also be accessed from the user layer by document consumers in the viewing function.

Repository Architecture

A typical repository has four primary parts, which exist in client and server applications, within a database, and in file system storage.

The user of such a system will usually only see the client application and know there is a server version. The database and file system are hidden from the user through the custom application. Figure 4-1 shows this architecture.

Figure 4-1
Typical EDMS
Architecture

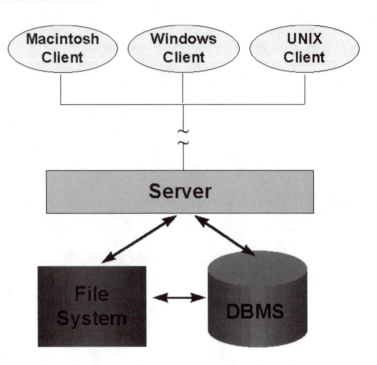

Client Application

The client application can be a standalone system or integrated into a larger system. Most repository vendors provide a standalone client application which can be used "out of the box," and run across multiple platforms. Most of these vendors also have some type of application programming interface (API) to allow building a custom client application. Many vendors provide working models of a custom interface using popular 4GL tools with their repositories which can reduce the time required to develop a custom application. A typical repository client is shown in Figure 4-2.

With the dominance the Web has on all information systems today, it is also exerting an influence on the client applications for the repository. The debate is focused on "fat" clients or "thin" clients. Here, fat refers to the proprietary client available from most vendors today, whereas the thin client refers to the use of a Web browser that will interact with the repository. This is accomplished via HTML

Figure 4-2
Typical
Repository
Client
Application
(Interleaf)

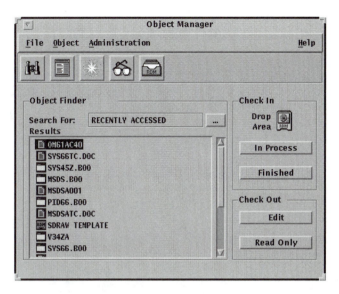

forms, a common gateway interface (CGI) and the repository's applica-tion programming interface (API). Thin clients are usually limited by the functionality and capability of the extensions to HTML that are used, and the new programming environments of "applets" (such as those made possible through JAVA and ACTIVE X). A thin client is presented in Figure 4-3.

When using a standalone client application, it becomes incum-bent on the user to know when to access the repository and when to access the local file system. If the user cannot discern when to use the repository or forgets to use it, valuable time can be wasted or critical documents can go uncontrolled.

The client, or its critical functionality, can also be integrated into other applications or systems. In one example the system performs its functions, perhaps searching and retrieving results. In the background a repository may be accessed to retrieve the desired documents or information. This is the ultimate in integration, where the user never sees, knows, or even cares that there is a repository.

In a slightly different approach, the client application can be used to intercept the calls to the operating system for files from desktop applications. Most vendors are using or are moving towards Open Doc-ument Management API (ODMA) as the standard way to access repos-itories. This standard ensures that any desktop application can interact with any repository client regardless of vendor. In this scenario, the FILE OPEN, SAVE, and FIND commands are usually intercepted and routed through to the repository. This is shown in Figure 4-4. The user

Figure 4-3
Web
 Repository
Client
(Open Text)

may see the client application or a tailored version of it at this point. Users will usually see little impact on their day to day work.

The widespread use of ODMA compliant desktop applications can allow users to perform their normal tasks without having to "remember" to access the repository. This is true for both saving and retrieving files. It also allows repositories that have been coupled to workflow engines to ensure that documents are routed to the correct individuals without relying on the author or editor to remember that step. The most effective repository will be the one the user never sees.

However, the repository and desktop applications are not fully integrated yet. Therefore, there is an advantage right now to building a custom interface; it can be tailored to meet the exact needs of the intended user. Functionality that is not needed by the users can be removed to simplify the interface. Also, the interface can be organized, labeled, and presented to fit the user's needs. Development of a custom interface or integration into an existing system can seem like an unnecessary and expensive task at first. However, when an interface can be simplified or embedded into a familiar application, focused on the job at hand, and uses familiar terminology, training and implementation costs can be dramatically reduced. If this system is to be rolled out to

Figure 4-4
Desktop
Application
Integration with
Repository Client
(PC DOCS)

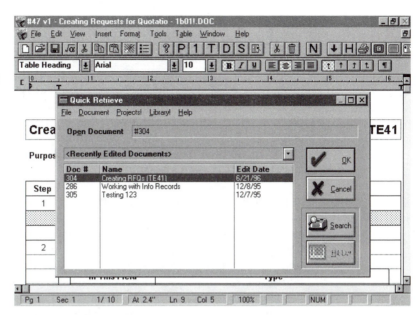

hundreds or thousands of users at once, the time saved in training each of these individuals can easily pay for the development of a custom interface or the integration into an another application.

Server Application

The second major element of the repository is the server application. Depending upon the client server architecture used by the vendor, the server can be simply the database server engine or a completely separate application, commonly referred to as two-tier or three-tier client server architectures. The differences are the same as with any client server system: tradeoffs between cost, performance, and capability. In some two-tier architectures the client is forced to do more of the work and is therefore "fatter."

In a true client server environment, the server application is the real work horse of the system. In a repository the server communicates with clients, the database, and file system in order to complete its tasks. It brokers information and requests from the clients, queries or updates the databases, stores and retrieves files from the file system It is the part of the system that, in conjunction with the database and file system, provides the three major repository functions: library services, version control, and configuration management. As mentioned above, these will be detailed in later sections. In some systems, the server may also "house" the workflow engine.

Database

The database is that part of the repository which stores all the information about the documents. Information about information, or in the case of a repository, "information about documents," is commonly referred to as *metadata* or information *attributes*. This information can include common items such as the date, author, and title of the document. The database may store other information about the document that is not provided by the user directly. Some examples may be draft or version numbers, or in the case of a document set, which chapters belong to a particular manual.

The database used in a repository can be either flatfile, relational, or object-oriented. For the most part, though, systems based on flatfile databases are no longer in widespread use. Currently most systems use relational databases, with object oriented slated to replace those in the coming years. The relational databases used by most EDMS vendors are the market leaders, such as Oracle, Sybase, Informix, and Microsoft's SQL Server, although some use proprietary DBMS applications. Some EDMS applications, however, are database independent, allowing a customer to choose which database engine they prefer, allowing the EDMS to adhere to each corporation's existing computing standards.

Still, today's robust relational databases are designed to store data elements that are typically of a fixed type and size. These databases can handle huge volumes of these elements totaling gigabytes or even terabytes. Compared with documents, however, each of these data elements are tiny. Generally speaking, databases are optimized to handle large volumes of small data elements. Therefore, the document storage is left to the secure file system, while the attributes are stored in the database.

File Systems

Today's operating systems and file servers are optimized to handle files. These systems are far better adapted to store files than a database. It is for this reason that most repositories are built with both a database and a file system. The database houses the metadata and other information about the document, including a pointer to the file or filename. The file system stores the file (document). This pointer is the critical link tying these two elements together, and this connection is under the direct control of the server application.

A secondary consideration beyond the issue of the best storage capability lies in document integrity. When both a database and a file system are used, the potential exists to lose synchronization between these two system pieces. If a database entry or file system gets corrupted, synchronizing the repository can become difficult. This multi-part repository also requires two sets of backup tools, one for the database and one for the file system. If the repository uses only a database the backup and synchronization issues are minimal.

Despite this complexity, most repositories are built on both a database and file system combination. If the repository is to be secure, the database and file systems must be also secured and controlled. For the database, this security is contained within the products themselves. However, for the file system to be secure, it must rely on a secured or controlled access system. For this reason most EDMS repositories have been derived from the UNIX environment, which offers greater security. Only with the advent of Windows NT have repositories been capable of moving off UNIX systems, while retaining the necessary security and control over the file system. The market dominance of Microsoft Windows and the price performance point of Intel based systems are making Windows NT a force in the repository end of the EDMS marketplace.

Scalability

An important consideration in the design of the repository is the ability to scale up to meet the needs of an entire organization. The more information that is controlled and managed, the greater the number of people that will want access to it. This "new found" availability will drive more and more requests from the system. Also, as will be discussed in the methodology part of this text, the goal is to bring on one part of the organization after another, where the size of the system will grow exponentially with the addition of users.

More and more users will need to control more and more documents, and do so across wider and wider audiences within the company. This will put severe demands on document storage and retrieval, as well as on networks. It will be important to look at the repository design for features that will support this growth.

Document storage and retrieval performance is tied to processing power and to database performance. In terms of computing power, we must look at the platforms supported: will that hardware provide the necessary power? Can the system take advantage of Symmetric Multi-Processor (SMP) machines? In terms of database performance, is the application built on a three-tier client-server architecture so the server and database processing can be divided and each server tuned for optimum performance?

The networking issue, primarily one of bandwidth will need to be addressed by either some type of file compression/decompression, or distributed data. The compression/decompression issue shifts the problem back to computing power not just on the server but also on the client, resulting in a potentially expensive solution. The more direct approach is to distribute the data across multiple servers within the organization. However if the data sets cannot be easily segmented, then they all may need to be placed on multiple servers, demanding support for replication. The question then becomes one of replicating the files, far and away the biggest data set, or both the files and the metadata stored in the database, another costly proposition.

Looking past the organization's immediate requirements and into the future will help identify issues that might affect the long term architecture of the system. If the entire company resides in one building the problem may be non-existent. However, if the organization is spread throughout the world, with hundreds of offices in dozens of states and countries, this issue is very real. It is also incumbent to look at what the repository vendors are doing as well; by the time the problem is big enough that the system must upgraded, the vendor may have offered a cost-effective solution.

Object Oriented Model for Document Management

In implementing a repository most vendors have built an object-oriented model for handling documents. They have used the basic concepts of abstract data typing, inheritance, object identification, and polymorphism to deliver many of the capabilities discussed in this chapter. This approach benefits both developers and users of an EDMS. However, the details of object-oriented concepts and models are beyond the scope of this book.

The results of these concepts are best illustrated through examples. One example of inheritance and abstract data typing in a repository allows users to create document classes, whereby all documents are defined as belonging to that class which has similar characteristics, such as key attributes or security permissions. This even allows end users to build "basic objects" and then leverage those entities by building classes of objects on top of the basic ones. Object classes allow system-wide changes to be implemented easily and quickly without having to manipulate each document or object individually.

The fact that an object is not restricted to a single file allows for multiple files to be stored as one object. This is important when there is a need to store the content of one file in multiple electronic formats or languages. It also allows workflows to be stored in the repository so they can be managed. Furthermore, workflows are often tied to document classes, and involve other objects such as route steps and groups of users.

Object identity is used to assign each object (document, file or groupings of these) a unique I.D. This allows these objects to be referenced by other documents without having to be copied, creating the problem of multiple "master" documents. Relationships and virtual documents make use of this concept.

Some of the most powerful concepts made available by the object model in document management systems are provided to the developer. Since they are very tool- and vendor-specific they are not covered here. However, it is noteworthy that the capabilities presented often make it faster, cheaper and easier to implement new functionality or customize existing systems than working within traditional environments. It also allows the vendor's development team to add new functionality more quickly as well.

Server Functionality

A repository is, of course, the core of any EDMS. It contains and controls all the documents and information about those documents. The repository can also drive the business work processes, as well as information sharing and distribution. The typical document repository residing on a server provides three primary functions:

- Library Services
- Version Control
- Configuration Management

Secondary functions provided by some repositories are:

- Conversion
- Searching and Indexing
- Workflow

These additional functions are not discussed here but are presented in Chapters 5, 6 and 8 respectively.

Library Services

Library Services are comprised of an entire set of functions within the EDMS application. Library services are also so-named because they typically model many of the services users would find at a public or private library system. The "librarians" in these institutions perform a variety of functions, including:

- Check-out and return (Check-in) of books and materials
- Verification of complete borrowing privileges

- Assistance in searching for books via computer catalogs and indexes.

These "library" functions should be familiar to most people and will therefore provide a general framework for the discussion of repositories that follows.

Check-In

The most basic function provided by the repository is the ability to enter or literally *check in* a new document. Upon receiving the request, the repository will verify that the individual providing the document is authorized to do so. Once the user providing the document has been verified, the repository must then determine where this information will be stored. This location is referred to as an information "vault." Vaults are usually physical directories within a secured file system, which is controlled by the repository.

The storage location can be determined in one of several ways. In some repositories the document's storage location is determined by the repository itself. In others it is based on rules established when the repository is constructed. Perhaps all documents of a particular type will be stored in one specific vault. Some documents are directed to a vault by user input during check-in. Finally, some documents are stored via rules which use metadata to define the appropriate vault for storage.

Once the file storage location is known, several actions occur in sequence. First, an entry for the document is written to the database portion of the repository. Second, the physical file is transferred to the vault. Figure 4-5 shows the relationship between the database, the vault, metadata and the document being checked in. In some repositories, the last action to occur will be the generation of a full text index of the document and the merging of this index with the complete repository's index. The details of this process are covered in Chapter 6, dealing with searching and indexing.

Attributes

Checking a document into a repository ensures that it is safely stored. However, simply storing a document is not sufficient for building a usable repository. It is equally important to be able to retrieve this document. Therefore, the check in process must include a step which fills out a card catalog. In the repository this information is the metadata. The term metadata usually implies that the data about the document was derived from the document itself. In document management this is very often not true. A document may be of the type procedure, but never contain the word "procedure." Therefore, for the purposes of

Figure 4-5
Actions
during the
Check-In
Process

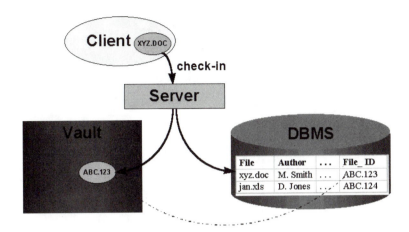

the library services discussion we will use the term "attribute" to describe this data about a document.

There are often two types of attributes. The first are the standard ones that would apply to virtually any document such as: author, title, subject, date, type, etc. The other type are custom and usually specific to each type or class of document. Attributes for an automotive repair procedure document, for example, might include: model, make, year, engine size, etc. This information is critically important to being able to accurately search the entire repository and quickly retrieve the exact document desired. An example of a document check-in screen is shown is Figure 4-6.

The implementation of each repository's attributes is different. Some repositories have a limited number of attribute fields. This can be an issue for some implementations. Other repositories allow for custom attributes, but they are custom to all documents, not specific document types. This is important to understand because a number of fields presented to a user for search and retrieval might not make sense. To extend the automotive example above, service procedures may require entering another document in the system on the repair of, say, a transmission. For this document, the model year and engine size may be applicable, but not the exact body style, and users who initiate a search for a related document must recognize this fact.

To facilitate the search, retrieval, and manipulation of documents, users must adhere to a standard set of values for an attribute. Most systems allow for the creation of a list of acceptable values, where "pick lists" are used to select the correct item for an attribute. In addition to controlling the values used in a field, it may also be important for that field to have multiple values, a feature often found in only higher-end document management repository products. Again, extending the

Figure 4-6
Check-in
Screen Showing
Attributes
(Documentum)

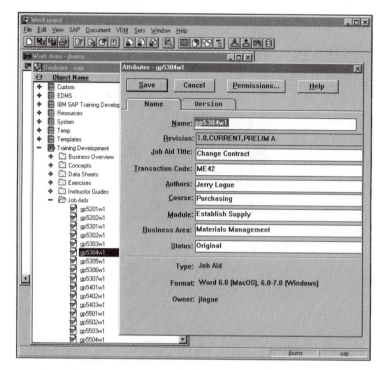

automotive example, suppose the repair procedure applies to both 1994 and 1995 model years? Without multi-value attributes, the document is entered twice or a second year field is added. If the document is added again, the underlying premise of a single master document is compromised. If a second year field is added, then the user must know which one to search or search both, not a good situation.

One last area for discussion of attributes is their connection with revisions. Often times attributes apply to a document over its life and rarely change. When they do change, they usually apply to all of the document's "ancestors" or revisions. There are cases where this is not sufficient and attributes may be different from one revision to the next. In this situation, the attributes must be revision specific. They inherit initial values from their predecessors, but can be modified. For example, in our automotive procedure the first revision may apply to the make "A." However, the next revision may apply only to make "B," the third revision may apply to make "A" again. If the attribute *make* did not have revision specific values the fact that revision two applies only to make "B" would be lost. It's unusual for attributes to require revision specific values, but it may be important for some organizations to have this repository feature.

In looking towards attribute management in the future, there are things that can be done today to ease the transition when the EDMS finally arrives. Many desktop applications offer a summary block, such as Microsoft Word as shown in Figure 4-7. These summary blocks enable the user to enter "attributes" about the document. These attributes can then be searched by many application tools available today. It is important to recognize that many repositories can extract the information from these summary fields and place them into attribute fields during check-in.

Figure 4-7
Desktop
Application
Summary Block
("attributes")

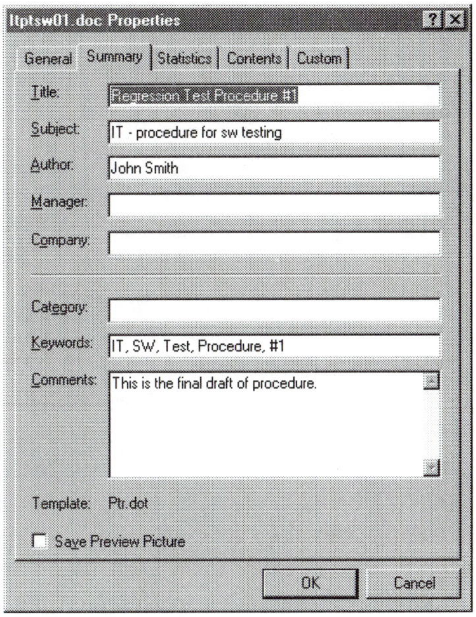

Filenames

Filenames are in essence the way documents are managed in a file system. Most individuals and many organizations have derived ways to name files so the contents can be identified without opening the document. These schemes can be simple or complex, and some workgroups have formally documented these schemes as standards. And trying to fit a complex naming algorithm into the DOS constraint of eleven character filenames is challenging. An example of a formal filenaming scheme using this pattern is shown in Figure 4-8.

The use of attributes that allow one to describe a document make filenames unimportant within an EDMS. While this is true, there are some considerations to be taken into account before eliminating any existing conventions or deciding not to create any new ones. Key ques-

Figure 4-8
Filenaming
Scheme

Filename: ABBCDEEE.doc				
Item	**Type**	**Description**	**Allowable Values**	
A	Alpha	Originating Division	A - Accounting D - Design E - Engineering *etc*	M - Marketing P - Production S - Sales
BB	Numeric	Originating Department	01 through 20	
C,D	Alpha	Doc Type, Subdoc Type	C - Corp Policies	A - Administrative G - General H - Human Resources
			L - Letters	A - Action E - Emergency I - Information
			M - Memos	G - General
			P - Procedures	D - ShutDown E - Emergency N - Normal S - Special U - StartUp
EEE	Numeric	Sequence Number	000 through 899 900 and up - reserved	

tions at this point are: When will the documents come under the control of the repository? And are there times in the document's lifecycle when the document will be outside the control of the repository?

The first consideration deals with the authors of these documents. Will they immediately check in a document to the repository after it is created? If so then filenames are unimportant. However, in many situations documents may live a life before they are entered into a repository. While having documents exist outside the control of a repository is not advisable, it is in fact a common requirement. In this situation, the filename is important, otherwise it will be difficult to keep track of which files are which within the operating system. Without a filenaming convention, a user would have to open one file after another until the desired file is located. This is a time consuming task which adds no value to the business's goals or objectives. If documents are named according to a strict standard, then often times attribute information can be derived by parsing the filename during check-in, thereby reducing redundant data entry.

Another consideration is whether the document may need to be checked out of the repository and left outside of it for a significant period of time. For example, in some workgroups files may need to be transferred to other parts of the organization where an EDMS is not in use. This means the files must be named in such a way that the user on the receiving end can distinguish one file from the next. Ultimately, the file is likely to be returned to the original workgroup. If the filename does not adhere to a standard, it may be difficult or even impossible to reconcile it with the original document in the EDMS.

In some repositories, filenames are assigned by the system and the user has no control over them. In cases where documents will not live outside the system, this is of little concern. However, in the case where the documents may have to exist outside the control of the repository, this is vitally important. In other repositories, filenames are used as the object names in the database. For still others, filenames are separate entities from object names. This is an important decision point in evaluating the fit of a repository to an organization's needs.

If an organization decides that having a filenaming convention is important there are a few items to keep in mind while developing this convention. First is not to include information in the filename that will change often, with revision numbers being a good example. Also, the standard should adhere to the lowest common denominator in terms of operating system limitations. DOS, for example, is the most restrictive in terms of file-naming conventions. Finally, if the repository is capable of launching the correct application when retrieving a document, the file extension, usually the last three characters after the dot, must be reserved for determining the application. For example, a Word document usually ends with the "DOC" extension. It is advisable, then, to make the filename complete in and of itself, and not to rely on directory structures to infer filename information. Files are often moved and if a document is moved outside its correct parent directory, it will need to be opened and evaluated to determine its content.

Filenaming conventions or standards are often the first step in a document management system. Even if an EDMS is years away, developing and implementing an intelligent and complete filenaming convention can be extremely valuable. Documents will remain organized and categorized, and thereby effectively managed until a formal system can be put in place. It is advisable to conduct training and periodic audits to ensure the standards are being followed. Many times filenames are used to drive the check-in and attributes for an EDMS only to discover that many files do not conform to the standard and hand-loading of documents is required.

Check-Out

Checking out a document is just like the check-out process found at a library. A librarian may assist patrons in locating the books they want using an online catalog. Users present a valid ID, and the librarian records their book selections, which they can take with them. In some cases, the specific books can only be checked out by certain people, so the librarian checks a list of authorized people before deciding whether or not to allow one to take the book. If users are not authorized to remove the book, they may be allowed only to make a photocopy of it.

The check-out process from the repository is virtually identical to that of the library. It usually begins with a search of the catalog for the desired document. This search may include an attribute search, a full text query, or both. Upon check-in the document was indexed by both attributes and a full text index to facilitate this retrieval. (The details of searching and indexing are covered in Chapter 6). After the search is completed a list of documents is then returned. This list usually offers two options, the ability to view the attribute information or view the document. In this way, the desired document can be located quickly and easily.

In actually checking out a document from a repository, there are usually several options available, because when dealing with electronic files there are usually greater requirements than simply "taking the document home." The options for check-out are generally:

- creating a copy of the document, or
- creating a controlled (editable) copy of the document.

In both of these operations, a copy of the file is transferred from the secured vault to a predetermined location on the user's or another's specified machine. This location is part of the "system configuration" for each user. An example of a check-out screen is shown in Figure 4-9.

Figure 4-9
Document
Check out
(PC DOCS)

When a copy of the document is created (transferred) this process is similar to the action of copying an electronic file within an operating system. Depending upon user permissions and document status, this file may be fully functional, or it may be marked "read only." Read-only is often used to signify that this document is not a controlled copy from the repository, and therefore may not be able to be checked back in. Of course a user can still make changes, then simply save the document with a new name. However, this new document cannot be checked in as a new version of the original, but can be checked in as an entirely new original document.

Appearing similar to the user at the desktop level, the controlled copy of the document is actually different than the copied version, but these differences are contained within the repository. Generally, the document is marked as "in edit" or locked within the repository. This ensures that all future requests to edit the same document are rejected, until such time as the document is "returned" or checked back into the repository. In this way, no document ends up being edited by more than one person at the same time. The repository will usually indicate to those requesting the document who has it "checked out" for editing so they can contact that individual if desired, which preserves the overall integrity of the system.

Some vendors create a new version when the document is checked out. Others when the edited document is returned to the repository. Checking out a document, the versioning model and when to create a new version of a document are usually tightly integrated. Every vendor's repository approaches these tasks a little differently. These documents are also closely coupled with workflow processes used in conjunction with a repository. More detail about these editing and revision or versioning processes will be covered in later sections.

Security

Security is also an integral part of any repository. Opening up the repository to "anyone" to do "anything" offers only a small advantage over using a common, shared file system. This security begins with the use of a secured file system under the control of the repository. Although the files are stored in a common file system, only those with access to the repository itself will be the users who can read, write, or delete these files. So with the file system secured, the only way to access documents is to go through the repository. This provides the first and most basic level of security: controlled access. Usually such users are given login names and passwords in order to gain access to the repository.

Beyond this first level of security are generally two methods of control. The first, and most simple, is to use the operating system's file permissions. This is often limited to read, write, and delete privileges. While this may be adequate in some cases, more control is often desired and required of a document management system.

Specific controls around the check-in, check-out, and versioning processes themselves become critical. Access controls are provided for basic functions and usually the repository will allow adding additional functions and access controls. Some of the basic types of access are outlined in Table 4-1.

Table 4-1: Types of Document Access

Access	Description
None	No access to documents or attributes
Browse	Can see that the document exists and see its attributes, but not the document itself.
View / Copy	Can see the document exists, its attributes, as well as open and view the document. Copies of the document can be made to user's machine or other designated location. In some systems these functions are separated.
Edit	Can make changes to a document in the repository. This includes both editing the contents of the document and it's attributes. Editing the contents usually requires copying the file from the repository to a local file system. Changes are made and the document returned to the repository. Attributes are edited directly in the repository.
Delete	Can remove a document from the repository entirely. Removing a document can have impact on relationships to / from that document. The goal of repository is to control documents; removing documents should be considered a highly unusual task.
Administration	Can accomplish administrative tasks such as archiving or moving files between vaults, or changing access privileges. The administration function is almost always assigned to the creator (user who checked the document in) and also to a system or department administrator.

Access controls require information about two distinct entities: documents and people. Document access controls can be specific to an individual document or an entire class of documents. This portion of the process is usually provided via users and groups. Some examples follow:

1. Let's review the access controls for the automotive procedure example presented earlier. Since this is a class of documents, these access controls apply to an entire group of documents, not only to an individual document. It is desirable for anyone in engineering to be able to make new procedures or edit ex-

isting ones. It is also important for anyone using the system to view these documents.

2. A second example might be the new test procedure John Brown just created. Since it is a new test procedure, John wants to limit control. He only wants engineers in the Test and Evaluation group (within engineering) to be able to see and copy this document. Only he can edit this document. All engineers can know this document exists.

3. Mary Smith is the financial administrator for the engineering department and has to create the departmental budget. She wants everyone in the department to know it exists, but wishes to limit viewing access to her department and other financial administrators in the company. Only her boss, the department manager, and she can edit it.

Table 4-2 provides the access control list for the examples given above. Below that, Figure 4-10 shows setting access control rights in a repository.

Table 4-2: Example Access Control Lists

Example	Example 1	Example 2	Example 3
Doc. Class	Procedure	Procedure	Budget
Document(s)	All	test123.doc	dept.xls
Users & Groups			
SYSTEM (All Users)	View / Copy	None	None
. . .			
ENGINEERING DEPT			
Eng Mgr	Edit	Browse	Edit
Engineers	Edit	Browse	Browse
. . .			
T&E Engineers		View / Copy	
. . .			. . .
Eng 7 (John Brown)		Edit	
. . .			. . .
Eng Fin Adm (Mary Smith	View / Copy	None	Edit
FINANCIAL ADM	None	None	View / Copy
. . .			

The access controls presented above are the basic ones found in a repository. When workflow is integrated into the EDMS the access controls must include more categories, such as: new revision, review, and approval. These are covered in Chapter 8 on Workflow.

Figure 4-10
Setting Access
Controls
(Documentum)

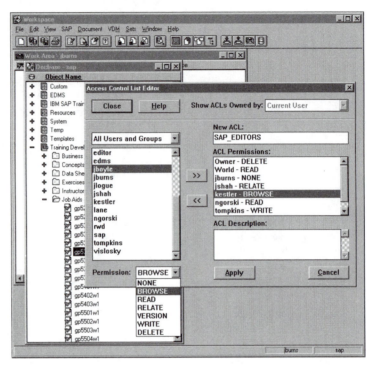

Users and Groups

Users and groups refers to the act of assigning and organizing individuals into logical bunches. An organization chart in a company defines a set of users, and the groups to which they belong. If there are a large number of individuals, they are then organized into a hierarchical structure of groups. At the highest level there may be a division and within that several departments. Each department may consist of several work teams, and each teams consists of several individuals.

Beyond the typical hierarchical structure, organizations often have teams for things like continuous improvement, best practices or projects. These are teams where members are pulled from across the organizational boundaries. These are often referred to as "functional groups." Another type of group not in the hierarchy may be classified by discipline, such as "engineers" or "CPAs" across a department or even an entire company.

Groups are used to simplify things like access-control or workflow-routing by using a predetermined, logical grouping of individuals that are responsible for completing a particular task or function. In our examples above, we had groups which followed the organization chart: the Engineering Dept, Test and Evaluation Engineers, and those that followed cross functional groups: Financial Adminstrators. It is easier to establish and manage access control via these defined groupings versus maintaining a list of individuals.

It is almost never a good idea to use an individual person for assigning access control rights. The better approach is to create a group for each job function within the organization because people often change jobs and move around inside an organization. They may retain their roles in cross-functional areas but change in the overall hierarchy. If individual names are used, the maintenance to keep the lists accurate and up-to-date can be overwhelming. By using groups corresponding to jobs, it can be as simple as changing the person assigned to a particular job, since most access control is actually with the job, not the individual.

All repositories provide a facility to create new users and groups, and users can usually belong to multiple groups similar to an organization chart, where people belong to teams, which in turn form departments, and so on. Groups can therefore be nested to form the same type of setup. Figure 4-11 shows a typical configuration of users into groups.

Figure 4-11
Configuring
Users and
Groups
(Interleaf)

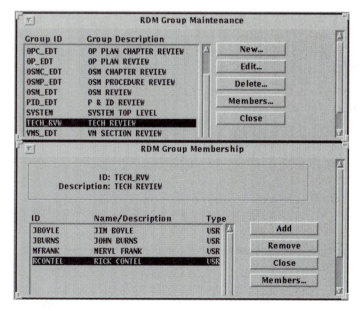

Creation and maintenance of users and groups is an important, yet sometimes burdensome, task. In most organizations, the EDMS is not the only place where users and groups are defined. Two places within the IS department's domain where users and groups are found are in networking and Email systems. Networking functions require that every user have a unique ID name or login and password just to gain access to the network. The same is true of the first level of security within an EDMS repository.

The Email system is perhaps the most extensive use of both users and groups. Users have unique ID's and they are grouped into both hierarchical as well as cross-functional groups. The IS organization is usually tasked with maintaining both the network and the Email system for both users and groups. Since the infrastructure is already in place to keep these lists maintained, the best solution is for an EDMS is to connect into these existing resources.

Versioning Control

Controlling versions of a document is the next major function of a repository. The process of controlling versions within a repository is usually a straightforward issue, at least from a technical perspective. Each time a document is updated, a new copy of the file is placed along side the previous version in the file system, and a corresponding entry is made in the database, including a version number. This enables the repository to provide a complete record of each version, along with when it was created, and by whom. This information maintains a full audit trail of revisions to documents over their entire lifecycle. Keeping these versions is simply an issue of storage space and archiving.

While technically straightforward, the process of versioning control can get complex when the needs of an organization are taken into account. And every organization has differing requirements for its document version control, which range from simply keeping the latest version to schemes with complex versioning, including branches and subversions. Configuring or using a repository to meet these needs can be challenging but also an effort in managing how business practices involving these documents are matched to their functions within the repository. Here integrated workflow software can ease this complicated task.

Version Numbering

The first issue in versioning control is the numbering scheme. In the simplest case, as each document is updated, its version number is incremented. In such cases, the version number (or revisions) of a document move from 1 to 2 to 3, or A to B to C, etc. While seemingly simple, this scheme raises several questions. Should users start with 1.0

and go to 1.1 or jump to 2.0? This is more a preference by the organization than a specific system requirement, except that almost every repository addresses version numbering differently.

Some repositories require that version numbers be integers, beginning with 1, which are then indexed automatically. Others allow the user to input the version number during each revision. While this allows for more flexibility, it also presents the possibility that a version number might be skipped, creating an auditing nightmare. In many organizations, a version control system may already be in place, and there may be a compelling need to match up with the existing version control sequence, for example starting with Version 11.

But for some versioning schemes, a simple number or lettering scheme is not sufficient. There may be a need for longer version identifiers, perhaps even for including the last names of people working on a document in a collaborative environment. This type of versioning scheme does not allow for automatic incrementing, but rather forces users to enter the version numbers when documents are removed or returned to the repository. The key is to determine what the organization needs, what the repository can support, and then marrying the two requirements together. This may require the development of a procedure for both training and guiding users in the versioning of documents

Versioning Schemes

Another issue to be faced is whether the versioning will be linear or branched. The linear case is the simplest and was illustrated above: A document moves from version *n* to version *n+1*. The version sequence can use letters or numbers, with each new version a direct descendent of its predecessor. But the branching scheme allows versions to have multiple descendants. For example, version 1.1 may give rise to both versions 1.2 and 2.0. In this case, each version is not necessarily a descendent of its predecessor, but still related. Both versioning schemes are presented in Figure 4-12.

Because there are clear advantages to each scheme, the key is to understand the various approaches and then match them up with the organization's requirements to determine which scheme best fits which need. In linear versions, each document is a direct descendent of the previous version and therefore updates build upon one another. There is only one latest copy of a document. This is the most common versioning scheme in most organizations.

In the branching approach, the system is far more flexible, allowing an author or other authorized user to create versions when deemed appropriate. Here each version of a document can take on a "life of its

Figure 4-12
Linear and
Branched
Versions

Linear Versioning

1.0 ➡ 1.1 ➡ 2.0 ➡ 3.0 ...

Branched Versioning

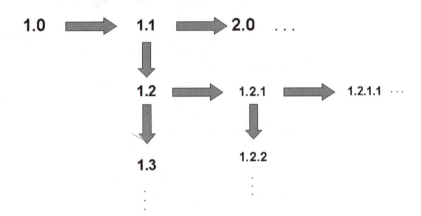

own". The organization should set some very clear standards as to when, and by whom, new branches can be created.

Another important point is with document revisions going out in multiple directions, some type of human intervention is usually required to reconcile the differing documents to bring them back to a single unified version, if required. In Figure 4-12 above, this would occur when versions 1.2.1.1, 1.3, 2.0 were combined into a new version, perhaps version 3.0. This process can only be accomplished by a person going through each version of the document line-by-line, a tedious, slow, and expensive process. Often times the goal of a document management system is to avoid the need for this reconciliation process.

There are cases where the branched model is useful. A common example of branched versions is found in software documentation. A user's guide may be developed and updated to coincide with each version of a software product. Version 1.0 is released and followed by version 1.1. Then the company may develop version 2.0. However, not all users can or even want to upgrade from 1.0 to 2.0. To support these users the company may develop another new release of the first version, this would be version 1.2. Depending upon how long the software lives the versions of the user's guide could branch out in many directions. The example cited here coincides with the branched version model shown in Figure 4-12.

Creating and Controlling Versions

Another consideration is when to create a new version of a document. In some repositories, this action is a distinct step a user must initiate, and they must have permission to do so. In other systems the versioning occurs automatically during check-in or check-out. This brings us to the primary question of when to assign a new version or revision number to a document. Simply put, there are three opportunities to create new versions: within the repository, during check out, or during check in. Each have advantages and limitations.

In creating a new revision in the repository, the function of creating a new revision can be separated from the permission to edit or check out a document. After a new revision is created, it simply remains in the repository awaiting further action. In other cases, the document may have an associated workflow, where actions can be started based on the creation of a new revision. This may even include routing it to an editor for changes. In many systems this task of "creating a new revision" is coupled with check-out or check-in.

The advantage of this process is that the repository knows exactly the progress of a document (i.e., that a new revision has been created, and its number). On the other hand, the down side is that if the persons making the edits change their minds, more work is required within the repository to remove this version. This is important if the task of creating a new revision launches other tasks such as notification of selected users that a revision is in progress.

The process of creating a new revision during check-out has similar characteristics to creating a new revision in the repository. The principle differences lie in the permission to create a new version and check-out a document are not separated. Also, if the document is automatically checked out, other processes may not be executed. However, tasks such as notification can be executed in parallel with the check-out process.

In a competing scenario, an editable copy of the document is checked out, but a new revision is created only when the document is returned to the repository. This approach enables the editor to determine what type of revision such as major/minor; or version/sub-version, during the check-in process when the changes are complete and the exact extent of the document modifications are known. This scenario simplifies the required effort if users change their minds about creating a new version and cancels the check-out process. Figure 4-13 shows the process of creating a new revision.

Figure 4-13
Creating a
New Version
(PC DOCS)

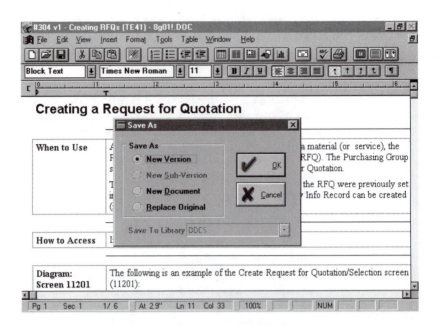

In both scenarios there are two additional considerations that are of paramount importance to ensure the versioning process models the business process. First is branched versus linear versioning. In the linear model only the latest version of a document can be "versioned" again. No previous version can be revised. This means that if a document moves from revision 1.0 to 1.1 to 1.2, it is possible to create a new version from 1.2 but it is not possible to go back and create a new version from 1.1. This ensures that each version of a document has only one new version and therefore all versions of a document are descendants of the others. In the branching model an existing revision can be versioned again to create a new version, thereby enabling branching. For example, version 1.1 might be versioned creating version 1.1.1.

The other key consideration is that of locking a document during the revision process. In this case a document is marked as "in edit" or locked within the repository. This ensures that all future requests to edit the same document are rejected, until such time as the document is "returned" or checked back into the repository. In this way, no document ends up being edited by more than one person at the same time. The repository will usually indicate to requesters who has the document "checked out" for editing so they can contact that individual if desired, which preserves the overall integrity of the document. While this is almost always the case, there are other scenarios.

Another scenario is to eliminate the locking component. This enables several people to make changes to a document simultaneously, but each one will become a separate version. One example of this may be the introductory material in a set of documents. A common set of "boilerplate" is created and made available for all to use. Each author can edit the document to meet their needs, but by keeping them all as revisions, it is possible to keep track of all versions of the introductory material.

An important aspect of this scenario is whether the system keeps track of ancestors and descendants. For example some repositories simply assign the next version number to a document checked back in, such as 1A, 1B, 1C, 1D. Both 1C and 1D may be descendants of 1A, but there is no way to tell that. In other models, a numbering scheme is used to help track descendants. Similar to the example above, the version numbers might be 1.1, 1.1.1, 1.1.2, and 1.2, where both 1.1.1 and 1.1.2 are descendants of version 1.1; version 1.2 is also a descendent of 1.1. This hierarchical numbering scheme assists users in identifying and tracing ancestors and descendants. Figure 4-14 illustrates this scenario. This concept is also important anyplace where branched versioning is used.

Most repositories allow, with proper permissions, the document versions to actually be overwritten. This is usually established for work in progress (WIP) documents. An editor may work on a document over a period of time, and can decide upon checking the document back in if a new version is required. If no new version is necessary, the document in repository is *replaced* by the new document being checked in. Since the previous changes are no longer available, this can be a dangerous proposition. There are, however, situations where it can be useful - the key being to ensure that the user fully understands this situation when it is presented.

Many repositories use drafts, subversions or minor revisions to track "inter-version" changes. Here major revisions or versions are often referred to as 1.0, 2.0, 3.0, etc. Examples of drafts, subversions, or minor revisions are 1C, 2.1, 3.3.1. Permissions can sometimes be different for who can create major versus minor revisions. Many times these inter-version schemes are used in concert with workflow. A key decision is whether the interim versions are kept until the document finishes its complete workflow, then purged or maintained forever. Figure 4-14 shows an example coupling workflow with versions and drafts.

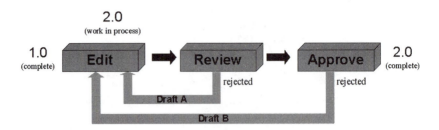

By bringing document work in progress, revisions, and workflow together, a repository can control the edits to the document. It also provides control over the movement of a document through the business process to its final version. Many scenarios require documents to sit in a interim state until they are approved for release, the point at which the document revision is complete. This concept of controlling a document's movement to a new "completed" version is critically important. In many EDMS applications, it is these "released versions" which are made available to a wider audience for viewing. In fact, many systems query the repository for newly-released versions and then copy them to a fileserver, such as a Web server, for consumption. One final note: often, the new release of a document may require many time-consuming or expensive activities. Key individuals must be notified and many users must receive training on the changes, and the way business is conducted may be modified. The cost of these tasks can make releasing a new version quite expensive, requiring it to be carefully managed.

Archiving

Depending upon the organization's requirements for versioning, new revisions of a document may be created frequently. Since the repository will store a new copy of the file for each revision, storage space can grow rather quickly. For this reason, most repositories offer an archiving function, whereby files that are not critical can be moved off to some near-line type of media.

A critical step here is to decide on a scheme for archiving documents. In some instances an administrator can go through the system and mark which items are to be archived. In others, it can be programmed to perform this function automatically. If the number of files or revisions will be high, the automatic routines are preferable. These can usually be driven by relative "age" of the document, the time since its last access, or even the number of revisions that are retained, with the number of revisions being the most common approach. For example, it may be necessary to keep only the most current version, or maybe one previous cycle. In this arrangement, when a new revision is created, the older version is either archived or simply marked for archiving.

Each repository has one or more of these schemes built into it, and all are viable. In the case of most repositories, files are copied to the archive media, and the database record is then updated to indicate that the document has been archived. This record is also modified to include the tape or disk number. This way, the repository can be searched for all versions of a document, but once requested, the system will indicate what archive is necessary to retrieve the desired document. This approach is usually feasible since the database records are relatively small and keeping all of them online does not require significant overhead.

The second step here is to decide upon archiving media: Will the documents be archived to disk, transferred to magnetic tape, or be written to optical media? These decisions require considering several factors such as number of files, the volume of files, the storage costs, the life of the media, and how often these files will need to be retrieved. As mass storage device technology changes, the costs, access times, and media costs will change dramatically. So it is important to understand the market's current offerings at the time of implementation of a system. Because an IS organization has similar needs in other areas of the company, these efforts (and decisions) can be leveraged to support the EDMS projects.

Configuration Management & Information Reuse

Configuration management is the control and organization of multiple parts of an entire system and easiest to understand from a physical perspective. Think about the construction of a simple ballpoint pen. It contains a body, a cartridge, a cap, and plug to cover the bottom of the body. The "bill of materials" for this pen includes all of these parts and, in essence, is the "configuration management" of the pen.

Now consider if the design of this same pen was changed. Perhaps the body was changed from clear plastic to white. This is, in effect, a new part or more accurately a new revision of the body. Now the entire pen assembly must be revised to reflect this new body design. Figure 4-15 shows in a tree diagram how the configuration management for the old pen and new pen compare.

Figure 4-15
Configuration
Management
across revisions

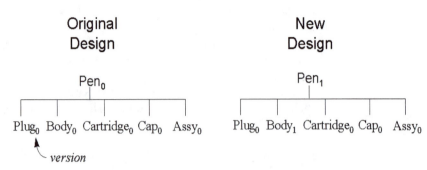

This entire field of configuration management for manufacturing operations is commonly referred to as *product data management* or PDM for short, and there are specialized applications, programs, and tools to address this problem. Several of the higher end EDMS repositories are even capable of handling this type of data and providing PDM solutions.

Returning to the pen example, we still need to imagine putting together the engineering repository for managing the design drawings for each part. The design for the original pen consists of five drawings or documents: four part drawings and one assembly drawing. These documents need to be kept together, and in the paper world we would file them in folder. Through the use of relationships (parent and child) we can create the same organization within a repository. The first container is created and it becomes the parent. Relationships are then made to point to the child documents. This container is often called a "compound" or "virtual" document. In the pen example, this first container would be the "design specification."

It is important to note that the child documents are not actually copied into this virtual container or document, but rather pointers are created in the database to manage these relationships. This allows these documents to exist in their appropriate vaults and have all the correct access and security controls. This virtual container is also placed under revision control, like any other document.

When a new design for the body is developed, the document will be checked out, edited, and then returned to the repository as Version # 1. A new version of the pen "design" (the virtual document) will then need to be created. In this revision, there is no actual content change, but in fact a change to a relationship. This new revision of the virtual document must point to the new revision of the body drawing. Figure 4-16 shows a tree type diagram for both revisions 0 and 1 of the virtual document for the pen design.

Figure 4-16
Virtual
Documents
for Pen Designs

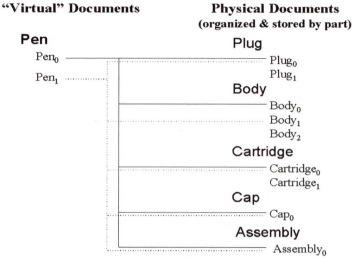

Note: Lines indicate relationships

Configuration management in a repository is a very powerful capability, but with it can come significant complexity. It is important to understand how configuration management can be employed to assist with the management of compound-complex documents, and several ways configuration management can be used are discussed below.

The most common use of compound documents by authors, that require configuration management in the repository, are documents that incorporate Object Linking and Embedding (OLE) technology. This technology allows a user to incorporate a spreadsheet or other object into a word processing document, yet keep this item(s) separately linked to the original source files. In this manner, if the original spreadsheet file is updated, when the word processing document is opened, it will automatically update the linked spreadsheet from the updated source file.

But when an OLE document is checked into a repository, the repository must detect these linked objects. It must then check-in the "master" file and all the associated source files for the linked objects. Next, it must create a document and the relationships to this master document and all of its linked source files. This also requires the repository to ensure that the linked documents are not checked in twice, but instead identified as linked relationships to existing documents within the repository.

This technical EDMS approach presents several challenges for an organization. First, one must decide whether a linked document which is placed in the repository is to be removed from the operating system's file system. By removing it, the document is more properly controlled, but if other documents link to it, those links will be broken. The second task is to carefully consider if the OLE linking process, while very powerful, violates the concept of controlled updates, where if the document is opened, updates are automatically made. While the user is usually given a choice, the document itself is updated without any type of version control. Here there are no right or wrong answers, just important factors to be weighed when implementing the EDMS solution.

The concept of always being up-to-date with document contents, similar to the way OLE works, is not lost within most repository configuration management schemes used today. In the earlier example of the pen, the virtual document (the pen design) had revision control, and so did the child documents (the drawings), while the relationships were revision specific. Rev 0 of the design pointed to Rev 0 of all the drawings. Similarly, Rev 1 of the design pointed to Rev 0 of all drawings, except that the body drawing was Rev 1. Yet some repositories also support revision-independent children.

With some virtual documents, it is desirable for them to always contain the latest version of the child documents, a process ensuring that when a document is updated to a new revision, all of its parents (virtual documents) are then revised and the relationship points to the new version of the child documents. This is a very powerful concept, but it must be carefully implemented. Since it is possible for virtual documents to be nested, as they are simply objects to the repository, this ripple effect could cause changes to a vast number of documents within the system.

A practical example of this scenario might be an operator in a manufacturing plant. First, the operator runs the plant by procedures contained in an operating system manual. Since each procedure is an individual document and requires its own version control process, the manual becomes a "virtual document" which contains (points) to the individual procedures. In this case, the operator is only concerned with using the latest and most up-to-date procedures. Therefore, it is helpful if the virtual document that represents the operating system manual is automatically updated with the newest revision for each procedure.

A third type of configuration management system is that based on "notification." In this case, one document may be developed based upon the contents of another. This does not refer to extracting a specific part of the document in its current form, but perhaps information contained in one document allowed the author to develop the second. In this case, it is important to explicitly state this relationship. This, in turn, allows the owner of the resulting document to be notified when the source document has changed. There is no requirement that authors change the derivative document, but rather they are provided with the necessary information to make this decision.

An example of this type of relationship can be demonstrated by extending the example above. Assume the procedures to run the manufacturing plant were based in large part on the equipment manuals provided by the vendors, and these documents are also contained within the repository. It would be prudent to establish a "based-on" or "notification" relationship indicating that the procedure "A" was based on vendor equipment manual "A." If the vendor equipment manual "A" was updated, then the author of procedure "A" would be notified that the vendor document had been updated. It is then incumbent upon the author of procedure "A" to review the changes to the new vendor document and decide if changes are required. This is a very powerful technique within a repository and is shown in Figure 4-17.

Figure 4-17
Setting up a Based on Relationship (Interleaf)

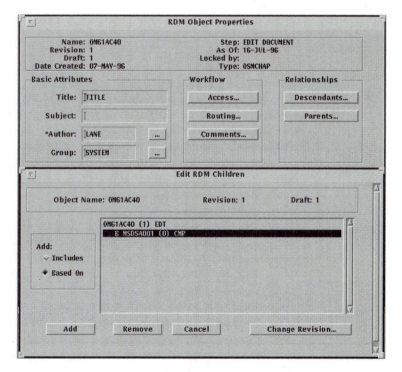

This same type of relationship can be used to set up notification of any person or group of people when a document is revised. The relationship can actually be set to trigger the notification on check-out, the creation of a new version, or any other action. In addition to notifying an individual, this trigger can be used to begin a process. For example, when a new revision is completed, a process could be started which would then convert the document into HTML and copy it to a Web Server so as to make it widely available.

Configuration management in a repository, then, is key to leveraging existing information. With the concept of relationships, documents can be created once and reused, in whole or in part, depending on the context or need. Considering the cost of creating critical business information, the cost savings by reusing information can be enormous.

Standards

As with any emerging industry, standards are vital to the successful growth of the market. There are two EDMS repository standards in various phases of development and publication. They are the Open Document Management API (ODMA) and a specification in development by the Document Management Alliance (DMA). Each of these address a different aspect of document management interoperability.

The ODMA standard is working toward a standard set of interfaces between desktop applications and document management client software. The intent of this standard is to allow any desktop application to communicate with any document management client without having to develop custom code from every desktop application to every document management client. This standard will enable desktop applications to be document management enabled.

The DMA specification is working towards a set of interfaces between document management servers. The intent is to allow any document repository to communicate with any other document repository without custom coding an interface between each and every repository. This allows organizations to have multiple repositories and to be able to share information between them without the user ever knowing or caring where a document is stored.

The power of each of these standards can best be shown in a diagram. Figure 4-18 shows how three desktop applications working with three document management systems would have to interact, where each line represents the integration that has to be completed. Figure 4-19 shows the same system using ODMA and DMA interfaces. Note that the number of integrations is reduced dramatically.

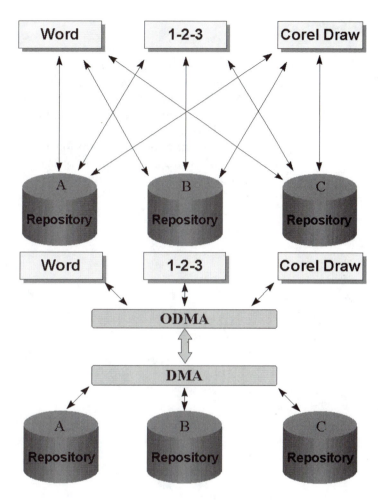

Figure 4-18
Document
Management
without Standards

Figure 4-19
Document
Management
with Standards

The ODMA interface should, therefore, receive widespread adoption and implementation rather quickly. It should require only modest changes to each desktop or document management client application to conform to the specifications and protocols. In fact, many systems are ODMA compliant today. However, the DMA specification will likely require changes to the architecture of many, if not all, of the repositories on the market today. For this reason, the DMA specification will take longer to be agreed upon by the industry as a whole, as well as a greater time to implement. These standards are not the only ones in the industry, but are the ones likely to have an impact in the near future on the EDMS market.

Summary

The repository is the heart and sole of any EDMS. It is imperative that key functions of any repository: library services, versioning and configuration management be clearly understood. These functions will be used to deliver a system which match es the business process of the organization, and therefore a careful mapping of user requirements to system functionality is critical.

The other important consideration for a repository is the client application. Choosing between a proprietary and a Web client, building a custom client interface or embedding the client functionality into an existing application is a significant item. This choice will have impacts on networking infrastructure, system design and even training of the users.

5

Conversion

To some, document conversion is a necessary evil today. If all of the creators, editors, reviewers, approvers, and consumers of documents used the same tool sets, there would be little need for document conversion. However, the reality is far from this; our global economy encourages competition and with it comes a world of document formats. Numerous hardware vendors, coupled with dozens of operating systems, running hundreds of word processing, drawing, graphics, and imaging packages leads to the proverbial Tower of Babble. "All the information is there," we are told; it just can't be readily found or shared.

In recent years, this problem has surfaced repeatedly and has even been addressed in straightforward ways: IS departments have mandated corporate standards for most types of applications, often called Common Operating Environments, and run from desktop and server operating systems, to corporate standard databases, to spreadsheets and word processing packages.

Another way this standards problem is being addressed is within software "suites." Companies such as Microsoft with its Office suite of tools have followed this trend to deliver complete and tightly integrated sets of tools that meet most users' needs, and are completely compatible. This helps to keep the number of different applications across an organization to a minimum. However, a lot of specialty (and non-standard) applications still remain, not to mention the mountain of legacy information stored in a variety of formats, everything from PCs to mainframe systems.

One of these legacy formats is almost always paper. So in trying to arrive at a common format for all information, the problem of converting paper to digital form must also be considered. Conversion of paper to electronic form, sometimes called information capture, scanning, or imaging, is a very different process than that of electronic document conversion. In fact, imaging is still by far the largest segment of the current document management marketplace.

In the context of this book, imaging is only a component of the EDMS, dealing with relatively small volumes or occasional instances of paper documents. If the document management problem is predominantly driven by *paper* source documents, the solution should be a document imaging system, not an electronic document management system.

Before discussing the technologies and issues in electronic conversion or imaging, two key points need to be made. First, in the ideal world there would be no need for document conversion. Converting documents from one format to another is *not* usually a value-adding process. Therefore, conversion efforts should be seen as a necessary evil. Conversion may be a necessary means to sharing the document's contents with another individual, but in and of itself does not add value.

Conversely, document conversion into a format that allows users to search and retrieve information or access it more quickly *are* value-adding processes. Also, as we will see in Chapter 9, delivering documents online using tools that enable electronic tables of contents, searching, hypertexting, annotations, etc., can make this conversion process the most important value-adding process within an EDMS solution. Despite this benefit, though, conversion should always be looked upon as an overhead expense, one that is to be minimized whenever possible.

Document conversion, whether electronic or imaging, cannot be devised and planned in a vacuum. Conversion processes and their requirements can have a significant impact on both document consumers and creators. The needs of the consumers should determine the desired document format. Then the authoring process needs to be reviewed with an eye towards delivering this desired format. If it is not practical to deliver the format directly, then conversion becomes an important part of the equation, a dynamic process filled with trial and error, as well as negotiation and acceptance, between the consumers and creators. Often, however, tradeoffs must be made in order to balance the competing priorities of consumer and creator.

To help make these tradeoffs and negotiations from the most educated perspective possible, there are several technical issues that should be well understood by all parties. This chapter will cover some of these, first for electronic document conversions, then for imaging systems. This chapter is then followed by chapters on creation and distribution, where again information can go through a value-adding process.

Electronic Conversion

Compound-complex documents today are usually comprised of a combination of text, graphics, and multi-media objects. Since each of these document components is fundamentally different, they must be converted using different tools and techniques. So there are no easy or all encompassing answers to conversion, and there are always a variety of tools to use, but they too change constantly as they grow and evolve. Some of the basics of electronic conversion are explored here, but any detailed issues are best left to be discussed with tool vendors and their products at the time of the conversion effort.

Standard Formats

Regardless of the type of conversion, standard formats should be used wherever possible, greatly simplifying the conversion process itself. Some of the more common standard formats for text, graphics, and multi-media objects are listed in the Table 5-1 below.

Table 5-1: Standard Formats

Object Type	Standard Formats
Text	ASCII - American Standard Code for Information Exchange SGML -Standard Generalized Markup Language HTML - HyperText Markup Language (subset of SGML)
Graphics	*Vector Graphics* CGM - Computer Graphics Metafile IGES - International Graphics Exchange Standard *Raster Graphics* TIFF - Tag Information File Format GIF - Graphic Interchange Format JPEG - Joint Photographic Experts Group
Multi-media	MPEG - Motion Pictures Expert Group

Where applications can output directly into these formats, the likelihood for problems in conversion are greatly reduced. However, most applications recommend the use of the "native formats," which are usually proprietary to the application. This helps to improve conversion performance, to reduce storage requirements and to preserve the proprietary file constructs and features.

One somewhat unique format that does not easily fit categorization in the above table is PostScript, for it is really a page description language (PDL), not a format, but still often thought of as a document format. But it is also the most widely used PDL for representing output intended for a printed page. Because most laser printers today are capable of supporting it, nearly all applications and operating systems have printer drivers that allow for PostScript output. And because PostScript is device independent, it is also platform- and application-independent as well. Since it is a page description language, it can render text, graphics, or images. This makes PostScript a very powerful tool for electronic publishing and conversion, as we will see later.

Conversion Process

The first step in any conversion process is to determine the formats involved in the conversion. The source format is often pre-determined. An organization may have thousands of documents in a specific format and be unwilling to change. On the other end, the "target" format can, and should, be pre-determined by end users. The key, then, is to find a "filter," the common term for a conversion tool to transform the document from the original format into the desired format that does the best possible job. This process is shown in Figure 5-1.

Figure 5-1
Conversion
Process

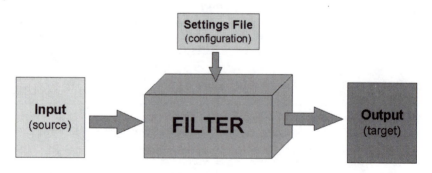

The key things to look for in any filtering process are accuracy and repeatability. It is best to take a wide variety of samples of the source materials, including the best and the worst section of text formatting, then run them through the filter. In determining accuracy, the most important criteria is content preservation, making sure nothing is lost. The second most important thing is format: Is all of the existing formatting being maintained?

If either content or format is lost, the cause should be pinpointed. Sometimes a simple adjustment to the filter or the input documents can work wonders in the conversion processes. If adjustments to the source documents are required, this sub-process can be reasonably accomplished by the authors or a simple automated pre-processing step can be introduced into the conversion process.

The second most important aspect of conversion is repeatability. This is why many samples are needed. There have been many occasions where two documents, seemingly the same, are then converted, resulting in one flying through the conversion process perfectly and the other failing. It is equally important to determine just how repeatable this process itself is. If the system must convert hundreds of documents per day, an annoying little problem in just a few documents can become a show-stopper in the production system. Conversion testing, therefore, cannot be overemphasized.

Graphics require some additional considerations in the conversion process. The most important consideration is to understand the document output format. For example, a document may contain a piece of line art, say a vector-based graphic. In converting this document, the graphic may be converted to a raster, essentially an image or dots on the page. If there is a requirement to scale the drawing in the final format, a raster image will not perform to the same spec as the same vector image. However, some filters do allow the user to control the graphic output format.

In some cases the graphics may need to be extracted, converted by hand or other processes, and then put back into the document. While this may result in a good final document, it is a manually-intensive process. Every effort should be made to find a way to convert this document in a more automatic way.

Style Mapping

Beyond the simple conversion of words or text from one format to the other, there are more advanced issues such as document structure and formatting. Many documents use "elements" inside the document, such as components, types, or styles to control the final formatting of a document. As you will see later in the chapter on electronic document delivery, these styles can become "electronic" roadmaps or tables of contents to the documents. It is therefore important that these styles or elements be preserved if they are to be used in the online delivery system.

Some filtering systems allow for "style mapping," that is the assignment of one style to another that may better fit the online document. This is critically important in using HTML on the World Wide Web. HTML is a "tagged" environment but still has a very limited set of widely recognizable tags. In order for the document to appear properly, or even function correctly in a hypertext environment, it is important that the document be properly converted in terms of styles.

In documents that make extensive use of styles, configuration files or maps can be set up to tell the filter, for example, to take style "Section" and output that as tag "H1", for Heading Level 1. These formatting maps need to be set up for every document template that is being used, and these must be thoroughly tested. Figure 5-2 shows an example.

Figure 5-2
Mapping
Styles
(Interleaf)

In documents where styles are not used, but formatting is, there are conversion programs that contain "visual recognition engines," such as Interleaf's "FastTag." It derives or infers a structure and organization for a document from things like font size, layout, emphasis, indents and numbering. These tools are not as reliable as style mapping but are sometimes the only alternative to doing the mapping by hand.

Conversion and Document Management

Most document management systems employ a full-text indexing system as a part of the repository and conversion toolset. The details of this text indexing process will be covered in Chapter 6, but there are some related considerations for document conversion that should be addressed here. In order to index these documents, the text must be extracted and provided to the indexing engine. Most vendors use a set of filters to convert documents into a format readable by the indexing engine. Since the filters are then part of the repository, they can be used in other ways.

Several repository systems, especially those with workflow tools, can create a step within a document workflow process that will use these filters to do the conversion. This new document version can be kept and stored as an additional format or as a "rendition" of the document. This allows the conversion process to be easily automated. It does not, however, remove the responsibility to test the accuracy and reliability of the filter.

In many places the use of "electronic paper" in the form of, say, Adobe Acrobat's Portable Document Format (PDF) is growing exponentially. It represents a document conversion process that provides nearly 100% accuracy and it usually preserves formatting as well. On the other hand, this approach does not support dynamically resizing a document to fit a window, etc. Creating a PDF document typically involves printing PostScript to a file from the native application, and then converting the PostScript file to PDF through a product called a "Distiller."

Since this conversion is a two-step process, and cannot be derived directly from the source documents alone, a more complex conversion process is still required. The native application must be launched and then used to produce the PostScript file. This file can then be fed to the Distiller. In at least one repository system, a separate server is actually loaded with the native applications and can be launched from the repository to create the PDF file. In this way the document repository can drive the conversion process in a hands-off fashion.

PostScript files can also be streamed to a printer to create a paper copy of a document without having to launch the document's native application. A repository could be configured to store both the native and PostScript versions of a document. Then the workflow process could kickoff either a printing or conversion process using the Post-Script file, enabling both on-demand printing and on-the-fly conversion, although the conversion process is usually slow for a "real time" system.

Through this variety of mechanisms, the repository can play a major role in the conversion of documents where necessary. And for the most part, these processes could be unattended, or used in just-in-time or on-demand situations.

Paper Conversion

Paper conversion, or imaging, is the process of transforming a sheet of paper into digital form. This process has been the mainstay of the document management market over the last ten years. Imaging has a wide variety of vendors and tools, all specifically geared towards the process of converting, storing, retrieving and managing documents. In the early days of imaging, much specialized hardware was required to deal with images, which often led to proprietary systems. As standards evolved and the performance of desktop machines improved, imaging has moved away from proprietary models. However, there are still a number of areas where specialized systems are "tuned" or "enhanced" to make working with images more efficient. These enhancements not withstanding, if paper documents are only a small portion of the document set, the tools for an electronic document management system can be used to manage these images as well. It will require that an imaging subsystem be established for the conversion of document to digital form.

An imaging subsystem consists of several key components:

- Scanner
- Image Capture Software
- Image Processing / Clean-up Software
- Optical Character Recognition Software

Not all imaging needs demand all these system components, but they are the most common. All the hardware and software may reside on one machine or may be distributed across multiple machines on a network. A functional block diagram of this subsystem is shown in Figure 5-3.

Figure 5-3
Imaging
Subsystem

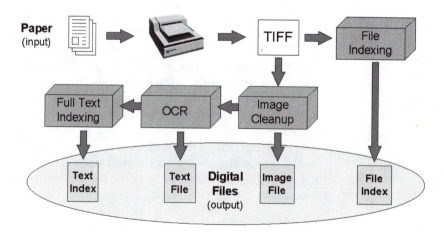

Scanner

The scanner is the physical piece of equipment that reads the sheet of paper and with the image capture software creates an electronic "picture" of the text. A scanner contains a "charged coupled device" (CCD) that reads the light reflected from the image. The resolution, usually in dots per inch (DPI), is determined by the number of light sensors or CCDs in the scanner.

There are many physical types of scanners, but only a few are commonly found in an imaging subsystem. The first is a flat bed scanner, where objects (sheets of paper, open books, magazines, etc.) can be laid on the glass bed where the images are captured. The second of scanner is an automatic sheet-fed model. Here documents must be single sheets, and they are then stacked, much like in an automatic feed copy machine. Also, just like a copy machine, an automatic sheet-fed scanner may be able to be used as a make-shift flat-bed model scanner, if the sheet feeder can be moved out of the way. A third type of a scanner is a "roll feed" model, which is usually used for large engineering drawings.

Two other considerations in selecting a scanner will be its type recognition and the resolution of its output. The "type" refers to the output desired from the scanner: black and white, gray-scale, or color. The "output" is a function of the scanner's design, not the software. The output from each CCD and the associated electronics will determine whether each dot on the page is seen as black or white, a shade of gray, or a color. This is also determined by the number of bits used to represent each individual dot. In a four bit scanner, sixteen colors or shades of gray are possible; an eight bit system gives 256 shades of gray or color. Twenty four bits is usually required for true color.

The resolution of the scanner refers to the number of dots per inch. The more DPI, the better the quality of the image. Today, 300-600 DPI is common in desktop scanning systems. In graphic and photo work, however, 1200 DPI is not unusual. It is important to note that this resolution is the "optical resolution" of the scanner based on the optics, not the electronics of the scanner itself. Many scanners employ electronics which can "interpolate" the image and thereby double or even quadruple the claimed resolution.

There is no doubt that the more bits available for gray-scale, or color and DPI available for capturing the image, the better the resulting image will be, but there are practical limits. A paper size of 8.5 x 11 inches, in true color scan at 600 DPI, can result in an image file of nearly 100 MB, not a very practical size file to deal with in a document management system. Note that increasing the scanning resolution from 200 to 600 DPI increases a file size by a factor of nine.

Image Capture

The image capture software is responsible for working with the scanner to feed documents and capture the output from the electronics to a disk. It is the mechanism through which the desired bit level, resolution, and output formats are determined. Most scanning software offers a variety of output formats, but the most common is TIFF, the standard for images. Image capture software also performs one other critical function: compression. A single page with a 16 gray scale image at 200 DPI can take up as much as 1.75 MB, therefore compression is a must. The most common compressed format is CCITT Group 4. Compression can often reduce the file size by a factor of ten or more, making images manageable.

Image Processing Software

When a sheet of paper is fed through a document scanner and the resultant image is created, a number of problems can be created. The first problem is a misalignment of the page. Everyone has seen this from a copier, where the page goes through the feeder off by a few degrees. In the case of a paper copy, people simple turn the page a little to read it correctly. Once that image is presented on screen, though, the only option is for the user to tilt his head in order to read it, not an ideal solution. And the scanning software has a range of how far it can "straighten out" the page before optical character recognition fails.

Another problem is the introduction of dirt. Dirt on the scanner glass, or even on the original document, results in black specks on a the resultant image. These specks require even more storage space and computing power to process and display them. Also, scanners are generally set up to scan in one direction, for example in "portrait." If landscape documents are fed into the scanner, the image output will be rotated 90∞ and be impossible to read.

Image processing software, sometimes built right into the image capture system, is designed to address these and other issues. It usually has "de-skewing" to straighten out the page. It also may have auto-rotate functions to rotate an image to the proper orientation. It usually has a "clean-up" or "de-speckle" function to remove stray marks and dots caused by the feeder, dirt and dust on the glass, or by using poor quality documents to begin with.

Optical Character Recognition

Up until this point in the process the imaging system has simply taken a picture of the page and put it into the computer as an image file. In order to be able to find and retrieve text on this page, it must be indexed into letters and words. First a user must give the document a filename and then earmark it with key attributes such as subject, title, author, etc. This can be a very time consuming and tedious process. Worse yet, if the person directing the indexing does not clearly understand how someone might look or search for this document, they may not index it properly.

It would therefore be great if there were a way to index this document automatically, and to some degree there is: Optical Character Recognition (OCR). Simply put, OCR is the process of a software application "reading" the image and interpreting the characters on the page, thereby turning the image into text, making the entire document available for indexing.

Optical character recognition is also commonly referred to as "intelligent character recognition" (ICR). In recent years ICR has come to mean the identification of handwritten text, whereas OCR is for the conversion of printed text. Many vendors of OCR software make claims of 99%+ accuracy in their products, claims that warrant reading the fine print very carefully, for those in the real world rarely see this accuracy in a practical sense. But OCR can achieve 99%+ accuracy on a letter for letter basis, with a brand new, fresh off the press 600-DPI laser printer. But is this level of accuracy sufficient for the organization's needs? If the intent is to capture the essence of document, for say background information, it may suffice. For supplying critical information to a knowledge worker performing an important task, it may not. Consider that even at 99% accuracy, if there are 4000 characters on a page, forty will be wrong and need to be edited.

OCR used to mean "pattern matching" against a predetermined set of font maps to match the correct characters. Now systems have been improved to use mathematical algorithms and expert systems technologies to help identify character patterns. OCR systems may even use techniques such as feature recognition, where certain curves, lines, or other letter features are identified and then compared to a knowledge base of known characters. Feature recognition is shown in Figure 5-4. In the latest system incarnations, vendors are even applying neural networks, which allow for faster and better character mapping as well as allowing the system to learn.

Once a character's mapping is complete, the next character is then tackled. Then character pairs and words are check against a larger dictionary set to improve the overall scanned text accuracy. Here common mistakes such as where the letter "S" is recognized as a "5" may be identified and fixed. The better the dictionary, especially in technical fields with lots of jargon, the greater the accuracy of the system. Of course, along with improved accuracy comes additional processing time to run through a larger dictionary.

Figure 5-4
Feature
Recognition
for OCR

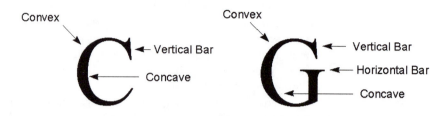

Finally, some OCR software packages are capable of recognizing a document's format. They attempt to preserve the formatting of the text and even the layout of the page. Many can also put this resultant text into a word processor format of the user's choosing. In some instances, the document returned by the OCR process is correctly interpreted, formatted, laid out, and perhaps even put back into the format of the original word processor that may have created it.

OCR processes that are used in the recognition, checking, formatting, and layout of text are very resource intensive. It is important that the CPU and RAM of the OCR system be properly sized. When the right system is not specified, the process can take a very long time or the quality will drop markedly. For example, it is not uncommon for the OCR process to take one minute per page. This is important, since many people buy scanners capable of running thirty or sixty pages per minute, only to discover that the OCR process can manage but one page per minute. This requires batching the OCR process or using multiple OCR systems.

The only way to guarantee nearly 100% accuracy is to put human beings in a verification and validation (V&V) process, where each line of each page is read and then verified. Fixes are made to the text and then the content is rechecked. Because the work is tedious, errors are common and often require several passes to reach the desired accuracy. This is a very slow and extremely expensive process.

Scanning Service Bureaus

If the needs of an organization for scanning are mostly at the initial stage, with little to no ongoing need for scanning, going outside of the organization for scanning may be the right answer. Scanning service bureaus are companies which specialize in document imaging. They typically work on a per-page basis and charge for each service, such as scanning, attribute or keyword assignment, OCR and verification. These costs can range from a few pennies to several dollars per page depending upon services needed, resolution, turn-around time, and the accuracy required.

Yet service bureaus can be a very valuable asset. The time the organization would have to invest in selecting, purchasing, getting trained, and managing the process along with the capital costs can easily outrun the cost of a service bureau for smaller jobs. But developers should be careful in how they define a "small job," as service bureaus are sometimes accustomed to getting jobs in the millions of pages. For large jobs, they will often set up shop inside an organization, reducing the effort and cost to copy or transport documents.

Imaging and Document Management

Document management systems can work well quite well with imaging systems. First, take the case of a multi-page document, where the imaging system will generate "n" images, one for each page. All these images need to stay together as a single document, as in an object-model document management system. Furthermore, the OCR process for this document produces one text document that includes the text from all pages. This file need also be placed in the repository.

When a search is executed, or an index built, the text file is used. But when displayed to the user, the images, and only the images, are displayed. This provides the benefits of OCR, without the expense of V & V. The use of document classes allows the text document to be identified differently than the images, which allows for proper processing, indexing, compression or launching the appropriate viewer to see either the text or the images.

Summary

Conversion, be it electronic or imaging, should generally be regarded as a non-value add process, one to be minimized if not eliminated whenever possible. However, conversion is often a necessary evil to broker between the competing requirements of document creators and consumers. When conversion does enter the equation it is important that it be carefully looked at for accuracy, repeatability and automation or the conversion step in the process can become a major impediment to a smooth running EDMS.

6

Indexing and Searching

Often document repositories are constructed with little or no consideration of the intended users, where the view of an EDMS as a component of a larger system is to fill it with lots of documents and provide a very powerful text search engine to allow users to find what they need. Anyone who has used the World Wide Web is familiar with this approach: A query is entered into a search engine and since it has millions of documents, it returns 12,329 documents containing 17,674 hits of the text string offered in the query. This approach is not exactly quick, nor very user friendly.

The primary method of locating a document by a user should always be the "logical navigation" through the information space or document set. If custom "views" are constructed for each user or user class, then this concept works rather well. However, there are times when a user may seek information that is off the expected path. The system should then at least assist the user in locating this information.

Here, the ability to search the entire document set can be very valuable.

Speeding Information Retrieval

As document repositories and online document sets grow, the speed of information retrieval becomes more important. Indexing offers a way of improving information retrieval by allowing a document to become more *granular* down to the word level. This speed increase results from the text retrieval tool (or engine), and not from having to compare words or phrases to actual text strings within a file, as is normally the case with traditional text search engines. Often, full text searches against millions of pages can be accomplished in a few seconds with proper indexing. This compares favorably with the "find" function in large word processed documents.

Accomplishing Automated Indexing

When a document is to be indexed, its contents must first be broken down into its constituent parts, usually down to the word level. The process of developing a full text retrieval system is dependent on organizing indexable words in such a way that they can be used to access information more quickly. When common words such as *and*, *the*, and other articles or prepositions are put into a "stopword" list (and therefore left out of the indexing process), only the remaining words within the document are actually included in the index.

Once this list of key words has been compiled, they can be further refined by reducing them to their actual stems or roots. The root or stem of a word is what is left once information about its gender, tense, and number are removed, as well as any other elements that modify the word within a sentence. A word is stemmed by recursively removing suffixes from the tail end of words until only three or more characters remain. The English language has only about 75 prefixes and 250 suffixes. The result of this method is that if you search by either a stem or modified term, you will still get the desired result.

There are two approaches to word stemming: heuristic and rule-based. A heuristic approach to stemming can determine a root very quickly by interactively removing suffixes like *s, er, ing*, and others, from the end of a string until no suffixes remain. This approach works very well for words like *compute(s), computer(s), computing, computable, computability, computation, and computational*. This approach does not work for words like *sable, sing,* and *seer*. The reliability of this algorithm improves if one requires that at least three characters remain in the root. But it will still group the terms *cap* and *capability* or *cat* and *catering* together. Dictionary-based approaches are slower and occupy more memory than heuristic approaches but they are more reliable. They record the permissible suffixes with each word in a large dictionary.

Compiling such a dictionary is time consuming. If a word to be stemmed is not contained within the dictionary, then the algorithm falls back to a heuristic approach

Once the stemming process is complete, important content-oriented words must then be measured in terms of their overall frequency or occurrence within a document. In some indexing schemes this frequency rate will, in turn, determine whether or not the words get included into the index. Much of this process of determining word frequencies can, in fact, be done automatically. However, terms that are used frequently in a document may not always be useful in an index, and consume additional storage, so there may be no point in automatically including them in an index. In the case of a true full text index all words, except the stop words, are included. Most text indexing systems in EDMS solutions are true full text indexes.

Indexing Methods

There are actually several ways to index a document (whether the process is done manually or automatically). It should be pointed out, however, that in order to index a document, it must remain static during the indexing process, for if the document changes dynamically, then it is entirely likely that new words would be added to the indexing model as old words are removed.

Inversion of Terms

A simple way to index a document electronically is to create an *inversion* of all the terms or keywords within the document, where the words are sorted and then stored in an external file alphabetically. In this file, each word has a pointer to all its occurrences within the document set. A search query can then be compared against this list of word pointers in order to find the target location within the document where the word exists. This process of term inversion can be optimized by using several different programming structures to organize the word lists and their pointers until finally an inverted file is created.

Inversion techniques, however, require a fairly large overhead in terms of disk space since the terms and all of their occurrences must be stored in external files. But once these inverted lists are created, finding the information by looking up the word in the list first and then listing the document, is a fairly speedy process, since the program is not doing a string match process but rather a location look-up activity.

It is often helpful to think about this index just like the index in the back of a book; it lists key terms and the page numbers to locate them in context. A full text index is an electronic index, just like a book's, except it includes every word in every document in the system or repository. It also knows the number of times the word appears and contains pointers that support quick retrieval of the document and even opening to the first instance of the word *inside* the document.

These word lists with their associated pointer information can then be sorted and used to extract statistical information about the words in the document and is combined with statistics from indexing other documents to get overall statistics about the entire document. From these statistics, one can then determine how many times a word is used, be able to assign it a value or degree of importance, or select it as a candidate hypertext term. This is how an index might be customized to fit a particular organization's needs.

At this point, the indexed information is reduced into something much more manageable and meaningful for the EDMS. In this process, some words may be removed in order to adjust the granularity of information. (Again, granularity refers to the smallest unit or chunk of information that can be retrieved from the full content retrieval system). Sometimes terms can appear many times in a document dealing with a particular topic or domain, yet have very little meaning or significance to the user performing the search. Such words, while not considered stopwords, really become nothing more than extraneous elements that are selected for indexing simply because of their high statistical probability of existence within the document, even though they furnish little in the way of content.

In any sufficiently large document, only about half of the words will occur once, and about half of the remaining occurrences are for stopwords. Thus, a good estimate of the actual number of occurrences of key words to be indexed in a near full-text index is about 25-30 percent of any of the actual key words within a document. The average word length of these words in English is about six characters, and using up to twelve bytes to remember each occurrence results in an overhead of about 50% over the original text. However, economies of scale can often be achieved with larger documents such that the indexing scheme expands the text by less than 50%, even when it uses fine-grained development systems.

Once compiled, the inverted index will now become a type of dictionary of words that includes all important terms, minus stopwords of course. This online dictionary will also contain statistics that indicate how often these words appear and the key words that appear in the document. It also contains information about how to find the occurrence of these terms using file offsets or pointers.

Thus, indexing, while enormously powerful for information retrieval, has a certain price in terms of overhead. But once information in a document is indexed, it can then be retrieved much more easily.

However, there are several different types of retrieval methods that can be used within an indexable system.

Indexing schemes

In a document repository the indexing function usually occurs as a background task, so the user never knows it is happening. In most systems it takes place immediately after a document is checked into the repository.

The document must be fed to the indexing process in a format it can accept. Most of the popular indexing engines, such as Open Text, Verity, or Fulcrum, can accept most major word processing formats. For uncommon formats, it is important to recognize that these tools only require the words in the document, and as long as the ASCII text can be extracted, the process will work well. Where a particular document format cannot be read directly, the filters in the repository, or even in a third party package, can be used to extract the text. Sometimes, the PostScript file, if available, for the document may be used to "feed" the indexing engine.

One key point to understand up-front is what graphic formats can be accepted by these indexing engines. In some cases documents may have embedded graphics, with callouts that should be processed. These callouts are often elements people hope to retrieve in a search and after all if it isn't in the index, it won't appear in the search results. Therefore the indexing engine should be able to extract and index the text in graphics or graphic frames inside a document.

Depending upon the document distribution model used in the EDMS, the document consumer may or may not use the repository's full text index. Where the distribution function is detached from the repository, as in the case of a Web, a new index must be built and maintained. In the case of most Web sites, this indexing occurs via a Web "crawler" or "spider."

A crawler or spider is given either a "home" URL or top-level directory on the Web Server. The engine begins with this document and checks it against the current index. If the document is not in the index, it is added. Otherwise it is skipped and the engine either follows the hyperlinks in the document to another document or moves down the directory tree. Again, the new document is added to the index unless already present, and the engine moves on.

Using a top level URL makes sure that all information this Web links to is indexed. It is a complete and full index. By using directory structures, if the Web server is set up properly, custom indexes can be built for specific areas or subjects, contained in a particular set of directories. These can be used to build departmental indexes on a corporate-wide Web server. Choosing one over the other or doing both is a function of the user's requirements for locating or searching for information. If users expect to search in a particular way, it is often beneficial to create a custom index.

Searching

Searching is a powerful capability within an EDMS. Every type of user is likely to search for materials, whether they be authors, editors, reviewers, or consumers. They may be looking to simply locate and view a passage in a document, or they may wish to update the document. The structure of the EDMS can dictate some of the searching capabilities of the system.

In the model where all users access the repository for a document, then the full-text index as well as attribute searches are available. If the documents are "published" to another system, such as a Web Server for distribution, then the document consumers will generally only be given access to a full-text system. In some distribution schemes, attributes can be passed to the document viewing system, but this is highly dependent upon the viewing system selected, and is not yet a common feature.

Independent of the type of user or search, the process of formulating the query and processing the results must be simple. Generally speaking, a user specifies a particular attribute and value for that attribute or a full text string to be located. Sometimes the search engine allows for the use of wildcards, such as ? or * to denote unknown characters or strings. This makes searching easier for the user. The interface should be simple and easy to understand. Figure 6-1 shows one possible search interface.

Figure 6-1
Search
Interface
(Documentum)

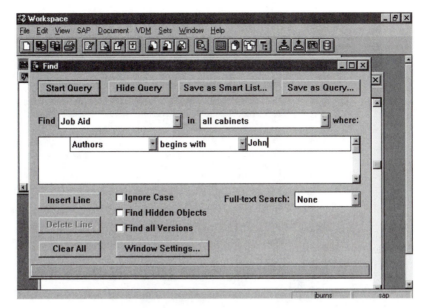

The next most important item to the user is the results interface. What can they expect to see after a query? Some online systems show an actual line of text around the found words or the first line of text from the document. More often though, the user is presented with a list of documents that meet the search criteria. Usually this list displays the title or subject attribute of the document, but sometimes this list can be customized to show other attributes. Figure 6-2 shows a sample search results window.

Figure 6-2
Search Results
Interface
(Documentum)

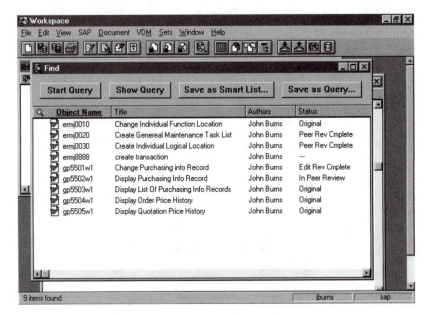

With document sets as large as they are today and growing larger every day, it is important to get the desired information as quickly as possible. Retrieval effectiveness is often judged by two parameters, recall and precision. Recall is defined as the proportion of relevant materials retrieved, or how much of all the right information you get. Precision is defined to be the proportion of retrieved materials that are relevant, or how much of the information you got is what you wanted. While these are important concepts they do little for the user in determining which document on the list is most likely to contain what they seek.

More pragmatically, most retrieval engines provide some type of ranking process to present the documents in a particular order, one that hopefully will assist the user in locating the desired information more quickly. Many systems present the document list in the order in which the documents were indexed in the system--first in, first on the list, etc. The most common ranking criteria are instances or matched-terms counts. Instances count the number of times words are found in a particular document. Matched terms is a combination of the number of times a word appears and how many of each of the key search words are located within the document.

Ranking algorithms can be helpful in quickly getting to the right information, but there are other ways. The most straightforward is to perform a secondary search, but against the results of the first search only. This helps to reduce the field very quickly. Some other types of search mechanisms found in many retrieval systems are as follows:

- semantics
- synonym
- Boolean
- proximity
- fuzzy word
- concept

Each of these are described briefly below. However, most importantly, developers must understand the full capability of the search and retrieval system and then ensure that this information is also provided to users, for it can greatly improve their productivity while it also reduces their frustrations.

The most simple add-on to an indexable retrieval system is to integrate synonyms. With synonyms, a pre-defined list is built to indicate that when searching for "book" also look for "publication." This action usually occurs behind the scenes so users never knows it is happening. If they do know it exists, they can request synonyms to be added.

Using semantics the system begins by prompting the user to choose a particular use or definition of a word. When all instances of the word are found, the text around the word is digested to eliminate entries that do not fit the intended meaning. For example, the word *stock* can mean a financial instrument, store merchandise, cattle, or inventory. Simply locating all occurrences of the word *stock* may produce a lot of undesirable hits. Semantic searching can therefore reduce this list of hits to only those that are relevant.

Boolean simply means the ability to join together multiple words or phrases into a single search. The most commonly used operators are AND and OR. But using the NOT operator can be very helpful in focusing searches. Proximity searching uses the distance between two terms to help infer meaning. For example, a user may want to search for "document management," but these two words are extremely common and will return a lot of false hits. Using proximity searches to search for "document" NEAR "management" may produce far better results. The terms NEAR and FAR are often user-definable.

Performing full text searches assumes that the words in both the search and index are spelled correctly, but as we know, this is often not the case. For example, in discussing conversion, optical character recognition was introduced, a process that often leaves many words incorrectly spelled, and the cost of clean-up is too high to justify in all but the most demanding circumstances. "Fuzzy" word and "concept-based" searches aid in retrieving information in these environments.

Fuzzy word searches use character and string pattern matching to find words that resemble the word or phrase presented to the retrieval engine. Similar in operation are "intuitive" or concept-based searches. The material is digested by the retrieval engine, and a number of techniques are used to discern relevance or "meaning." This meaning is then transformed into a new search, and the results are returned to the user.

In some areas, predefined concepts are used to read live feeds, like news wires, and pass only the stories that match the concept to the assigned individual. Again, this amounts to presenting the user with a custom view of information based on user-determined criteria. This is an excellent example of delivering the *right* information to the *right* person.

Summary

One of the main advantages of using indexing and search and retrieval technologies, such as those described above, is that within the electronic document collection they aid users in finding relevant information quickly and easily from a potentially vast document repository. Thus, the real power of these so-called full-text or content-based retrieval systems depends in part on the quality of the documents themselves, the richness of the index that has been created, and the types of search strategies that are employed.

7

Creation

Creating documents has been one of the most popular uses of the personal computer since its introduction. The focus of word processing over the last fifteen years or more has been to deliver paper output. How the tools got us to that point was not considered important. Many fine looking and useful documents with complex layouts were literally the result of many pages of output, scotch tape, and paste-ups. So long as the process was reasonably efficient and the job got done, what did it matter?

With online document management and delivery, however, it matters a great deal. Now authors must be concerned with the document's content, format, and even its electronic structure. Consideration must be given to how the document will appear both online and in paper forms. Authors have more powerful tools to ease the mundane tasks of formatting and layout, but much more is still required of them. Consequently, document creation is a much more complex task requiring planning.

Planning and Design

When deciding to put information or documents in an electronic form, developers often have the tendency to jump right in and start composing documents. But by taking the time to do some preliminary planning, they can save themselves considerable time and energy at the same time that they can make online documents more readable.

Planning the document development process involves several factors. Developers will need to consider the differences between what appears on the printed page and what appears on the screen, and how that makes a difference in the structure and design of the document. The differences between accessing information in a printed manual and getting the same information online means that the material might be organized differently for the two media. And though some tools automate the process of building online documents, the degree to which automation can be effective depends on the amount of time spent prior to beginning to build the electronic document.

Designing for Online Use vs. Printed Use

Many document developers find that users react to printed information differently than they do to online information. This is partially because it is much easier to find needed information online than it is to find it in print forms. Another reason is that information sometimes appears differently online than it does in its printed form. These differences in access methods and appearance mean that documents can be designed differently for alternative media. Of course, developers don't always have the luxury of being able to write and design information or documents strictly for online use. They may have to maintain print copies of the material in tandem with online versions.

Consider what the reader sees

Readers see the same information differently, depending on whether they are looking at it online or in print. This is because of the way the two media deal with nonlinear information. Nonlinear information is information which is related to the primary information being presented, but is not essential to it. Nonlinear information can consist of sidebars, explanatory tables, footnotes, illustrations, revision histories, related topics, and more. In contrast, print uses visual cues to differentiate the nonlinear information from the main topic being presented. Sidebars are presented next to the main information, with boxes around them, so we know that they are separate from the text. Explanatory tables are often set in smaller type, and footnotes appear at the bottom of the page with reference numbers. Most of these visual cues are not available to us when we read the information online.

Usually text is presented in a single text window, while illustrations appear in their own, independent windows, unless they are integrated with the text as compound objects. There are no headers or footers to provide cues as to where we are in the document. Balancing that, readers have tools not available in print for finding exactly what they want. For example, they can use hyperlinks to go to related information; they can use the interactive outlines to jump to other related information; or they can use full-text searching to find what they want.

Consider Hyperlink Information

Hyperlinks are the online equivalent of cross-references in a printed manual or book. If readers are interested in finding out more information about a topic, they click on the link and are taken to its destination. Although some tools make it easy for users to determine where the sources of links are, document builders can make it even easier for readers to use hyperlinks. They should try to make it clear to readers what they will see if they follow a hyperlink to its destination. This makes it easier for them to determine whether or not to follow the link. Ideally, the link source would show the title of the section being linked to.

Consider using visual conventions

By setting up visual conventions throughout all electronic documents, developers can make documents easier to use. But many of the visual conventions used in printed manuals aren't available in online manuals. So the key is to determine which visual conventions are used in the printed versions of materials, and then set up equivalent conventions for the online versions. Developers can then let their readers know of these conventions in a "How to use this electronic document" section of an online manual.

Consider document sizing

Part of the planning process to go online is determining the overall organization of an online document ahead of time. As developers put more information online, this step becomes essential. The capabilities of some tools to combine files into online documents which can be hundreds of megabytes in size, its ability to link among different documents, and to search across multiple documents mean that organizational choices are almost limitless. However, choosing the right sized document, based on how the documents will be used, will greatly improve the usability of online publishing products.

Consider how many files are needed for the online manual

Online documents can encompass literally thousands of separate text files. No matter how many files are used in an online document, the document looks like a single stream of text to the reader. While it may be tempting to make each online document a single file, there are several disadvantages to doing this, particularly in large documents. If a large online document consists of a single file, only one person can edit that source file at one time. In cases where material will be revised, it can be advantageous to allow different people to edit different portions of the document at the same time. Developers should also consider what must happen when the document is reassembled in a different format after editing. When a document is updated, will the development tool attempt to reestablish all the pre-existing headings, links and views? This process could never be perfect. If a single file is used, then the entire document must be updated, even if only a few words have changed. This increases the likelihood of lost links and headings. But if the document is broken down into many files, then only those files which have changed are updated, which reduces the amount of work necessary.

Consider the purpose and content of the information

The intended use of online information, and its contents, will affect how developers organize the information into different online documents. Remember that the Index and Search functions of all tools will usually show instances of a word or phrase within a given document. So if documents are excessively large, or contain information presented in different contexts, using the Index and Search becomes more difficult, due to the large number of search hits, or the number of false hits.

Consider how the information will be used

Another consideration is how the information will be used. For example, let's look at a company which makes a product needing documentation. There is an installation manual, a user guide, and a repair manual for the product, and obviously the three manuals share some of the same information. If developers combined the three manuals into one large online document, it would be possible for readers to find out all the information available about a particular part or process. And linking related sections together is easier than if the information was in three separate manuals.

On the other hand, consider the audience for the information developers put online. If the installation manual is used by the install-ers, the user guide only by end users, and the repair manual only by repair technicians, then it would prove confusing to each audience to combine the manuals, since they would see and find information they had no use for.

Authoring Requirements and Standards

In an earlier chapter, in discussing conversion processes, we pointed out that the process of authoring and delivering documents involves negotiation. It is a give-and-take process. It is paramount that the consumers of documents, those who use them to derive and add value for the organization, be in the driver's seat. While they are the ones who define the need, they are not the ones who define the solution. It becomes the EDMS development team's responsibility to work with the authors to redefine the creation process or develop a conversion methodology to meet these needs.

The needs of the user community for documentation will generally point to one solution or another for authoring. In the case where electronic paper, or an on screen image of a paper document is desired or sufficient, conversion is a very viable option and little or no changes are necessary to the existing creation tools or processes.

In more dynamic environments where documents need to be flexibly formatted on the screen, or smaller and more rapid delivery of documents is needed, then conversion to formats such as HTML makes more sense. To facilitate this conversion, the way the document is authored may need to change dramatically or the conversion process will require hand tooling of each document, a slow and expensive proposition.

In other environments where documents need to be dynamically assembled or re-purposed into many other documents, a more structured approach may make far more sense. Also, if issues of delivery over multiple platforms, operating systems, and even applications is required, then the authoring environment may need to change to a highly structured approach such as SGML (Standard Generalized Mark-up Language). SGML is not typically used for "internal" publishing efforts unless the organization has already adopted SGML for external publishing efforts.

The SGML Decision

The movement to SGML is not a trivial one. It requires a great deal of planning, and typically a whole new suite of tools. One of the advantages of SGML is that with this additional up-front planning, the downstream processes of re-using and compartmentalizing information will offer many benefits.

Many companies and organizations, in an attempt to standardize their document collections, are requiring that their document resources be put into a standard format that can be easily archived, retrieved, or transported into other application platforms or environments over time. The preferred choice today is SGML, which many large organizations and professional societies (such as the aerospace, pharmaceutical, and automotive industries) have already selected as their internal document standard.

Essentially, SGML allows documents to be codified and then broken down into elements that can be tagged with certain content identifiers. In other words, SGML is not a page description language for formatting, layout, and style like, say, Postscript. Rather, it offers a way of cataloging units of text such that they can be manipulated within an electronic document delivery system or even delivered in a print-based medium.

SGML essentially has two major components: the document type definition (or *DTD*) and the actual SGML-encoded text structures. The DTD tells an SGML system what the document looks like conceptually: that is, which components it will have, which units of allowable text can exist within the document, and so on. The tags or embedded codes within the SGML source document basically identify each unit of text according to the DTD (whether that be a heading, a paragraph, or some other type of document element). In other words, there cannot be an SGML document without a related Document Type Definition (DTD) defined in advance.

Many complex DTDs are published today (such as in the aerospace and automotive industries), but many more less sophisticated DTDs are being developed for corporate documentation systems in order to provide some level of SGML structure to otherwise randomly associated (or loosely collected) texts within an organization. Moreover, a number of SGML development tools have proliferated in the marketplace, and these typically include SGML structured editors, authoring systems, viewers, filtering, or conversion programs for getting proprietary word processor files into an SGML format.

In fact, the thrust toward SGML has been sufficient enough to have companies such as Microsoft and others come out with their own SGML export and import utilities or products that will work with their otherwise proprietary word processing systems. So a key question for managers today is whether to jump head-long into SGML technology or take a wait-and-see approach. Clearly, with the major online publishing vendors leaning in the SGML direction, it would make sense to at least keep in touch with SGML technologies as this particular marketplace matures.

The underlying structure and complexity of SGML often demands a very specific and sophisticated document management repository. In SGML the granularity goes below the file level, and the repository must support this construct. This book and the approach delivered here is focused at file based document management. SGML requires a different approach to managing these documents. From a technology perspective some of the document management systems discussed later in this book are capable of managing SGML, but the approach used is different.

Creating Documents

In many organizations individuals are not willing to move to an electronic document management system until such systems have been proven to be effective across a variety of circumstances and organizational functions. For this to happen, it is important that documents cease to be stand-alone entities and become tools for transmitting *knowledge*, not just *information*, across an organization. Here, the knowledge contained within online documents can have a leveraging effect, where its re-usability or re-purposing can support numerous workgroups in the organization. This being the case, it is useful to compare traditional documentation or document systems, and those that are based on a more intelligent model.

Organizational Knowledge in Documents

What many managers fail to realize is that documents are not simply static collections of texts, but rather tools for embedding organizational knowledge and transmitting it across an organization. Three types of knowledge can found be within documents, which are discussed in more detail below:

- Structural Knowledge (How a document is constructed)
- Domain-specific Knowledge (What the document contains)
- Contextual Knowledge (How document sections relate)

When documents are referred to as having embedded *structural knowledge*, what is meant is that there is usually a great deal known about how they are constructed. This means that issues of hierarchy, sequence, subordination and coordination of text sections, and navigational mapping cues or indicators (such as "See Also" references and footnoting) can be used to help bring greater usability to online documents by exploiting these explicit document structures. In other words, if a company or individual has spent a tremendous amount of time structuring documents, then this structural information should also go into the resulting online product. Moreover, because the new product is an electronic document, these structural elements can often be used to greater purpose, such as re-combining information to suit new audiences or user needs.

In other instances, *domain-specific knowledge* within a document can be used to help structure online information and make it more functional overall. Here issues such as *general* vs. *specific* information, *procedural* vs. *background* information, and the *functional role* of a document can all be used to help leverage information contained within an EDMS. In other words, once domain-specific knowledge has been identified, it can used to help compartmentalize information accordingly.

And finally, *contextual knowledge* contained within online documents can be used to help users navigate through information spaces more effectively. Here, meta-textual information such as *links, references, annotations, mixed-media* types of information (graphics, text, video), *dynamic document functions* (such as on-the-fly text updating or database field embedding with a document), and *preferred user presentations* can all be used to make an online information product or EDMS more responsive to user needs.

Tools for Creation

Early attempts to put documents online often required significant efforts in converting and editing the documents. Source documents in native formats were often converted to the format of a hypertext or online authoring tool. The documents were then edited to clean up conversion problems and enhancements added. These often included tables of contents, glossaries, outlines, hypertext etc.

The output from these systems was often quite good. The problem was maintenance. Even a few years ago, a corporate document may have gone unchanged for years. However, the time and effort required to develop these systems made maintenance a significant issue. As changes did arise, many of these systems collapsed under their own weight, primarily due to the limitations on keeping the online information current.

In today's world where change is constant and where updates are issued in days or weeks, this approach is not acceptable. Today the electronic documents must be capable of going to both paper and online with a minimal amount of effort. Recall that conversion is a non-value-adding event, and should be minimized. This requires some changes to the way documents are created.

In certain situations an approach such as SGML is viable, and it is widely believed that SGML will become the authoring standard of the future. In the here and now though moving to SGML overnight is not practical. What can be done to bridge this gap or at least address the need to leverage the intellectual assets stored in the documents?

The first step is to create a list of acceptable authoring tools and formats for text, graphic, image and multi-media formats. Often these standards are managed by MIS and culminate in a list of accepted or approved tools. By including both tools and formats, unusual requirements can be met by exception to the approved tools list, but still comply with the formats list. Adopting standard formats was discussed in the chapter on conversion.

Second, most organizations have a significant investment in authoring tools and a knowledge base in the authors on using these tools. The recommended approach is to leverage the existing tools and skills by taking advantage of new and existing capabilities in these tools. By exploiting these capabilities, and improving the skill set of the authors, document creation can be leveraged for both paper and value-added online delivery.

With most documents still primarily text-based, the biggest return on investment can be found in leveraging tools that work primarily with free text. And the two largest features to be exploited in word processing systems are the use of "styles" and "templates." These features have been around for many years, yet surprisingly few people have taken full advantage of them.

Styles

Styles are markers used in a document to control document formatting. A style is a set of formatting rules defined with a specific name. The user can select a section of text in a document and apply a pre-determined style. This text will take on the formatting of the style definition. Styles are a very powerful concept.

If properly used, styles ensure consistent formatting throughout a document. For example, in this text all the section titles have the same style; that way we as authors don't have to remember what typeface, font size, indenting, etc. to use for each section title. We simply choose the correct style and apply it. Should we decide to change the format of the section title, there is no need to change each instance throughout the document; simply redefine the style.

Styles, with a little bit of planning, can become much, much more than formatting controls. One common example is to use defined heading styles: Heading 1, Heading 2, etc. to indicate levels of organization within a document. Many word processors can use a set of styles to create a table of contents (TOC) for a document, complete with page numbers. It can literally be two clicks of the mouse to update a TOC after a document has been edited.

Styles such as Heading 1, Heading 2, etc., are very helpful in these instances but can become much more powerful. By giving styles names that make sense to the author and refer to what the element contains, styles help define the structure of a document. Using the Heading 1 and Heading 2 example, replace those style names with Chapter Title and Section Title respectively. Now it is clear when to use the style, and the document now contains structural knowledge. By inference the document now knows of itself, and is therefore "intelligent." An example is provided in Figure 7-1.

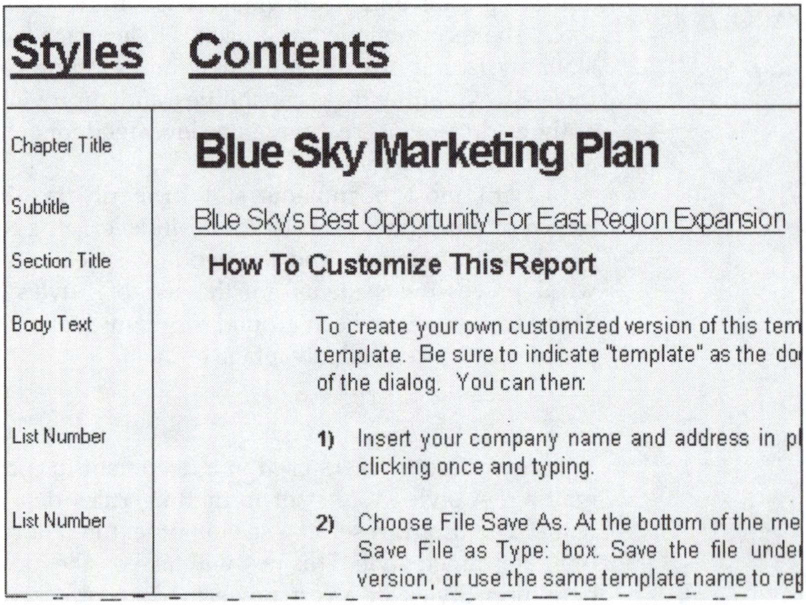

Figure 7-1
Styles in a
Word
Document

Styles	Contents
Chapter Title	**Blue Sky Marketing Plan**
Subtitle	Blue Sky's Best Opportunity For East Region Expansion
Section Title	**How To Customize This Report**
Body Text	To create your own customized version of this tem template. Be sure to indicate "template" as the do of the dialog. You can then:
List Number	1) Insert your company name and address in p clicking once and typing.
List Number	2) Choose File Save As. At the bottom of the me Save File as Type: box. Save the file unde version, or use the same template name to rep

This type of structural knowledge provides an immediate payback in making a document far more usable in online systems. Many conversion packages have the ability to convert and manipulate documents automatically based on styles. Commonly these styles are mapped to automatic outlines or tables of contents. Also many systems can automatically generate hypertext links and references based on style information. This can make the transition to value-added online documents much easier. One long-term payback is that documents are becoming semi-structured, a first step towards structured solutions such as SGML.

Templates

Templates are special types of documents that provide a variety of tools to help create and complete a document. The useful tools in the document authoring environment are boiler plate information, a basic layout, and styles. These tools are useful to the author in that they can make documents easier to create and contribute some basic quality control features to the document.

Styles, as discussed above, can enable consistent formatting and structure to a document. However, it is important that these formatting and structural features be used in all documents of a particular type or class, regardless of author. A template can contain pre-determined style definitions so that a template can be used by any author to generate documents that have similar structures as well as look and feel. This way the final copy of a document will look the same electronically and on paper regardless of who created it.

Templates can be very powerful tools for online document authors. The most common issue with documents is the need to serve two masters, paper and screen. One common trick is to develop two templates one for paper the other for online delivery. The first template, the one used for paper, is created to deliver the document in the desired paper format. The second template is created by copying the first template. The first of two changes is to the reduce the page size from 8.5 x 11 to a size that fits on a screen, perhaps 7.5 x 5. The second is to enlarge the fonts, and maybe remove the italics to make the text more readable. Simply by applying a new template a document can be transformed from one purpose to another.

Boiler Plate text is information that may need to appear in every document of a certain type. An example may be a legal disclaimer or notice in the beginning of all manuals. Rather than have each author enter it again and again and risk errors or omissions, the standard text is placed into a template and becomes boiler plate. When an author creates a manual based on the template, this text will automatically appear. Headers and footers are other common examples of boiler plate text.

Finally, many documents are a combination of forms and content. A memo is a good example; it has a *From:*, a *To:*, a *Subject:* and then the body. A template can be constructed to hold these basic form elements, then the user simply adds in the addressees in the *From:* and *To:* sections, along with the *Subject* and the contents of the memo. This is valuable because the user does not have to remember what types of information they need to put in the memo or the layout.

Templates can be constructed to hold any or all of these items. Templates can hold many other items, but they are very specific to the application and are usually geared to assisting the author with the more mundane tasks of word processing. Templates combined with styles, along with a bit of training for the authors, can make creating consistent electronic documents much easier.

Creation and Document Management

Most of the discussion thus far in this chapter has been on how to change the way documents are created in order to simplify their delivery within an online system. There are some equally important and very often overlooked elements of document creation that must be blended with the document management aspects of an EDMS. These topics will now be covered in detail.

Managing and Controlling Paper

Two of the great benefits of an electronic document management system is that all the information available is current and controlled. The distribution end of the document management system is designed to keep all the electronic documents up-to-date. However when paper is introduced, the ability to guarantee the latest version becomes nearly impossible.

In some systems, the distribution system is restricted from printing, but this often not a practical solution. Another approach is to require that users destroy paper copies after they are finished. The downside to this is that it requires the individuals to remember to do this, not a very reliable approach. Other schemes have ranged from limiting who can print, to ones as far fetched as using disappearing ink.

Each organization must take stock of its needs and requirements and manage this issue. One of the more useful approaches to this problem is to have the print engine place the current date in the margin of the document along with a warning statement. For example, the words

"Controlled document. Paper copy only valid for 24 hours from 3/13/97, 3:07pm"

at the top or bottom of the page may be sufficient. This requires modification to the distribution systems print engine. This can be a trivial or very involved task, but when it comes to keeping control of paper documents, there are few alternatives. Of course, training people in the organization to recognize the danger of paper is also critical to success

The other part of controlling paper comes in the authoring process. Once a document is checked out of the repository and an author begins to edit the document, it can be just as important that paper copies generated by the author are controlled. Where the authoring community is small, training can be effective to some degree. A system-wide approach is often the best choice. In the authoring environment, it is usually not possible to restrict printing, so another approach is needed.

Again the idea of some type of watermark or annotation on each page may be the best solution. In some cases, the absence of the official mark may be sufficient. In other systems where paper is often widely handled, the lack of an annotation may not be sufficient. In some systems, background watermarks are used only to indicate drafts. Figure 7-2 shows one such watermark. This requires very tight integration of the authoring tool with the document management system, and many tools do not provide the ability to integrate this type of functionality. For most organizations another approach must be used.

Date Fields

Many documents contain dates for a variety of reasons. Most word processing packages enable the user to dynamically assign the current date to a date field. For example, a business letter may contain the date of origin. Since the letter may be in draft form for weeks, and what is desired is that the current date be used when the final version is printed, many people use a date field. Every time this document is opened, this date field is updated to reflect the date of the current computer system clock.

This is helpful in the creation process but presents issues from a document management perspective. If another user decided to view a copy of the document in its native format, the date would change when the document was opened. This user either believes that this letter was issued today, or knows it was not, but then does not know what date it was issued. Date fields should therefore be given due consideration before being used in documents to be controlled in an EDMS.

Version

In many organizations version numbers are already in wide spread use for document control. Users can check an electronic or paper copy of a document and identify the version number and cross check it against the list of current documents. This is a very viable approach. To simplify this cross checking process the version number

Figure 7-2
Draft
Watermark
(Microsoft)

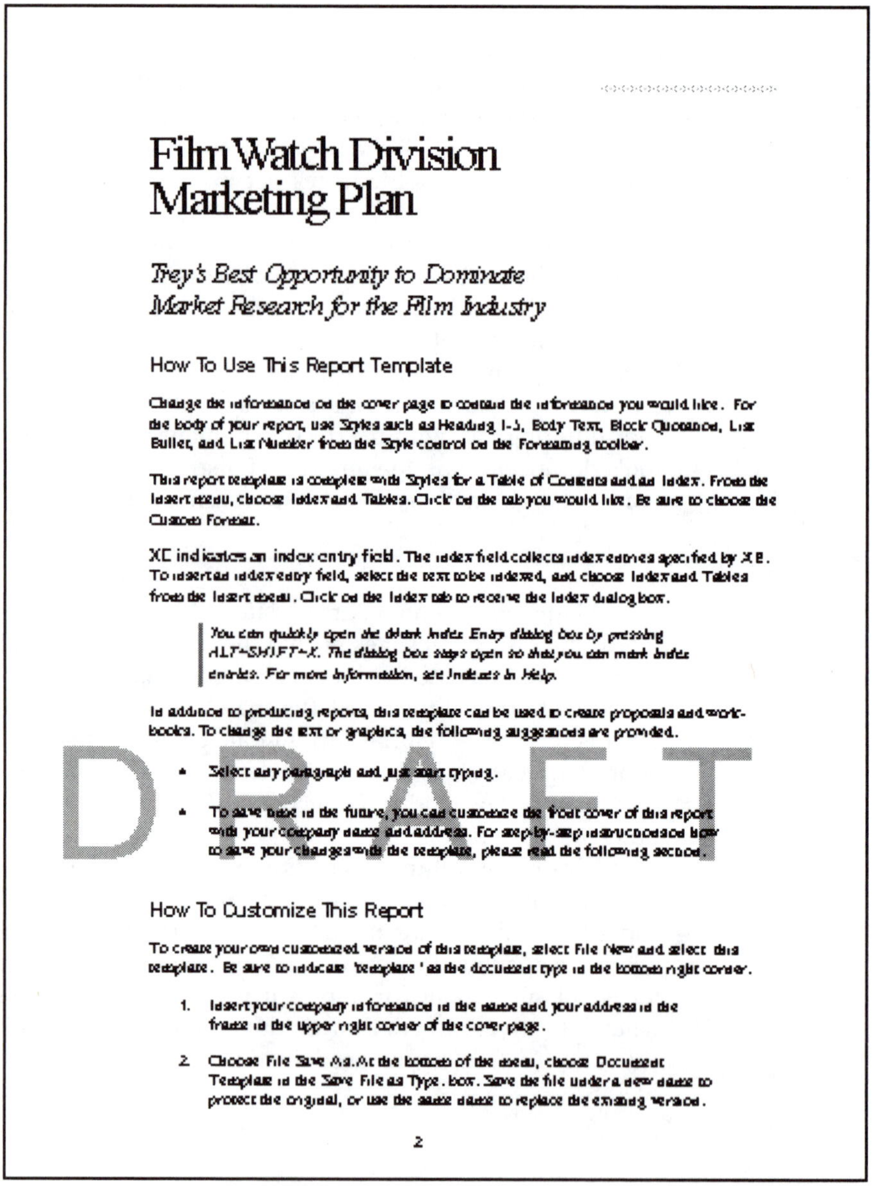

Film Watch Division
Marketing Plan

Trey's Best Opportunity to Dominate
Market Research for the Film Industry

How To Use This Report Template

Change the information on the cover page to contain the information you would like. For the body of your report, use Styles such as Heading 1-3, Body Text, Block Quotation, List Bullet, and List Number from the Style control on the Formatting toolbar.

This report template is complete with Styles for a Table of Contents and an Index. From the Insert menu, choose Index and Tables. Click on the tab you would like. Be sure to choose the Custom Format.

XE indicates an index entry field. The index field collects index entries specified by XE. To insert an index entry field, select the text to be indexed, and choose Index and Tables from the Insert menu. Click on the Index tab to receive the Index dialog box.

> *You can quickly open the Mark Index Entry dialog box by pressing*
> *ALT+SHIFT+X. The dialog box stays open so that you can mark index*
> *entries. For more information, see Indexes in Help.*

In addition to producing reports, this template can be used to create proposals and workbooks. To change the text or graphics, the following suggestions are provided.

- Select any paragraph and just start typing.

- To save time in the future, you can customize the front cover of this report with your company name and address. For step-by-step instructions how to save your changes in the template, please read the following section.

How To Customize This Report

To create your own customized version of this template, select File New and select this template. Be sure to indicate 'template' as the document type in the bottom right corner.

1. Insert your company information in the name and your address in the frame in the upper right corner of the cover page.

2. Choose File Save As. At the bottom of the menu, choose Document Template in the Save File as Type box. Save the file under a new name to protect the original, or use the same name to replace the existing version.

2

is often put in the header or footer of a document so that it appears on each and every page of a document.

When an EDMS is introduced a new issue around version numbers appears. The version number is always a standard attribute of the document repository. The version numbering and sequencing schemes are built into the repository. This attribute becomes the official version number for a document. If the version number is typed into the footer of the document by the author, it now needs to be maintained.

When documents were really controlled and updated by one author/owner, this was not an impossible task. In collaborative, networked environments with a decentralized control structure, however, this proposition is hit-and-miss at best. Somehow the document authoring environment must be capable of extracting information from a repository.

One common type of approach is to keep the version number in a data element or field in the document. A reference to this field is placed in the header or footer as appropriate. During check-in and out this field value is updated from the repository. This approach, like watermarks, requires some integration of the authoring tool with the repository. Dealing with the version number should actually be easier than a watermark. The development and support for the Open Document Management API (ODMA) standard may make this task easier and more transparent across applications and repositories.

Production Process

It is important to recognize that when a complete EDMS is put into place, the use of key technologies can revolutionize how work gets done. In using a document repository to control and drive the document production process, authors and others in the document production process can be freed from a number of low value add tasks freeing up time for the creative and high value add process.

By steering the author's interaction with the repository instead of local files and network drives, the writer is freed from having to keep track of filenames, locations and status. The repository will handle these tedious tasks. The repository, if coupled with workflow, will automatically route and track documents through the production processes. This means multiple review and approval steps, cycles, collection/administration of comments and feedback. It can drive the paper and electronic distribution processes by printing and converting documents when required. It also eliminates the constant nagging question of where is the "such and such" document; the system can tell the interested party directly, without walking the halls, asking everyone in sight or rifling through people's in-boxes.

Summary

All of this leads to the potential to streamline, reengineer and reorganize the document production processes. By using an EDMS, the document production process can be transformed from a loosely organized group of people following a set of guidelines, to a smooth-running, precision-controlled information factory. When documents consume nearly 15% of an average corporation's revenues, this offers real and measurable benefits to the organization as a whole.

8

Workflow

Workflow, simply stated, is a business process: the flow of work through an organization. But a more practical and less circular definition is the division of a business process into a sequence of actions or steps to achieve a desired outcome. In the context of document management, workflow can be defined as the movement of a document through this series of steps to meet a desired business objective.

Every organizational person is subjected to, and interacts with, workflow, usually everyday, all day. Phone calls are received, information is provided, and actions are undertaken. Expense reports are filled out, approved and paid. Documents are reviewed, redlined, edited, approved and published. Each of these are examples of workflow; however, not everything we do is workflow.

When is the work we do not part of workflow? A lot of the work we do is informal and collaborative, brokering information and skills among sets of people. There is a broad set of steps, but no sequence. The people involved are not defined, and these people are given little or no specific actions to take. Email is often mistaken as "workflow." It can be an enabling part of a workflow, but often messages and documents are routed from one person to the next without knowledge of an overall process or even a desired outcome. The use of Email and collaborative environments are very valuable in our organizations today, but should not be construed as workflow.

Workflow technology is aimed at streamlining the execution of the business processes. It seeks to eliminate wasted time, the time documents spend sitting in an in-box, the time spent gathering information to take action, and the time spent moving the document from one person to the next. It also includes the ability to track a document through a process. This information supports determining exactly where in a process a particular item is at a particular time. This same information can also be used for identifying and fixing bottlenecks in the current processes.

Document Management and Workflow

Document management without workflow is an opportunity missed. Document management in and of itself is valuable, but with workflow it enables the reengineering of the business processes, offering a far greater return. Unfortunately, reengineering has driven many organizations to build large, complex systems to move information within and between organizations. These systems often focus on data and not on documents, leaving the "other" 80% of corporate information unused. In cases where these systems do focus on documents, they tend to be "fixed" systems that are not adept at being changed to match the next generation of business processes. In our world today change is the only constant, and any system must be capable of handling this constant change.

Workflow technology is the system that brings the people and the documents together in concert with a business process to drive an accomplishment toward a final result. Workflow is then comprised of four primary elements:

- Process - the sequence of steps
- Actions - what's to be done
- People- who is to accomplish these items
- Document - the focus of the process

In some circles and systems, workflow is referred to as the 3R's: Routes (process), Rules (actions), and the Roles (people). Each of these elements is presented later in this chapter. These systems allow for continual change by modifying any of these process elements.

A classic case of document management and workflow comes from ISO 9000 certified organizations. At the highest level, the ISO standard requires an organization to:

"Say what you do, and do what you say."

In the design group of many certified manufacturing companies, this forces the definition of a structured workflow for critical documents such as design specifications, engineering drawings, etc. These documents need to be controlled and managed through versions, but must also follow a prescribed path for reviews and approvals. The standard also specifies that quality records, proof the process was followed, be maintained. Organizations look to both document management and workflow together to provide this capability. A document management repository controls the documents; a workflow engine controls the review and approval process; and the auditable history kept during check-in/out, versioning and work processes all come together to fulfill the ISO requirements.

Figure 8-1 shows a complete work flow model for an engineering specification in an ISO 9000 certified organization. Note that it shows the document class, process, actions, and people: all elements of a complete workflow.

Figure 8-1
Workflow for
Engineering
Design

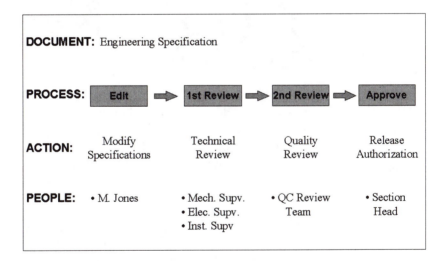

Integration With Repository

From a functional perspective, workflow is the layer that sits between the repository and the users of a document management system. From an architecture point of view, workflow technology can be an integrated part of the repository or an add-on application. These are shown in Figure 8-2.

Figure 8-2
Relationship
Between
Workflow and
Repository

Functional Block Diagram

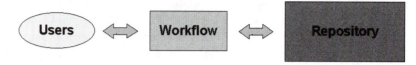

Architecture Diagram

Third Party or   **Integrated**
Add-on Workflow   **Workflow**

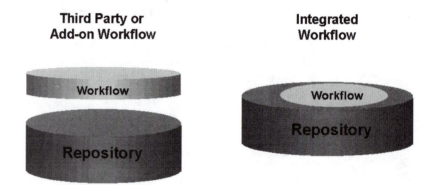

Most of the major vendors in the EDMS arena have either developed their own workflow systems within the repository or have integrated third-party products. The choice is not binary, but rather one of shades of gray. As presented over and over, the best way is to determine the organization's requirements and then select the products that fit best.

In the case of products where workflow is an integral part of the document management system, this offers several advantages. First, the integration can be very tight, so the workflow engine has full access to all necessary components of the repository such as users and groups, access controls, versioning models, and the document attributes. Another advantage of this approach is that there is one less client to deploy, one less interface to learn, and one less place to "do work" from a user's perspective. A third and final advantage is the ability to treat workflow as "document object" which can be revised and edited over time, with these changes being controlled and tracked just like a document.

On the other hand, systems where workflow is an add-on component offer other advantages. The most obvious is that users don't have to pay for things they don't need. Many organizations decide to leave workflow to a later stage, choosing instead to focus on using the repository to control of the organization's assets. Second, individual vendors can focus on what they do best, one on the repository--the other on workflow, and a system can be constructed using best of class for each product area.

It is important to recognize this difference in vendors products, because the costs will reflect this difference. If one vendor has integrated workflow and repository functions, this must be compared against the cost of a repository-only system, plus the cost for the workflow add-on.

Workflow in conjunction with a repository, whether integrated or a third party add-on must be integrated to work together. There are several key areas where the systems must work together well for the integration to be successful:

- Users and Groups
- Security
- Versioning
- Attributes
- Documents
- Relationships

Some of these areas are to prevent duplication of effort and thereby avoid the issues of synchronization and replication of the data. Others are required to get the system to function properly in a document driven environment.

Setting up and maintaining users and groups along with access control lists is a significant effort. In some cases this information is pulled from other IS systems such as networks or Email systems. Forcing an EDMS application to maintain separate lists for the repository and workflow is unacceptable. Also, information about documents in terms of attributes or relationships can be important to the workflow process and should not be duplicated.

Versioning and workflow components are probably the most tightly-coupled technologies within an EDMS. The workflow engine must "understand" each of the various versioning models, and be able to maintain the integrity of these models. The workflow model must understand when a new revision is created and how this relates to the check-in and check-out functions. After a document is checked in, it is the workflow engine which will then direct the document through the required steps in the business process. If the business calls for the document to remain at the current revision until the final step, the workflow engine must ensure that this requirement is met while conducting the check-in and check-out processes during the document route.

The workflow engine must also understand if each of these steps must be tracked for audit purposes and keep the records if necessary.

This function should not be duplicated in the repository by keeping track of each and every check-in or check-out. Often, the versioning of one document will begin another workflow for a related document. The workflow engine must be able to use the versioning as a triggering event. This requires access to the relationships that "connect" one document to another.

The workflow engine may also need to pass information about the document, or attributes, to the people in the workflow process. If this is the case, the workflow engine must have access to, and the ability to read from and act upon, the attributes of a document. Finally, the workflow system must be capable of transferring documents from secure vaults of the repository to a user's desktop and launching the appropriate application in order to simplify the user's interaction with the system.

Relationships offer an astounding array of possibilities for workflow activity in concert with document management. If a document is the parent of several children, and one of those children is modified and passed through a workflow process, what happens next? The options are a) nothing--not a good choice, as we are giving up valuable information about the system; b) notify the owner of the parent document; c) use this as a trigger to begin a workflow for the parent. This last option is the typical response where the parent document may be an entire manual and the child documents are chapters.

Process

A workflow consists of steps and the sequence of those steps necessary to reach an end objective, which is usually the business process. Associated with each step will be the people and the actions they are expected to take. Developing this workflow is the process of business process reengineering (BPR) and is addressed in our methodology section.

From a technological perspective, it is sufficient to state that a "process" must be defined in order for the workflow to be built, for there must be a model for the software to follow. In the process domain of workflow, there are two fundamental types of process: structured and ad-hoc.

Structured processes imply that a document will follow a predetermined set of sequenced steps in order to reach an end point. Figure 8-1 showed a structured workflow. This set of steps is usually defined for a type or class of documents. This ensures that all documents of a particular type will follow the same steps, and that the author or creator does not decide what steps this document will follow. This provides integrity to the overall business process; we know there is a controlled way for a document to reach its final endpoint. For example, all documents of type "procedure" will go through steps A, then B, then C. The author is not given the latitude to decide that B is not necessary.

Ad-hoc is exactly the opposite of structured. It allows for the workflow process to be created "on-the-fly" based on whatever the author or anyone else in the process decides. Ad-hoc is actually the way a lot of daily work gets done. It is a collaboration, but one where the document being tracked is not driven through a pre-determined process. Remember even an ad-hoc workflow requires an endpoint, it just does not have a defined path to get there. An ad-hoc workflow is very hard to depict since it is created "on the fly."

Each of these approaches is a viable method of workflow in a general business process. However, earlier in Chapter 3, the definition of documents within an EDMS as mission-critical implies that there should be a pre-defined set of steps for the document to reach its end objective. For example, it is not desirable for design documents for new products to reach manufacturing without the consent of the marketing, finance, and R&D departments.

In any real-world EDMS application, ad-hoc workflow does have a place, but it must be limited and controlled. When the document is at one step in the workflow, it may be advantageous to add a new person/workgroup to the work process. One scenario is to Email, call, or send the document to them and incorporate their comments at the current step. However, this does not formally capture that the document was reviewed by that workgroup. For example, if "marketing" may have wanted "legal" to review a new product plan for patent infringement issues, it should be required that this step be formally documented along with any comments they provide. This provides a formal audit trail for the document. Using Email outside the electronic workflow system does get the job done, but provides no audit trail or history.

In dealing with business critical documents, the workflow should be pre-determined. This workflow should function as the minimum route for the document. The system should prevent anyone from removing or changing these basic steps for a document. However, the author and others involved in the process should be able to add additional steps along with designated people and actions. These changes should be to a specific document workflow and not the entire class of documents. If the change affects all documents of a class, then the structured workflow for this class should be revised.

Actions

For each step in a business process or workflow there must be a defined action. What is it you want the individual to do at this step? In most systems, a pre-defined message can be built and sent to the user along with the request for action to assist them in performing a particular work step. There are generally two classes of workflow used as part of an EDMS. Review and approval is one; the second is a catch all for all the tasks not directly related to releasing a document.

The review and approval processes are usually focused on getting a document from the author or editor through to distribution. This usually entails reviews and finally approvals. These processes range from extremely simple, where one person reviews and approves the document, to the very complex. A document may go through three sets of departmental reviews in parallel, then two cross- functional teams review in series, then off to a corporate editor for smoothing, back to the author for concurrence, followed by five sets of serial approvals. At any point, rejection by a user may kick the document back to the author to begin the cycle again.

This "other" class can take many forms. Common forms include conversion, notification, or external program calls. One form might be a production process where a document is converted from source to PostScript, sent to the printing department and finally hard copies are joined with other documents and mailed out. Another example may involve the conversion of, say, a Word document to HTML, which is then routed to a WebMaster who adds additional hypertext links, and finally the document is copied to a Web Server.

In some cases, a workflow may combine both types of steps. A common occurrence is the review and approval of a document, so it is ready for distribution. The document may then continue on through the workflow process for distribution, involving conversion, printing, posting or mailing. Joining these two forms can have enormous benefits in streamlining the business processes, reducing cycle times, or providing almost instantaneous electronic updates to document sets.

People

Of course, people are the key to any workflow process. But they must understand the overall workflow and how they fit into the scheme. Equally important is that the users understand the action to be taken when a document arrives. Beyond educating the users in the process and actions to be taken, the only technical challenge regarding people is defining their roles in the workflow system.

Similar to the users in a repository, it is not generally a good idea to use actual individuals in a workflow. People change jobs, roles, and responsibilities often. It is better, then, to have a job as a node on the work process map, and not an individual. By using a job, only one list of tables needs to be maintained, matching jobs with individuals names.

Another key issue for workflow, not often seen in a repository only application is the concept of an "agent." An agent is someone defined to act on behalf of another individual. Persons may have a peer defined as their agent to act on their behalf when they are away from the office. In a paper world, we are used to rifling through a colleague's in-box to find an important document and keep it moving on its way; this is the electronic equivalent.

Workflow is perhaps the most difficult part of implementing an EDMS within an organization. The issues are not technical but human. By developing work processes and putting in a software application, we are, in fact, creating rules that users must abide by. Before, things may have been left to chance, now they are highly structured. Users must be educated on the gains and benefits from this system such as streamlining the process, one place to receive work, etc.

To achieve the benefits of a workflow system, it *must* be used, and used religiously. If a complete electronic workflow system is established, and someone decides to bypass it by going to paper and routing that back to the author, the workflow is a lost cause. Once an electronic workflow system is breached by paper, the ability to track the steps and comments as well as drive the remainder of the process will fail. This system must be very carefully crafted and introduced into the organization to be successful.

Features and Functions

Crafting a system that meets the needs of the business and the acceptance of the users requires an understanding of the features and functions of the workflow package. This is divided into two parts: the issues around building and maintaining a workflow system, and how the user interacts with this system.

Building Workflows

There are several considerations in determining the workflow requirements for any organization. First are the types of workflow approaches used. Generally speaking, there are four types of workflow:

- sequential
- parallel
- branching
- time driven

Many of these are combined into one workflow process to more closely model a business process.

Sequential workflow is linear set of steps, each one dependent upon successful completion of its predecessor. The second type is parallel, where a document may be passed to multiple people or processes for action at the same time. This has the benefit of reducing cycle times over a sequential process, but introduces the issue of reconciling the results of each parallel path, as illustrated in Figure 8-3

Figure 8-3
Linear and
Parallel
Workflow

Sequential (Linear)

Parallel

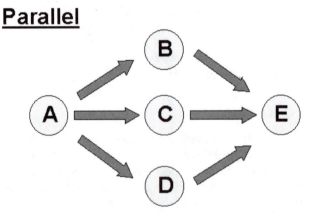

Branching is a conditional type of workflow, where paths to be followed are chosen based on some criteria. This can be the decision of a human or an automatic branch based on some predetermined criteria. Often, the automatic branching is driven by data provided either in the workflow process or by the attributes of a document. An example might be a person who approves a policy decision based on the financial impact of that policy: If the impact is under $5 million, the department manager approves it; if it is over $5 million, the VP approves it. This is illustrated in Figure 8-4.

Figure 8-4
Branched
Workflow

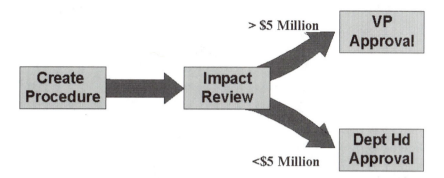

The final workflow type is time-driven and is often used to keep a process moving. A time period is defined for a step, along with the action to be taken if that time period is exceeded. This action can range from moving the document past the current step and on to the next, to notifying the person again, or notifying the author and the assigned person's supervisor. For example, a document may be routed to persons who are given one week to respond. If they don't respond within a week, a notice may be sent to the author of the document that the due date has passed. This helps key individuals set priorities and enables them to keep a process moving. This is a complex task for many workflow systems, and each implementation will vary widely.

The following example, Figure 8-5, combines sequential, parallel, and branched workflow for both review and approval. The example is the production of a procedure document. The process begins with creation, either an entirely new procedure or as a revision to an existing one. First, it can only be edited by the author. Second, it is reviewed by mechanical, electrical, and instrument design engineers, then by the head of the department. The approval is then dependent upon the level of complexity of the procedure (simple or complex), assigned by the department head. If the process is complex, a usability review is added. The procedure is approved by the section manager.

These several examples suggest that workflow can be best depicted graphically. Therefore, any good workflow engine should allow for graphical creation and viewing of any workflow process. These processes must be available to the administrator who creates the workflow, but also to the users who receive a document for action. Users are always better off knowing where their actions fit into an overall process. Figure 8-6 shows the interface for graphical workflow in one system.

Figure 8-5
Example of
Procedure
Workflow

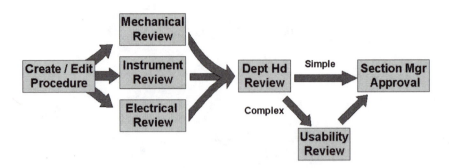

Figure 8-6
Graphical
Workflow
(Open Text)

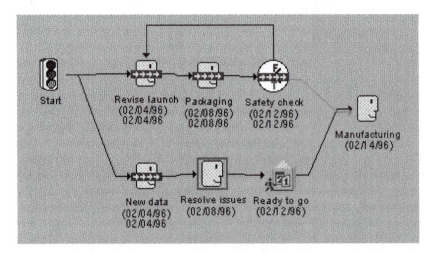

Another important part of creating or building a workflow is how to select the actions and people for each of those actions. It should allow the creator to use the same users and groups in the repository system and to create new ones where warranted. Deciding when and how to begin a workflow process is important. Will it be when a new version of a document is created, or some other automatic trigger in the system? Is there a way to initiate a process manually? These are important questions for both the business process and the software itself.

Finally, the system should allow for creating a library of workflows. These workflows should be treated just like documents in the repository and allow them to be accessed and version-controlled. Workflow should be able to be associated with a particular document class or type, yet allow individual instances of a document type to follow a similar set of workflows. This aspect offers flexibility but as with all flexibility, it presents the possibility of abuse and must be carefully controlled.

User Interactions

With many workflow initiatives having failed before any significant benefits are achieved, significant attention must be paid to how the user interacts with the workflow process and potentially the system. This interaction usually begins with an "in-box" where tasks to be performed are presented.

Most of the interfaces are "Email" like, including a listing of tasks to be performed along with information about the action to be taken, the document(s) attached, the person the information is coming from, etc. Figure 8-7 shows a typical workflow in-box. This in-box is part of the document management client interface in an integrated system, and in a workflow client interface as an add-on.

Figure 8-7
Workflow
In-box
(Documentum)

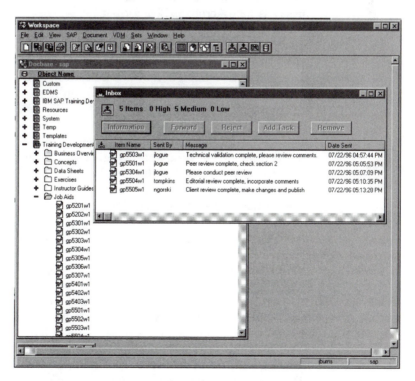

Unless users' primary jobs are document production, they normally do not open the document management client application every day, let alone several times a day. This presents the issue of work being routed to them via this in-box, but they do not "work" from this in-box. Most users these days live by Email, and many of them keep their Email box open all day, every day. To address this gap, most workflow systems will notify a user of an assigned action via their Email system, alleviating the requirement to check multiple in-boxes for "things to do." Documents are *not* routed for actual work in the Email system because the workflow/document management repository cannot maintain positive control over the document if it is handed off to another system like Email.

Users, in working with their in-boxes, should have the ability to perform any number of functions relative to the documents. The actions prescribed as a part of this step should be as simple as the click of a button to review, approve, etc. Another is the ability to see the workflow, the attributes about the document, and the document itself. The workflow should be graphically displayed. The document should be in a viewable format which the intended viewer should be familiar with; this could be a native document or a visual representation of one in, say, Adobe Acrobat's PDF format.

A user should also have the ability to easily delegate this work to another person in the organization. Equally important is the ability to add additional ad-hoc workflow. This workflow should be metered such that at its completion any results are returned to the initiator of the ad-hoc process before being passed on to the next step in the pre-determined workflow.

In coupling workflow with document management, the most popular use of this technology is to review and approve a document. Electronically reviewing, approving, or otherwise working with a document presents several challenges. How can comments be added easily by a user, captured, and made available to all interested parties? Couple this requirement with the fact that the document may have been produced in any number of packages ranging from a Windows-based word processor to a UNIX-based CAD package and the problem gets complex.

There are no easy answers to this issue and it usually requires adopting an additional application. In one approach the documents are converted either prior to or during the routing to a common format. Each user is then provided with a tool in which the document can be viewed. In another case, each user is provided with a generic viewer which can convert many common formats and the documents are converted by the client's workstation on demand. In both cases, conversion accuracy is paramount. Even missing one or two words can change the entire meaning of a document.

Once a document is delivered in some type of viewable format to the user, this user must be given tools to provide comments. Often, this includes redlining and adding extra-textual notes so that the document can be marked up for changes. These are usually annotation "layers" which sit on top of the document and hold the comments separate from the actual document itself. The key is to be able to capture these comments and provide them to the people in the other steps or back to the author/editor to make the changes. In some instances each user is given a different color for comments and the author/editor can then view these layers individually, in groups, or even merge them together. An example of online comments is presented in Figure 8-8.

Figure 8-8
Online
Comments
(Adobe)

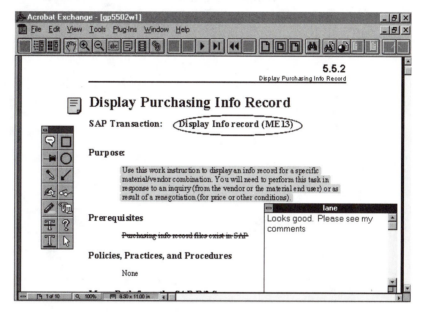

Implementing a review and approval system which can be technically accomplished and managed, as well as meet with user acceptance, is therefore no simple task. Involving the users who will do the online review and approval processes is critical to building a successful system. Recall that if the electronic review or approval processes break down and paper intercedes, the workflow process is dead, along with all of its benefits such as audit trails, reduced cycle times, and enforced business processes.

Summary

Implementing an EDMS and not addressing workflow is solving only half the problem. Workflow is the key to improving performance by eliminating low value add tasks and streamlining business processes. Workflow often goes hand in hand with business process reengineering and can lead to dramatic return on investments if properly utilized.

The key to implementing workflow is not technical, but rather the people and their resistance to change. The most critical aspect of workflow is making it match the way the knowledge workers operate, not making the workers operate the way the system does. Careful analysis upfront, coupled with strong implementation are two ways to minimize risks and maximize the use and therefore benefits of workflow in the organization.

Distribution

Distribution in the world of EDMS is the act of delivering the needed information, usually in document form, to the end user who will use or consume it. This is perhaps the most important part of any EDMS application. The creation of a document is the process of capturing organizational knowledge into a permanent data form, but it is the *use* of that knowledge that generates value to the organization. Recall that a successful system is defined to be one which

delivers the correct information, to the right person, at the proper place and time.

In considering how to deliver the information to individuals, several key topics must be addressed. First is the organization and presentation of information. Also, the types of technologies used to view electronic information are important. Finally, the architecture of the distribution process, including its relationship to the repository, is critical to selecting and building a solid distribution mechanism.

In an electronic document management system, the tendency is often to focus on the electronic delivery of information only. However, there are large parts of many organizations where paper is either the only *viable* means or is still the *best* means to deliver information to a consumer. So before we present the details of electronic publishing, let's look at some of the elements to be considered in paper delivery systems.

Paper Distribution

Paper is rapidly being displaced by electronic delivery, but it still remains a large part of all organizations. Why? Some reasons are practical, others technological. First, electronic delivery means having a computer and some way of receiving information. There are still lots of people in many organizations that do not currently have computers, so the thought of spending several thousand dollars per person, per year, for a computer, training, and support, requires a compelling reason. Second, if information is not very dynamic, or if the cost of using outdated information is low, then paper may be sufficient.

Also, paper is often a superior medium. It is very portable and people are familiar with it. Most people use documents their entire lives. It will not be for another generation until we have people who have truly grown up in an electronic world. So people are still more comfortable reading paper than screens.

On the technology side, paper does not require batteries or power cords. It also provides superior resolution. Typical printers today, laser or inkjet, operate at 600 dots per inch. Most monitors are in the 72-100 dots per inch range, with the best monitors at 150 DPI. This gives paper four times the density, producing vastly superior resolution and clarity, making it easier to read.

Initiating Distribution

EDMS applications can facilitate the use of paper in organizations where it makes sense, and in several ways. The first is to drive the distribution process of paper itself. When a document is finally completed, through the review and approval process, the workflow engine can initiate the distribution process. In an earlier chapter on conversion, we pointed out that this effort was focused on transforming the document from one format to another. However, this same workflow engine could also kickoff a process that prints the new paper version of the document.

Printing one copy of a document and notifying the right person in the reproduction group may be sufficient for some organizations. However, other significant gains are possible. Paper documents are often distributed to a large number of people via inter-company or even regular US Mail. In these cases, it is possible to create an electronic distribution list and then merge the document and this distribution list to the production printer. These machines are often capable of printing documents, creating a mailer page, and shrink wrapping the entire package, all without manual intervention. Since distribution lists are tied to a document, it makes sense that this list be tied to an EDMS.

Many organizations already have this electronic mailing list and the necessary print capabilities to perform this task. If the EDMS and the workflow engine can track which distribution lists go with which documents, and then can feed this system with the document and the distribution lists, this process can be automated. However, this is not always a viable solution because of the cost of printing and distributing large volumes of paper; updates are often made via change pages. Here a set of replacement and new pages is generated, and sent along with instructions for adding, replacing, and removing pages from the original document to the user community. When working with an EDMS which maintains granularity at the file or document level, and not below, this process cannot be automated and human intervention is required.

Paper (Print) On Demand

Producing, shipping, and managing paper is an expensive task. Often, large documents are produced in bulk and then warehoused. By printing in bulk, economies of scale come into play and reduce the cost of production. These documents are then stored and shipped to the people who need them when requested. There are two problems with this approach: the cost of shipping and the fact that a document may become obsolete *before* it is shipped. The cost of shipping, especially in "just-in-time" businesses that necessitate overnight deliveries, can be enormous.

Technology affords some solid solutions to this problem. Many printing equipment vendors have created document production systems which can print the document, insert tabs, and then bind the finished document, all without human intervention. These systems can often make small production runs practical both from a time-to-produce as well as cost perspective. Though this can also alleviate the problem of obsolesce, it may not address the shipping cost issue if these systems are centrally located.

If an organization has regional offices where this type of production system is practical, then the shipping cost can be eliminated. The document can be electronically transmitted from a central repository for pennies. This would allow, for example, a user in Japan to request a copy of a document stored in the U.S. and then have it printed "on demand." This makes document delivery truly just-in-time.

While these systems are powerful, there must be a tight integration with the authoring tools and repository to make this happen. This level of integration is usually only found in professional publishing systems such as those offered by Interleaf or Frame. This entire process must be very carefully mapped out, and involving the printing vendors is crucial to its success.

Benefits of Electronic Document Delivery

Electronic document delivery has several advantages over paper for many organizations. Some of the more notable ones are:

- Lower cost of document distribution
- Easier maintenance and updates to the documents
- Faster access to documents
- Greater nonlinear access to information
- Customized views of the document set
- Better quality of presentation

These benefits are essentially brought about by applying new technological approaches to working with traditional textual materials. For example, by combining database programming approaches with hypertext navigational tools, access to pre-processed information is dramatically improved, where hours of search time can often be reduced to minutes or seconds by using train-of-thought browsing methods. Add automated indexing and the speed of retrieval of specific text passages is again boosted dramatically. And online publishing systems within a GUI environment offer windowing techniques, scaleable font technologies, and graphics engines that can render a quality of presentation of documents that, in some ways, is superior to print media and much more flexible. What's more, new text processing tools that combine these features can automatically process existing documents into online publishing and other applications that result in lower production costs and ease of distribution and maintenance of documents that are delivered in a compressed, online form.

In terms of electronic document distribution, the benefits of delivering text-based materials online (say through a centralized file server or network) are also impressive, even if only the cost of document delivery for this new medium is considered over paper-based products.

Aside from the economic benefits of this technology, we also need to consider that online documents have now become an integral part of the workplace, replacing the outmoded context where people were comfortable for many years with paper-based products as information or knowledge delivery tools. In other words, there is now a cultural or paradigm shift taking place that is pushing today's knowledge workers inexorably into the world of online information delivery.

Advantages of online publishing also include lower production costs for information products defined in terms of both dollar savings and reduced time investments for individual staff members. For example, with online publishing, many intermediary steps that are often used in paper-based document production processes are eliminated, such as paste up, blue lining, etc. Also, online publishing removes the most expensive part of the print publishing process itself: the need for scarce and expensive pulp wood. For example, it may cost between $1-3 or more per paper-based book for the cost of the paper itself depending on its quality, along with the printing and binding process; whereas, a single disk-based publication can be created for less than fifty cents today, and the text-based information that it contains may be enough to fill several print-based volumes.

Online distribution products have the added advantage of being "always in print," especially when they are archived within an information systems environment. Because there is no need to maintain storage space for physical objects (i.e. the books and documents that live on the shelf), the material can be stored in a compressed form on disk, always ready to be copied or re-used in some other way, and ready for revision or output on demand. In other words, once an order is placed for a document, the most current version of that information is delivered to the user immediately.

Faster text delivery is also an advantage of online publishing efforts. While paper-based publishing is time consuming and wasteful because of its additional steps, online publishing saves a tremendous amount of time since source texts remain in their native electronic formats, while online information products are produced in a minimum amount of time, and often in "just-in-time" setting. With online publishing, there are significantly less production delays and staff time is not spent on "wrapping" the content for publication, but rather on delivering it quickly and efficiently.

It should be pointed out that while the focus of this book is on *corporate* EDMS applications, many experts in the area of *commercial* publishing, such as that found in the news and entertainment industries, believe that online distribution systems have the necessary characteristics to cure many of their own industry's problems today, such as high inventory costs, dealing with shorter production life-cycles for information products, reducing the high distribution costs of paper-based materials, eliminating wasteful product returns, and constantly dealing with insufficient shelf space in newsstands, bookstores, and libraries to give new information products a chance to sell.

Adding Value through Online Documents

Despite the many additional features or benefits that electronic document delivery might bring to an organization, one thing is certain: online documents are going to have to be extremely user friendly, esthetically appealing, and readable as they try to match the portability that paper documents have. Once this significant step is achieved, we can then begin to look at how electronic publishing enterprises can "add value" to existing information.

Simply put, *value-added* documents contain the original content of a printable text but add to it--in its electronic form--the organizational, presentational, retrieval, and navigational elements or structures that make any given text or document more accessible, portable, maintainable, integrative, or cost-effective to produce and disseminate. Moreover, these benefits can occur within the creation, production, distribution, revision, and use of an online document. In fact, a most desirable model for online publishing is one where documents can be transformed into their most cost-effective electronic versions while still adding value to them at virtually no additional costs for end users.

While this value-adding process is most closely tied to online publishing and electronic document delivery features such as electronic tables of contents or outlines, indexes, and hypertext linkages, it is also demonstrated through the integration of graphics and tabular information, as well as in the ability to attach icons, toolbars, or other navigational devices to otherwise static texts. Other value-added features might be improved searchability--typically through Boolean search techniques--where sophisticated text location and retrieval engines allow users to find pin-pointed information nearly instantaneously.

And finally, value can be added to online documents in the area of screen typography, where the availability of scaleable font technologies, with corresponding laser output of 1200 dot-per-inch or more, is becoming commonplace along with the expectation for this type of print quality to be found on-screen. What is powerful about most electronic publishing tools today is that they allow readers to set up their own preferred formats and presentation styles for how information is going to look on the screen. For example, someone with poor vision may pick a very large font and then have the text automatically reformatted to accommodate a personally-sized window that is preferable to them.

Organization

Estimates routinely place a corporation's most valuable asset, its employees, at wasting 20 - 40% of their time. What are they doing?

Usually looking for information. Combine this with the fact that organizations spend nearly 15% of their revenue on documents, and the
problem is clear. Worse yet, if these knowledge workers don't find
what they are looking for, then what will they resort to? Use whatever
information is available and risk an error? Create what they need from
scratch? Neither direction would be acceptable.

The most important aspect of delivering information online is its
organization and presentation. It must be very carefully laid out. Common organizational schemes are hierarchically-based, usually by
topic/subtopic, or contextually organized by sequence, or organized
by relationships. Almost all documents can be arranged hierarchically,
but this is not always the easiest way to find or present information, for
it assumes the user knows something about the document's relationship to the topic at hand. While often true, this may not be the most
useful or expedient method for accessing document content.

Organizing a document in a non-hierarchical fashion requires
additional work; one must determine the context for the document as
well. Once this is known, then one can pursue the relationship of this
document to others. The key to presenting a contextual organization of
documents is knowing the person using them, the consumer. Each user
will think about the documents differently. It is therefore important to
capture and understand this so-called "mental model" of document
relationships and sequences. This cannot be done from afar, but only
by working with the end users of a document; they must be interviewed, observed, and even involved in building this mental model.

But while technically feasible, it is still practically impossible to
develop a model for each individual user. It is, however, possible to
develop a profile for a "class" or "group" of similar users. It can be
expected that all "customer service representatives," for example, perform roughly the same tasks, in nearly the same way, using the same
information. So capturing this information about end users provides the
inputs necessary to build so-called "custom views" of the information.

In order to build custom views either by user type or class, the
online document delivery system must be capable of dealing with two
types of information: navigational and content-oriented. The navigational information can be the custom view itself, sometimes best
thought of as Tables of Contents that contain information relevant to
only a particular user group. They contain some type of organizational
and contextual knowledge about how the information fits together.
The content is the actual documents which are to be viewed in order to
extract knowledge. Also included in this system must be a hierarchical
view or navigation, so that other information not routinely accessed by
a user in the custom view can be found. Figure 9-1 shows these various
layers of management for a Web based delivery system.

Figure 9-1
Navigation
and
Content Lay-
ers

Mixed

**Navigation & Content
(HTML)**

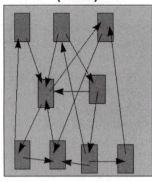

Layered

Navigation (HTML)

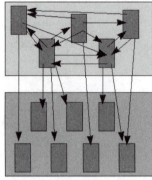

**Content
(Native, HTML, PDF)**

Separating these layers allows customization of the information to better server the users. It also has a tremendous side benefit, maintenance. If the navigation or context of the document can be separated from the content, then the content document can be updated and replaced without requiring any additional effort to keep the context correct. Many times this contextual knowledge is embedded deep inside the document, making maintenance considerably more difficult and practically eliminating any chance of automating this process.

It is often the maintenance of a system that results in its ultimate demise. Relatively speaking the cost of building most systems pale in comparison to the costs to maintain them and this is especially true for the online portion of an EDMS. Giving maintainability the attention it deserves early in the process goes a long way to building a lasting and therefore successful system.

Presentation

There are many different ways to present materials, either by navigation or content, to the user. In the past there were tools, often referred to as hypertext authoring systems, where documents were manually converted, edited, and modified, adding significant value in the process. While these offered many benefits, they suffered from the effort required to maintain these documents. Where document content is static, these tools are still quite valuable.

However, the pace of change is making these solutions impractical for the majority of applications. Organizations are now looking for ways to add value to online documents with minimal effort. While there are many types of tools available on the market today, they can be grouped into one of two general categories or types of presentation. The first, commonly referred to as Electronic Paper, presents a rendering of a page on-screen. The paper and on-screen documents are identical. The second category is an Online Document, where a document follows the metaphor of a book or manual, but where the concept of a page no longer exists.

One other approach is to leave the documents in their native format. By making the files read-only, changes to the materials can be prevented, thus providing some security. This solution will only work where everyone who needs a document has the application that created it. If an organization is 100% standardized on a common set of tools, this approach may be viable. It certainly has advantages by eliminating the conversion step.

Architecture

In displaying materials to an end user, the presentation method selected and its tools are inexplicably linked to the architecture of the system. The capabilities and limitations of the tools chosen will depend heavily upon the underlying architecture. There are several approaches/architectures in use today. The pro's and con's of these architectures should be considered along with the tool's capabilities when deciding on the overall EDMS architecture.

The most basic architecture for an online publishing solution is to create, convert, and then publish. This case has no repository, and therefore suffers from the problems of insufficient document control. Figure 9-2 shows this architecture. While most of the issues of document control are faced by the authors, the consumers are also adversely impacted. They must rely on a person to know when a source document has been changed and then ensure that the document is converted and placed online. Since this process is almost always informal, with a document set of any real size the process breaks down. The user is then left with out of date information.

This is the model most commonly in use today. It is the typical model used in most Internet and INTRAnet sites. The source materials already exist. A Web server is established and users are given a low-cost browser. The Webmaster is responsible to receive any "new" content and oversees the conversion of this document. It is then posted to the Web, and hyperlinks to/from the document(s) are added. In another slight variation of this model, the authors handle the conver-

Figure 9-2
Typical
Online
Publishing
Architecture

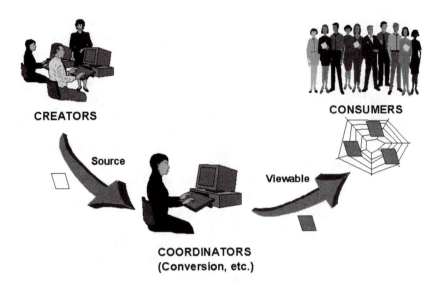

sion, and the Webmaster posts and links the materials. Either way someone, the author or the Webmaster, must keep the site current.

Only now, after the creation of an uncountable number of Web pages, is the document management problem becoming apparent. For the past year or two organizations have focused on hiring Webmasters, setting up conversion teams, and trying to stay ahead of the demand to post new materials. Keeping the original content up to date and in synch with source materials is only now rearing its ugly head.

An alternative approach addresses this situation. In this approach to online publishing, documents are stored, managed, and controlled in a repository. This provides the authors and other contributors, as well as reviewers and approvers, the capabilities they need to guard these valuable assets. A publishing step is then created where documents are extracted from the repository and are published through an online viewing system.

Ideally this process would be automated, and in some cases it can be. Typically, in places where electronic paper is an acceptable format, this process can be automated. In online document sets, some manual intervention is usually required. However, if this process is driven by the workflow engine it can be managed. Figure 9-3 shows this type of publishing architecture.

This solution also allows the source documents and online documents to remain in synch. If an update is made, the change will be reflected in the online document set. This could be a couple of hours or even weeks later, depending on the need to get the new information out to the end users. This solution allows for documents to be "viewed" in a format where an inexpensive browser or viewer is all

Figure 9-3
Publishing
Architecture

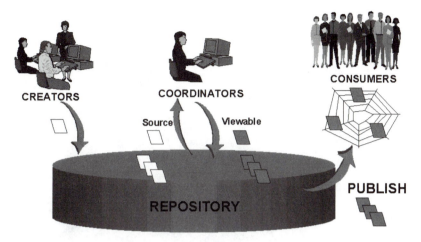

that is required by the consumers. It does, however, leave the converted or viewing documents uncontrolled; this is often not a big issue,
but there are special situations where it can be important.

Finally, in this distributed approach the consumers do not have
access to the full power of the repository. Full text and attribute
searches are not available. Often, another full-text index is built using
the content of the online documents, resulting in a duplication of
effort. Because the online documents are detached from the repository
the attributes are not available as they are not supported in most file
systems or viewing applications.

The third architecture in use today is called the repository-viewing approach. In this situation, the documents, both source and viewable formats, are stored in the repository. The conversion step can be
automated or not, depending upon the capabilities the repository (just
like the Publish Architecture), but all documents reside within the
repository. Users actually access the repository directly to view the documents in an appropriate format. This approach is shown in Figure 9-4.

This approach is not all that common, mainly due to the cost of
the clients for accessing the repository. It does, however, provide all the
capabilities of the repository such as full text and attribute search. It is
a good model, since all documents in source and viewable formats are
controlled and kept in one place.

The last architecture is actually a combination of publish and
repository-viewing architecture, best referred to as the access architecture. All documents, native and viewable, are stored in the repository.
The conversion process may be automated depending based on the
tools selected. However, to overcome the cost and complexity of proprietary clients, many repository vendors have added a component to
the repository that allows Web-based viewing access to the documents.
This is shown in Figure 9-5.

Figure 9-4
Repository-
Viewing
Architecture

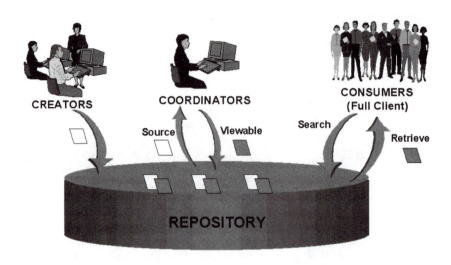

Figure 9-4
Repository-
Viewing
Architecture

Figure 9-5
Access
Architecture

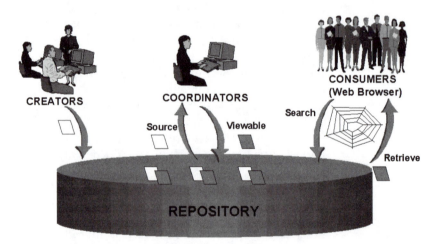

This new approach offers some very interesting alternatives to the others. It allows inexpensive Web browsers to act as viewing clients against the repository. Attribute and hierarchical relationship information is usually presented as the interface through which users can "drill down" to find what they want. The complete search capability of the repository is usually made available in these "clients."

There are a few significant advantages and drawbacks to this approach. The major drawback is not technology, but people. Most organizations have spent a great deal of time setting up Web sites and hiring/training Webmasters. They have been focused on the more traditional model for online publishing. This approach changes that to keeping no documents on the *http* or Web server, but rather keeping them all in the repository. It is an issue of human change, and just as quickly as the Web site is set up, this approach asks for it to be dismantled.

Yet there are significant advantages to this approach. First, if the goal is to make the contents of a repository available to a wide audience, then this is a quick and relatively painless approach. Second, document specific security is now available. But the real power is in the ability to exploit the relationships and attributes of a document repository to create truly custom views. Much of the navigation layer discussed earlier (which is created to reveal different organizations of the materials dependent upon the user) is actually a set of rules applied by the person developing the custom table of contents. Now through the use of attributes, relationships and queries, the rules can be implemented dynamically.

For example, one navigation view may be to show all the procedures relating to the billing functions of a system. Another view may be to show all the training material related to a topic. In a document repository these are either pre-defined queries or transversing relationships to find the parent, child, or sibling of a document. By connecting an interface to the repository for viewing, much of the navigation layer can be created on the fly from the information a document knows about itself. In this way there is *significantly less* work in online publishing, but it does require that relationships and attributes be kept up-to-date. However, this requires only one place to keep the information current, not two.

Tools and Technologies

In choosing tools for document viewing there are several considerations to take into account. The most basic one is the choice between:

- Electronic Paper
- Online Documents
- Native Format

Each of these has distinct advantages and disadvantages as addressed below.

Electronic Paper

Electronic paper provides an on-screen version of a paper or printed document. It has the advantage of familiarity to users, but only if they have used the paper documents before. Many of these systems can become highly automated, as the conversion accuracy is nearly

100%. These solutions are not tied to the how the document was constructed, so the solution is independent of good structured content.

The downside to electronic paper is that what works well on paper does not always work well on-screen. To see a full page a user will typically require a 20" monitor or larger, not yet a common occurrence, but one that should be considered if going to online distribution. Because screen resolutions are much less than paper, documents that are readable in paper (10 point) are not readable on a screen unless the fonts are enlarged (14 point). Usually these viewers cannot resize the document inside a window, so the effect can be like looking at a document though a keyhole.

Electronic paper is often useful where documents are located electronically, but then printed to be used. It is also very helpful in situations where the on-screen must look exactly like the paper, often for regulatory reasons. It is valuable where the document authoring process cannot be controlled. The most popular application for electronic paper is Adobe Acrobat's Portable Document Format (PDF), as shown in Figure 9-6.

Figure 9-6
Electronic
Paper
Acrobat PDF
(Adobe)

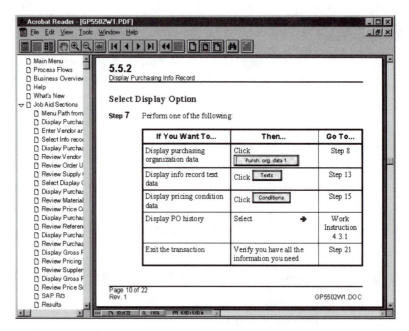

Online Documents

This second category of documents are those that abandon the page metaphor of typical paper documents. Without a doubt the most popular format for these documents is HyperText Markup Language

(HTML). It is the format for the World Wide Web and is a relatively open standard and therefore adopted and supported by many vendors. HTML is a subset of Standard Generalized Markup Language (SGML) which is also a widely used standard.

HTML is supported by a wide variety of browsers available in the marketplace, at a relatively modest cost. HTML, like SGML is an ASCII based language and is therefore platform independent. It is a compact format that works well with low bandwidth connections. HTML also supports graphic formats, but does require additional bandwidth to make these truly useful.

Browsers using HTML abandon the concept of the printed page. This works well on a screen by giving the user an apparently seamless presentation of information. Browsers also allow users to configure how the information will be displayed in term of fonts, sizes, colors, etc. Here the user, and not the author, determines the presentation of the document. Browsers can typically be configured to launch pre-defined applications to view document formats they cannot display directly.

HTML is a very simple standard and therefore provides very limited formatting capability. Often document layout is very important in conveying information to a user, and HTML really limits the presentation in these instances. Also, paper documents often use headers and footers as landmarks within the document, and this construct is not supported in HTML. Conversion to HTML often requires fairly structured input documents in order to map content to the styles used in the HTML-supported tag set.

Online documents can make electronic viewing far more palatable to the document consumers. It is the ideal choice for documents where the contents are likely to be used right online. If a window is resized for viewing, the content will resize with it, reducing the "keyhole" effect. It often requires some modifications to the authoring process or some serious efforts in the conversion process. Recall that conversion is a non-value add process by itself. The critical factors are usability of the documents and the conversion process.

Native Documents

In organizations where *everyone* has the same tool set, documents can be delivered without conversion. This is a significant advantage for organizations who have truly standardized on a set of tools. While compelling by eliminating the conversion process, it does have drawbacks.

First, the process can be somewhat slow, as loading a full application such as Word takes significantly longer than a simple browser or viewer. Also, it demands that all users be familiar with the package.

Another drawback is that users can then make derivative works by saving the file under a new name. This may or may not be acceptable.

As the use of the technology and HTML browsers proliferate, many vendors are looking to create simple helper applications to view their documents. These viewers enable one to view native documents with 100% accuracy, but limit what the end user can do other than view and perhaps print a document. Microsoft, for example, has developed viewers for both *Word* and *Powerpoint*.

While this approach may work for some organizations it is not a viable alternative for the majority. For this reason it will not be discussed further.

Features

Choosing the right technology, electronic paper or online documents, is not an easy task. Often, a combination approach is best. However, there are a number of features to consider when making this choice. This decision can be done on a document-by-document basis, for classes of documents, or for entire organizations. Below are listed some of the most important features in these applications.

Searching - The system should have an indexing, search, and retrieval component or be able to use/connect to the repository's search system. Consideration should be given to full text, keyword, or attribute-based searches. The ability of the tool to highlight the specified text and move to the next and previous occurrences is important.

Zooming - Since many systems give the user a keyhole view of the world, the ability to magnify, both up and down, on a document is very useful. This is often true on graphics where detail is limited when the graphic is, say, only 2" x 3". How much magnification is therefore a key consideration.

Hyperlinking - Any system should support the ability to cross reference inside and across documents. The fact that hyperlinks exist is the user's only concern. How the system creates and can facilitate the creation of these links is crucial to the long term viability of this system. Also, the ability to make links actually execute programs, such as queries against the repository are also very important.

Annotations - The system should allow users to record notes or comments on a documents. These can be either text notes or marks in a transparent layer that is placed over the document. These notes should support both private and public notes as well as a way to identify the author of the note. There should also be some mechanism to capture this information and feed it back to the authors/owners of the documents.

Outlining/Tables of Contents - The ability to quickly identify and get to the exact information desired is critical to success. Tables of contents often provide such a mechanism in paper and this element refers to the electronic equivalent. Click on an outline and the book opens to that section. This is an important feature to the end users, but, similar to hypertext, how the tool creates these items and whether or not it can be automated are vital to the long-term success of the system.

Bookmarks - Users should have the ability to mark commonly used places in an electronic book, just like they do with yellow sticky notes in paper books. Similar to annotations, consideration should be given to both public and private bookmarks. This can supplement the outlining-TOC features and give users the ability to really customize. Also, some thought should be given to the status of bookmarks and annotations when a document is replaced with a new version.

Printing - Printing a document from the system can be good or bad depending upon the situation. The tools should be able to restrict or enable printing of one, some, or all documents. If documents are printed, the system should enable use of a watermark or notice of expiration to help manage the paper documents. Also, the ability to print while zoomed can be a nice or even critical feature.

Integration Capabilities - While document viewing can be a standalone application, sometimes it is very important that this function be embedded into another application. Some applications provide very thorough API's to enable integration, while others provide a simple command line interface to enable data exchange. This communication must go both ways into and out of the viewing application. Some viewing applications provide no interfaces to or from the product.

In choosing the best technology for document distribution, the feature sets cited above must be taken into account, along with the general approaches of electronic paper (PDF), or online documents (HTML). In making this decision, there are several key questions to be asked--and answered. While there are no absolute answers, there are some guidelines that can be used to control the selection process. These guidelines are presented in Table 9-1 below.

Table 9-1: Example Guidelines for Choosing Online Format

Topic	Issue	Favors: Online Document Format (HTML)	Favors Electronic Paper Format (PDF)
Authoring			
	Adherence to styles and templates	X	
	Large documents		X
	Unusual layout (i.e., multi-columns)		X
	Many or excessively complex tables		X
	Many graphics		X
	Frequent updates		X
Conversion			
	Limited resources or desire automation		X
	Require links internal to other documents	X	
	Many hyperlinks	X	
Distribution			
	Presentation		
	User definable presentation preferences	X	
	Base font less than 12 pt or lots of Italic	X	
	Page layout is Important		X
	Functionality		
	Need to zoom or view small elements		X
	Frequent printing		X
	Screen real estate is limited	X	
	Primary Use on Screen	X	
	Primary Use on Paper (print & use)		X
	Need to search text in graphics		X

Distribution and Document Management Issues

Beyond the obvious connection between the repository and distribution or delivery system, there are other issues where electronic document management and online documentation meet. The two most important are hyperlinking and notification. It must be noted that there are no clear-cut answers to either of these issues and there are as many vendor solutions as there are business problems. It is incumbent on the organization to define its needs, then look at the vendors' options and implementation in addressing the needs.

Hyperlink Management

In the context of corporate publishing, document management comes down to file-level management. That is, files are the smallest entity to be managed, or the smallest level of granularity is the file. Our discussions, therefore, do not extend to the domain of the document's contents or to the elements it contains. Yet, typically hyperlinks are physical elements inside a document. This presents a problem for the EDMS developer, for hyperlinks are important and need to be managed as well, yet they are elements below the established granularity threshold.

Hyperlinks are created in several ways. They may be placed in a document by the author, either directly or through the use of codes, which are then transformed into hyperlinks during conversion. This requires an authoring environment that supports normal document authoring but also hyperlinks. *Interleaf*, for example, is one such environment. Other tools such as *Word* provide the author with the ability to enter field codes which can be converted to hyperlinks in *WinHelp* during conversion. However, most hyperlinks are entered, by hand, after the document is converted. This presents the biggest problem, because they usually must be entered manually every time the document is updated.

Hyperlinks are a form of knowledge representation; they show the relationship between one document and another. They may also relate an element inside one document to an element inside another. Hyperlinks are therefore important and should be managed and kept current. However, most hyperlinks are file system and path dependent, so keeping the links pointing to the correct document is a difficult task.

There are several approaches to hyperlink management. The first is really an assistant, where a tool runs over the online document set and checks all links and provides a list of broken links. Another approach is to look at hyperlinks in a totally different way. In almost every case, hyperlinks are not a random pointing of one passage to another, but rather a set of relationships among or between documents. For example, they may be used to move between the pages in a document and the table of contents, or between, say, the operating and maintenance manuals for a specific piece of equipment.

Looking at it from a systems perspective, there is usually a fairly well defined set of logic that is followed to create a hyperlink. This premise offers two solutions. The first is to use an actual programming environment, through an API, to develop simple applications which make a system call, or query, in place of a "hard coded" link. The second is to use these logic rules to build relationships between the documents or classes in the repository and build an external application to use this "knowledge" to provide the functionality of a hyperlink.

The more that can be done to provide the desired functionality externally, rather than internally in a document, the more maintainable the system will be. Several vendors are working on approaches to hyperlink management in a repository, but no ready solution is available today. The most promising one is to build an application that goes into the document and extracts the link information, replacing it with the unique document ID from the repository. If the hyperlink was executed in the repository, the document would be retrieved. If a publishing model was used, the document ID would be replaced with the filename and path during this publishing step.

Notification

In today's paper world, users get notified when a document is updated. This typically occurs when a package of paper hits their in-box. It may be a new document or change pages. Whether the changes are incorporated and used are another issue, but the paper showing up in the in-box is a kind of notification. Notification is critically important for the document users or consumers; they have no other good way to know when changes are made. There are similar needs for electronic documents as well.

For electronic document notification, there is active and passive notification. Active, as the name implies, is the concept that every user on the "distribution" list will be positively notified that a change or update has been made. This is usually done via Email. One of the key problems with this approach is that a user may receive hundreds of Email messages. Of course on the flip side, this may entice the user to keep themselves on only the distribution lists that are truly important to them.

The passive approach is to make the change and update information available to the user, but they must seek it out. This is equivalent to the List of Revisions found at the beginning of a document. This list includes revision numbers, dates, changes, and reasons for those changes. In the Web world of distribution, this often becomes the "What's New?" icon.

In either case, notification can be driven from the document management system. For active notification, most repositories can send notification messages, via Email, to users or group of users when certain actions occur. For distribution, it is usually at the end of the step in which the document is made available for viewing. In other cases individuals may want to be notified when a new draft begins; this can be triggered automatically as well.

For passive notification, authors can be trained to update the "List of Revisions Section" for a document when the document is modified. Another alternative is to require certain information be entered (attributes) when a new version is requested or completed. This information can then be extracted from the repository and published along with the document. This is the ideal case when the Access model is used.

The more the repository prompts the author/editor for the desired information, and then presents it automatically to the end user, the more successful the system will be. This is yet another example of understanding what the user, not the author, needs and building the EDMS into that system framework.

Summary

Distribution of documents to the end users or consumers is the most critical part of any EDMS - it is the place where information is transformed into knowledge and value is added. It must be recognized that each user or group of users will demand a "custom" view of the document set in order to be efficient and productive in their daily tasks. The system must be designed to meet this need.

Constructing a delivery mechanism that is tailored to the users requires a detailed understanding of those users needs. Those needs must be met, but also balanced with a system that is maintainable over the long run. The user requirements must also be balanced with the proper architecture, tools and technologies in order to arrive at an effective and viable system.

EDMS Methodology

Building a successful system once can be either the result of skill or luck. Doing it repeatedly, however, demonstrates real skill on the part of the development team and/or project manager. In order to do it repeatedly with different people, teams, situations, and tools requires an efficient development process as well. This section of the book focuses on providing just such a process for building an effective EDMS application.

Of course, the key to a successful, performance-enhancing solution is to focus on the user. This is the place where information is transformed into knowledge and the maximum value-added components are realized. Embracing this concept is critical to the methodology presented.

Building and implementing an EDMS is a systems integration effort and as such relies heavily on system development principals. The focus on the user changes what requirements get prioritized and how to carefully define them. But once these are collected, the problem is then one of software engineering. Therefore, our methodology, particularly at the design and development activities, is based on traditional software development techniques and methods.

The high-level model for this methodology is presented in Figure III-1. It has a strong resemblance to a "waterfall" approach for software development. However, the level of effort devoted to each of the phases is different than that of the typical custom application development project. There are quite a number of differences in the details of each phase of the methodology compared to traditional approaches.

This section presents a chapter that outlines the overall development methodology followed by chapters covering each phase. The most critical phases in this effort are Analysis and Prototyping, each with an entire chapter devoted to them. The remaining phases are covered in somewhat less detail as they follow more closely a standard systems-development process.

However, no process can be cast in stone, and this holds true for what is presented here. This methodology should be seen as a baseline model for development, one to be molded to match the circumstances of the EDMS project. On the other hand, it is equally important to recognize that the process is one based on substantial experience and therefore should not be quickly cast aside if it does not fit exactly. The goal of this process is to guide the EDMS development team around pitfalls in order to expediently complete the project.

The methodology presented in this section is by permission of RWD Technologies, Inc., and may be covered under copyright, trademark, patent or other forms of intellectual property protection.

Figure III-1
Methodology
Overview

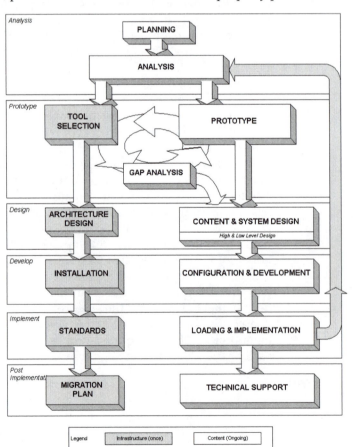

10

Methodology

Developing and implementing an EDMS based solution in an organization requires a methodology. This methodology is to ensure that the right questions are asked, the right technical issues are addressed, and that the entire EDMS implementation team, including the selected organization and vendors, are all well aligned on the steps required in the process. This chapter will outline an optimal methodology for implementing an EDMS.

No methodology can be blindly followed without regard for details and specifics of each organization's situation or without a detailed understanding of what is involved in each major step. The following chapters provide significant detail on each of the individual phases within the methodology. Armed with this overview and the details that follow, we expect that the methodology can then be tweaked, modified, or adapted to individual situations.

In order to frame this methodology some concepts and ideas from Part I will be revisited, presented briefly again, and then discussed in a somewhat different light. The focus now is not theoretical, but rather practical--how these issues help to shape the methodology. In fact, it is these principles that form the basis for the methodology presented.

Three critical elements need to be addressed in order to understand this methodology:

- Philosophy
- Business Approach
- Technical Approach

The philosophy is aimed at providing a common foundation or vision of how to approach the problem. The business approach is to provide an overall framework for the EDMS implementation, specifically one which will support the technical approach. The last one is the technical approach which gets down the detailed phases, tasks and deliverables required in order to successfully implement an EDMS.

Philosophy

Philosophy is an unusual subject to find in a practically-oriented book such as this. However, it is in fact the most important part of the entire approach to solving the EDMS problem. This philosophy will run through each and every facet of the methodology and is the key item which separates this approach from others currently in use. This philosophy, simply stated, is to focus on the *user*, not the document.

Document Centered Approach

As we have shown earlier, it is still novel to state that the focus of a *document* management system is the *user* and not the document. Historically, we have focused on the control of documents with such things as document numbers, revisions, authors, filenames, etc. Following this pattern we have developed systems that do electronically what we have done with paper over the years. Using the simplified model developed earlier we can look the typical approach to document management. This is show in Figure 10-1

In looking at the flow of a document over its lifecycle, it gets created, managed, published, and then revised. This is exactly how EDMS systems of the past have been built. They start with the document and follow it along its life. How does the author want it to be controlled? How does the author want the document to be published and distributed to its intended audience? How often will the author update the document? All of these questions can be asked and answered by the author.

Having one individual who can answer all the pertinent questions about a document makes implementing a system much easier. Developers locate all the authors, ask them what documents need to be

Figure 10-1
Typical
Approach

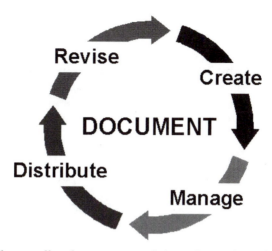

controlled, as well as how to control them. In a relatively short period of time, developers can derive all the information needed to build the EDMS system, and furthermore they will have likely exceeded the needs of the authors and receive high marks for the system.

The Paradigm Shift

What makes this solution obsolete is the paradigm shift we have seen over the last few years. A document was once considered to be a set of words on the page, and in advanced thinking it included graphics. No longer can a document be defined this simply. This new paradigm has changed that definition.

A document is a container, bringing together information from a variety of sources, in a number of formats around a specific topic to meet the needs of a particular individual.

Presentation of related information on a specific topic is the representation of knowledge. Consider this: No one actually goes looking for a document; rather, users are looking for the knowledge they believe to be embedded in a particular document. The document is simply the container that holds the knowledge they seek.

This change in definition brings about a dramatic change in the goal and objectives of an Electronic Document Management System, as well the approach to implementing one. To begin this new philosophy we must understand how value and knowledge are created, and then map that against the document paradigm, then finally into a document management system.

A New Approach

Earlier the concept for an EDMS was reduced to a four phase model, Create, Manage, Distribute and Revise. The key to this philosophy is the focal point for this process. In the past it has been the document, as defined by the author. In the new paradigm it is knowledge as defined by the user. Therefore in the new paradigm the user, or consumer of the document, will be at the center of the system. This is illustrated in Figure 10-2.

Figure 10-2
User-Centered
Approach

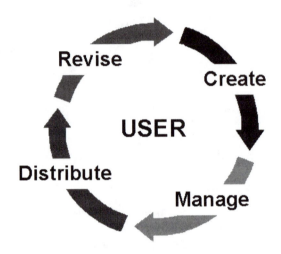

To put this all into context, let's look at an example. Consider the dilemma of trying to file (i.e. manage) the final paper copy of a technical specification which has just been completed. Should it be filed by who wrote it? Who approved it? The groups which use it? The type of equipment referenced? The topic or subject itself? In the old paradigm we usually chose to file it by author, and that was it. While it might be possible to file it in multiple places with paper, it would require numerous copies of the document, a complete set of cross referenced files, and many times the storage space, offering in the end not a very efficient solution. This problem is compounded when the document is updated frequently. Recognizing the difficulty of this situation, a standard way to file documents was usually created and questions on locating the document were directed at the author.

With an EDMS we can easily file electronic documents into a wide variety of categories. Now the question becomes, Where are all the places the document should be filed? This answer is no longer driven by who created it, but rather by who uses the document. In order to determine who uses the document we need to look carefully not at the document itself, but rather its contents. Who best knows what content is or is not useful than those who use it?

If the goal of an EDMS is to make information (ready to become knowledge) available to those who need it, not those who created it, then the focus must shift to those who need it: the users. This is not to say that the authors do not have considerable understanding of who should be using a document and why, and therefore participate in the process, but rather allows the system to be set up and focused with the user, not the author in mind.

Finally, in an ideal world we could build an EDMS that allows everyone to have their own unique view of the knowledge stored in documents. While many vendors are making great strides towards that end, there are always tradeoffs to be made. This philosophy of focusing on the end users requires that these tradeoffs be made not in the interest of simplicity, or limitations of the tool, but rather in the interests of the users.

Many of the people involved in implementing EDMS systems are from the vendor/supplier community. This results in most of them having a focus on the technology and not on the user. All tools have certain limitations, and all users have their requirements, which often place the two at loggerheads and something has to give. It should be and must be the tool, and not the user. After all the side of the road of information systems development is littered with projects that were abandoned by users, because they were just too hard. The user must take center stage.

Focusing on the User

This new approach, focusing on the user, is consistent with the concept that an EDMS is not an end unto itself, but rather an enabling technology. This is also consistent with the stated goal of an EDMS, which is to

Deliver the correct information to the right person at the proper place and time.

This concept stated earlier as "performance support," provides the information to users in order to support them in the performance of their jobs.

The idea was presented that value added in the document process comes primarily when the document is *consumed* or used, where information becomes knowledge in turn driving action. There is value in collecting, organizing and transforming data into information, but there is far more value in the consumption of the information. It is therefore imperative that the user be the focus.

When we looked at this before we presented a performance based approach that is best illustrated graphically. This is presented in Figure 10-3.

Figure 10-3
Performance
Based Analysis
Process

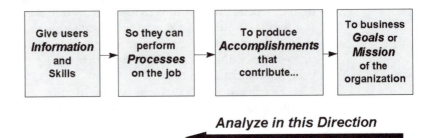

Analyze in this Direction

This process works back from the goals and objectives toward the information required by the users. If we assume, and for the sake of this text we have, that this information is contained in a document, then this analysis ends with defining what information must be delivered to users. By implication, the proper place and time can also be identified.

The next logical step is to look at the document lifecycle, developed earlier. For simplicity's sake at this stage, the revision phase of the model has been eliminated. This simplified model is presented in Figure 10-4.

Figure 10-4
Simplified
Document
Lifecycle

Superimposing these two models, document lifecycle and performance based analysis, they would meet where the document is delivered (distributed) to the user. This would indicate that the proper approach is to work back from goals towards the documents required by the user in the distribution process. Then by extension, the proper approach is to begin at the distribution of the document and work back towards the creation process.

This approach is consistent with the idea of remaining user, not document, focused. In a document-centered approach the process starts on the left and moves to the right. In this process, it begins at the distribution and works back. This philosophy is illustrated in Figure 10-5.

Figure 10-5
Philosophy
for this
Methodology

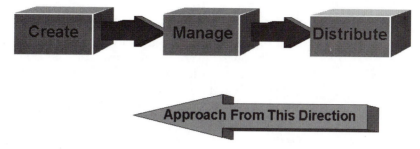

Business Approach

Certainly one of the larger, long-term goals of any EDMS is the ability to leverage or share information across the organization. Typically policies, procedures, and business processes have been developed inside departmental boundaries. This is also very common with information systems, where stovepipes are built: each department has its own systems which make sharing or integrating information more difficult. Figure 10-6 shows these stovepipes in a typical organization.

Figure 10-6
Departmental
Stovepipes

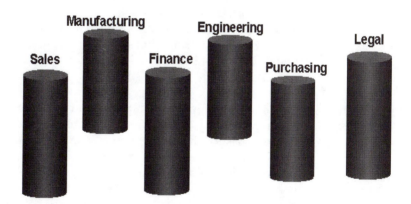

Information Sharing

One approach to achieving the goal of information sharing is to build one huge EDMS system that addresses every department's issues. This is technically feasible, but it would take far too long to implement and projects of that size often die under their own weight. They take so long to reach the first set of results, the departments have gone off and developed their own solution, in isolation perhaps. The best way to approach this from the business perspective is to choose an EDMS tool and make it the foundation layer upon which each department solution will be built.

By sharing the same foundation, it will be possible to integrate the systems to share information. Next, if a similar approach is taken from one department to the next, it is likely that the second department can leverage immediately from the content of the first. This starts to bind the stovepipes into a larger system. This concept is illustrated in Figure 10-7. From a technical perspective it does not matter if the foundation consists of one large enterprise wide system or independent instances of an EDMS - the key is that they can be seamlessly integrated.

Figure 10-7
EDMS
Architecture

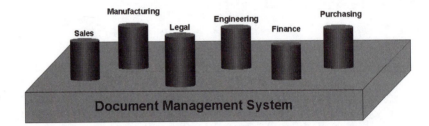

Over time as more and more departments or lines of business join in the effort, the stovepipes will cease to exist and the system will meld into one EDMS. This EDMS will then meet the original goal of leveraging and sharing information across the business units. The information will be looked at by those who uses it, not those who created it, creating an environment where supporting the performance of users is the ultimate goal.

With this type of architecture, an EDMS infrastructure must be put in place early in the effort. To be able to choose the right tools and technologies for this infrastructure some of the business requirements must be determined. This is where the EDMS process departs from traditional software development methodologies. The system is built one organization, workgroup, or line of business at a time. In the lines of business, the implementation is focused on the content and system configuration. The high level overview of the business approach is shown in Figure 10-8

An EDMS can be thought of like building a condominium. Some planning is done to layout the design. Based on the plans a few units may be sold. However to really make it a success a model unit must be built - to show the potential buyers. The individual units are then built according to specifications. However, the building is not really complete when the construction crew finishes - it is only half done. The owners move must move in, and set up their furnishings for it to really be complete.

Figure 10-8
Building an
EDMS

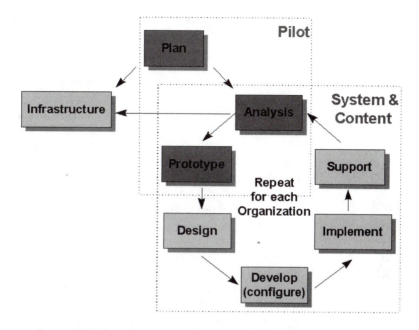

In an EDMS - planning is the initial design. The choice of a pilot organization is the pre-sold unit. The infrastructure is the equivalent of putting up the building. The analysis and prototype are the building of the model. The repeating of the system and content design for each organization is the building of a tailored unit for each owner. Loading the system with content is the equivalent of the owners moving and furnishing the units.

From a more practical standpoint - this approach can be divided into three distinct parts, Planning, Infrastructure, and System/Content. It is important to note that generally speaking Planning and Infrastructure are executed once. The System and Content are repeated for each organization or line of business within the company. There are times where the Planning or Infrastructure may be revisited and updated with new information as things change or the system grows.

Briefly, planning is used to define the overall project scope, objectives, team and to select a pilot organization. The first stage of system and content, analysis, is used to determine the needs and requirements for a particular organization both in terms of users and documents as well as from an information systems perspective. These requirements then drive the infrastructure and system development. The infrastructure might include items such as workstations, servers, and networking as well as document repositories, conversion, workflow, and viewing tools. The system and content step is where the tools are customized and configured to meet business needs. This step also includes loading documents into the system and rolling the system out to the users of that organization.

It is recommended that the process be executed in several phases starting with a pilot. During the initial analysis, one representative organization is chosen for pilot implementation. This can be carried out in parallel with putting the infrastructure in place. On the one hand this allows for the processes and infrastructure to be tested thoroughly and improved where necessary; on the other it allows the project team to create its first, albeit small, victory. Trying to develop and implement an EDMS for an entire company in one step is extremely difficult not to mention risky.

In Figure 10-8, note that the first three blocks, Planning, Analysis and Prototype are shaded differently than the rest. These comprise the Pilot stage. An organization is selected, some analysis is done and a prototype built. After this prototype is built and used for some period of time, an evaluation is made. This evaluation includes whether the system would be effective at accomplishing the goals and objectives; if the tools selected are appropriate; and what changes are required to go into production. Then the infrastructure can be fully implemented, and the pilot system revamped to support production.

Once the pilot is complete, the various organizations or lines of business can be prioritized for implementing a complete, corporate wide EDMS - one organization at a time. It is also important for both the project team and the business units to recognize, from the beginning, the roles and responsibilities each group has. The project team will get the system put in place and a working process up and running. It will also assist in developing a complete implementation plan for each organization. However, loading the business-critical documents for the organization falls to the business unit in question. Each business unit must commit the necessary resources to get the system up and fully operational, as well as take over the day to day control.

Technical Approach

The technical approach outlined here, and detailed in the next several chapters, must be considered a guideline. There can be no hard rules, as the technologies keep changing and at an accelerating pace. Companies, organizations, and people continually change to adapt to the new workplace as well as master these new technologies. Our shift to an information society that competes in a global marketplace will never demand less from us, only more. Therefore, it is important that this methodology and approach be treated as a living process, constantly growing, evolving, and adapting.

The technical approach must be flexible to deal with different tools, people, organizational structure and ever-changing requirements. Each person that adopts this approach must recognize that it must be modified to fit the situation. Gone are the days of autocratic behavior and a mandate to do it "this way." However, it is equally important to recognize that this methodology was born out of necessity, and grew from the experience of numerous projects, as well as industry research. It has been tried and tested and has held up well. So it should not simply be tossed aside when it doesn't fit the situation. Serious contemplation should occur to understand why it does not fit the situation at hand. After due consideration the process should be then modified.

Any one who is familiar with software development processes may recognize a resemblance in this process to a waterfall methodology. This is, in fact, true. The two processes are similar and a lot of this methodology has its roots in the this software development process. Despite similar origins, there are a number of distinct differences that set this methodology apart from the standard waterfall software development process. Perhaps the most notable is the repetitive nature of an EDMS project compared with a traditional software development effort.

In a traditional software development, the requirements for the entire user community must be collected and understood - the system must be developed, even if in phases, from one common design. It is built and delivered once. There may be phases or enhancements, but in effect the system is developed and delivered once. In an EDMS it will developed and delivered once for *each organization* in the company. The EDMS is in essence the empty condominium building and the organizations move into it only after each unit has been custom designed and developed. Therefore the EDMS team never seems to finish, but rather move from one unit to the next.

There are other, but perhaps less obvious, differences between this methodology and traditional software development. These will become apparent in the details of each phase.

Overview

The diagram in Figure 10-9 shows an exploded view of the EDMS methodology. It is divided into six major phases. They are:

- Analysis
- Prototype
- Design
- Develop
- Implementation
- Post-implementation

Figure 10-9
Technical
Approach

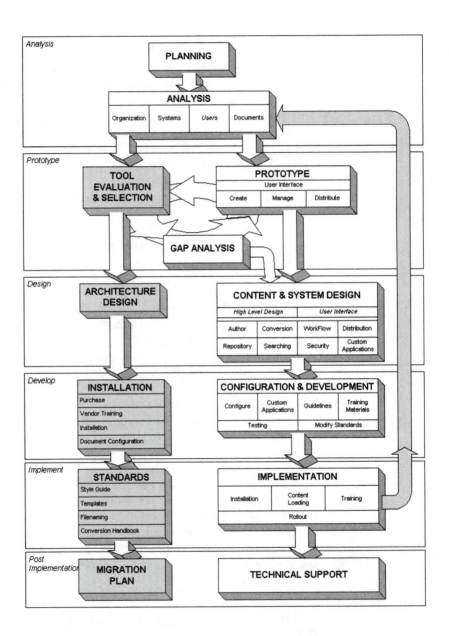

It is important to note that the tasks involved in putting the "infrastructure" in place are shaded in gray and run down the left hand side of the page. It is expected that these activities need only be accomplished once. However, it is anticipated that these elements will be revisited periodically as the system evolves. It is also expected that the Planning task be accomplished only once as well.

The tasks in the white boxes, which run down the right side of the page, comprise the analysis and system & content parts of the process. It is expected these tasks will be accomplished once for a pilot system, and then again for each organization or business unit.

The following sections provide a brief description of each element in the six phases and describe the inputs and outputs of each phase. These are explored in much greater detail in the ensuing chapters. Again, it is important to recall that this methodology is to be considered a guideline to help steer the process of implementing an EDMS for any company or organization.

Analysis Phase

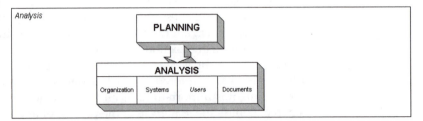

Planning
Purpose/Description: To determine the high level needs, goals, and objectives of an EDMS. It evaluates the needs for the different facets of an EDMS system, including Creation, Management, and Distribution. It also determines the key members of the implementation team, and an organization for the pilot EDMS system.

Inputs:	Outputs:
• Problem to be addressed • Missions and Goals • People (Users, Authors, IS) • Documents / Information used • Basic Work Processes • Systems / Applications in use • IS infrastructure & standards	Report detailing the following: • Benefits / Objectives for EDMS • Performance Measures / Criteria • Needs for Creation, Management, and Distribution facets of EDMS • Selection of Organization or Line of Business for Pilot • EDMS Team Members Project Plan

Analysis
Purpose/Description: To gather the requirements of the EDMS for the organization selected. This requires an understanding of what the organization does and how it does it. Each group of users or business functional groups must be understood in sufficient detail to determine where and how documents or information impact these jobs. The documents which carry the knowledge and work processes of the users must be completely and clearly understood.

Inputs:	Outputs:
• User Interviews, Observations, Focus Groups, etc. • List of Documents Created and Used in the Organization • Volume of Documents: number, pages, file space, etc. • Document Usage Survey • Work Process Maps, Procedures, Descriptions, Job Functions • Determination of Information Creators and Consumers • Number of Users and Locations • Common Operating Environment Specs. • Hardware / Network Specifications • List of Applications Used	A Systems or Functional Requirements Specification which outlines the functionality for all facets of the system. It may include or be replaced by the profiles. A series of profiles which document the information gathered in the analysis which supports the requirements specification. It also supports tool selection, prototyping and design phases. These include: • Organization Profile • Environment Profile • User Profile(s) • Document Profile(s) • Capacity Sheet

Prototype Phase

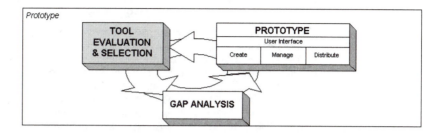

Tool Evaluation & Selection
Purpose/Description: The goal of this step is to evaluate the currently available tools on the market against the requirements uncovered in the analysis step. This requires a general knowledge of the major tools on the market and their capabilities. Vendors may be asked to provide a capabilities statement, demonstration or presentation. Technical capabilities, platform support, open architecture, and cost are among the key considerations. Another key aspect to be considered in selecting tools is the level of integration required between the individual applications which comprise the system or the systems to which they must be connected inside the business organization.

Inputs:	Outputs:
• System Requirements • Product Capabilities • Vendor Presentation / Demonstration • References from other users • System Architecture • Integration Between Products • Platform / Environment Support • Pricing / Licensing Schemes	A recommended application, or set of applications, to address all the needs established in the system requirements. This may include benefits and limitations along with pricing to make the determination between one vendor or another. This may also include actual functional testing of each candidate product. This would require the development of a test plan and formal evaluation criteria.

Prototype Phase (continued)

Prototyping

Purpose/Description: The prototype has several goals:

1. Translate the written requirements into something users can see and touch. This ensures that the requirements accurately reflect the needs of the users.
2. Help identify missing or additional functionality that is required.
3. Establish a common vision between all members of the team.
4. Allow for initial testing of the recommended tools.

While prototyping is often looked at as "a nice thing to do if you have the time," it is actually CRITICAL to developing an EDMS. Often the concepts involved in EDMS are foreign enough to most users that they don't truly recognize the impact until they "see" the results. Equally important is that the EDMS is likely to drive the re-engineering or re-inventing of the organization involved. Recognition of this fact often falls on deaf ears until it can be "seen and touched" by the actual users.

Inputs:	Outputs:
• System Requirements • Recommended Tools • Sample Documents • Small Test System • Small Group of Prototype Users including consumers, creators, coordinators, EDMS team and IS people	A working model, with limited content and function, that shows how the system would work. Some functionality and integration may have to be "mocked" up to keep the time and costs for prototyping at a reasonable level. This model is likely to identify changes to the systems requirements. It is likely items will need to be added, removed and modified based on what is learned during the prototyping. These changes are captured in feedback and comment reports.

Prototype Phase (continued)

Gap Analysis
Purpose/Description: Rarely will any tool or set of tools exactly meet the requirements of a given set of users. There are often many tradeoffs to be made in selecting one tool over another. Often requirements are ranked or prioritized to ensure that the most critical ones are met in selecting any tool. The purpose of this step is to identify the "gaps" between the users' requirements and tools selected. This gap analysis can then be used to drive selection of a new tool, finding an add-on application, designing a custom one, or agreement to leave this requirement unfulfilled in the current system. The gap analysis should include a set of potential ways to fill these gaps.   Identifying these gaps can result in changes to tool selection and/or the prototype. This often becomes an iterative process in which the tool selection, prototyping and gap analysis evolve to a point where the benefits derived do not justify the added time and expense. Two to three iterations is usually sufficient to catch all the major gaps.

Inputs:	Outputs:
• System Requirements • Recommended Tools • Prototype • Representative Users for Interviews • Expertise with the Various Tools • Understanding of Planned Enhancements to the Tool	A gap analysis report which identifies which requirements cannot be fully met by the chosen tools and two or three potential ways this gap can be filled. The first gap analysis will likely be used in rough form, to drive changes to selected tools and prototypes. The final gap analysis will be used to decide if functionality should be custom developed or shelved until a later version of the EDMS.

Design Phase

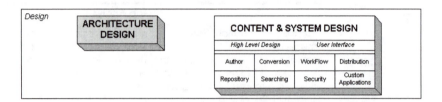

Architecture Design
Purpose/Description: The purpose of this step in the process is to lay out the overall architecture and design of the system. The first part of this is to determine the hardware requirements for each application, especially the server pieces. The second is to understand the networking and data transfer requirements between the client/server and the other servers. This document lays out the hardware required, the applications to run on each server and the networking required between them.

Inputs:	Outputs:
• Environmental Profile • Organization Profile • Current IS Infrastructure and Standards • Current System Hardware Specs. • Current Network Topology • Product Specifications • Understanding of Basic System Flow • Tool Recommendations	A report that details the following: 1. System Diagram showing applications, hardware and networks 2. List of Client and Servers and which applications will reside on each 3. Hardware Specifications for each Client and Server 4. A list of new machines and upgrades required to support these new applications

Design Phase (continued)

Content & System Configuration Design
Purpose: The design document is the translation of the requirements and information gathered in previous steps of what needs to be accomplished into how it will be accomplished. It consists of two major pieces, High Level and Low Level Design.

The high level design lays out the major pieces or functions of the system and how they will work together to meet the objectives of the system. This includes how information or documents will flow through the system, and where processes will be automated or manually accomplished. The high level design is developed at a level that can be understood by anyone on the team.

The low level design lays out the details of how each piece of the system or task will be accomplished. This document lays out in exact detail how each item will be completed and will be geared to the specific tools selected to comprise the system. This document is geared toward a technical specialist or developer to use to construct the actual system.

Inputs:	Outputs:
• System Requirements	• High Level Design Document:
• Prototype	- System Descriptions
• Recommended Tools	- Functional Block Diagrams
• Architecture Design	- Work Process Maps
• Organizational Profile	• Low Level Design Document:
• Environmental Profile	- Custom Applications
• User Profile(s)	- Authoring
• Document Profile(s)	- Conversion
	- Repository
	- WorkFlow
	- Searching
	- Distribution
	- Security
	- User Interface Design

Develop Phase

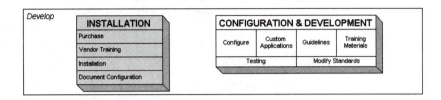

Installation
Purpose/Description: This step gets the infrastructure in place for developing and deploying the system. This step is comprised of three basic steps: setting up the hardware and software, getting trained on the tools and systems installed and documenting the resulting configuration.

Inputs:	Outputs:
• System Architecture Diagram • Recommended Tools & their Specs • Vendor / Third Party Training • IT & Vendor Support	A completely installed and tested infrastructure / system, and a document that details the installation configuration.

Development
Purpose/Description: The development process is where the design document is brought to life. For an EDMS solution this means mostly configuring the tools to meet the specifications outlined in the design document. It also means following a traditional software development process of coding, and testing custom applications. Both these items are then put through integration testing. Finally the work procedures or jobaids are developed for the system users. If required, modifications to the system standards are also made.

Inputs:	Outputs:
• High and Low Level Design Documents • Installation Configuration • Recommended Tools • Sample Documents	A set of tools that have been configured to meet the design specifications along with a set of custom applications to complete the system. Documentation in the form of jobaids, or work procedures also must be included.

Implement Phase

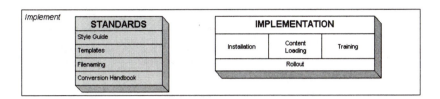

Standards
Purpose/Description: The standards are intended to provide a consistent set of guidelines to follow when accomplishing a task. This task can range from how to name a file, to a detailed outline of the process for managing change to documents throughout the organization.

Inputs:	Outputs:
• Existing Standards • Common Operating Environment Specs • Sample Documents • Layout or Formatting Guides • Change Control Processes	There can be a wide variety of standards established based upon the organization's needs. Some common standards are: 1. Style Guide 2. Templates 3. File and Directory Naming and Structure Conventions 4. Management of Change Process

Implementation
Purpose/Description: The implementation phase is where the system becomes real. It begins with training the client organization on the work processes, configuration, and custom applications that were developed. Then document loading and conversion begins. Once documents have been loaded, creators and consumers are trained, and the system goes live. The document loading and conversion may continue for weeks or months.

Inputs:	Outputs:
• System Design Document • Complete System • Actual Document Sets • Training Materials • Guidelines	A deployed, operating EDMS system and a well trained organization (users, authors, DM team). A prioritized list of documents for conversion and loading may also be developed

Post-Implementation Phase

Post Implementation	MIGRATION PLAN	TECHNICAL SUPPORT

Migration Plan
Purpose/Description: Since most EDMS systems are "bought" and configured, rather than built, one of the key issues in managing this system is the upgrade process. This plan is what outlines which upgrades from the vendor are desirable, which are not of interest and how will this upgrade process will be managed.

Inputs:	Outputs:
• Tools being used as part of system • Vendor's Product Release and Upgrade Plan • Vendor's Maintenance Agreement • Gap Analysis	A plan which outlines the guidelines for implementing new versions of the various tools from the vendors. It includes time for planning, testing, switchover and retraining.

Technical Support
Purpose/Description: This task outlines the need for and designates who will provide technical support. This can be in-house resources such as a corporate help desk or the EDMS team. It can also be a vendor or third party firm. Technical support must be provided for the end users of the system as well as the EDMS team itself. Different groups may receive support in different ways from different places.

Inputs:	Outputs:
• Service Agreements • Maintenance Agreements • Corporate Help Desk Policies • Training: Internal and Vendor	A plan which details how technical support will be provided, by whom and how it can be accessed by each user community.

11

Analysis

The analysis phase of the project is the first and most critical of all the phases. While a complete failure in any phase will cause the entire effort to fail, even a small miscalculation in the analysis process can have the same effect. The goal of the analysis process is to understand the business need for an EDMS solution and to gather all the necessary details to support building a solution that meets the stated business objectives. If the wrong objectives are outlined, then even if they are met the system will usually not succeed. Similarly, if the wrong information is captured in the requirements specification, it is extremely unlikely the right tool will be selected, nor will the system be able to meet the users' expectations.

The analysis phase can be divided into two tasks: Planning and Analysis. Planning deals with the high level issues of the project, the what, why, and who. Analysis is more detailed oriented and seeks to understand the organizational environment, as well as its people and documents, in sufficient detail to construct a complete EDMS to address business objectives.

Planning

The planning stage of a project looks at the overall business situation and determines the extent and type of issues that exist and how they might be addressed. Once this is understood, the goal is to put together a plan for the development and implementation of an EDMS. This plan may come in several phases, one for analysis and prototyping, followed by one for a pilot implementation, and finally one that directs the implementation for the entire organization.

Developing a Project Plan

A project plan or "charter" must address several key areas:

- Goals and Objectives (including success criteria)
- An Organization for the Pilot
- The Development Team
- The Process

In order to establish goals and objectives and choose an organization for a pilot, the entire company and the various organizations within it must be viewed from an EDMS perspective. Then a team must be assembled to lead this effort and likely the follow-on efforts with other organizations within the company. Finally, a process, hopefully one similar to the one presented in this part of the book, must be outlined and agreed to.

All of these elements must then be rolled into a project plan. This plan must cover each of the elements above, along with other details such as schedules, participation from organizational members, and checkpoints/reviews along the way. A suggested Table of Contents for a project plan is presented below.

Table 11-1: Sample Table of Contents for a Project Plan

Section Title	Section Contents
1. Introduction	1.1 Background 1.2 Objectives
2. Statement of Work	2.1 Scope of Work 2.2 Deliverables
3. Project Control	3.1 Assumptions 3.2 Risks 3.3 Risk Mitigation
4. Technical Approach	4.1 Work Breakdown Structure 4.2 Phase 1 . . . 4.3 Phase 2 . . . . . .

Table 11-1: Sample Table of Contents for a Project Plan (Continued)

5. Project Management	5.1 Project Team
	5.2 Roles and Responsibilities
	5.3 Communications
	5.4 Reviews
6. Schedule	6.1 Gantt Chart

Understanding the organization in EDMS terms

Understanding the overall organization or even individual lines of business within the organization requires an understanding of what that organization does. There are many types of companies and lines of business within these companies that do many different things. The question becomes, what is the business problem to be solved with an EDMS? Is it better distribution and access to information? Is it the ability to leverage existing information and re-use it in other ways? Is the objective to reduce the cycle time for a product by better collection and assembly of key data?

The end goal is to understand how the organization performs relative to the phases of an EDMS. Recall that earlier we developed a simple model of a document management system, shown here in Figure 11-1.

Figure 11-1
Major
Phases of
an EDMS

What needs to be done in this stage of planning is to look at how each of the master phases--Create, Manage, and Distribute--are used within the different organizations. This is best illustrated by examples. Most organizations will fit into one of the standard models given below.

Standard Models

An organization can perform a quick cut at determining its EDMS needs by looking at the number of individuals in the organization whose primary function falls into one of the three categories: Create, Manage, Distribute. Where creation is the bulk of the effort, the organization fits into the Publishing Model. When the majority of users are involved in accessing the information, the organization fits into the Consumption Model. When there is a nearly equal number in each phase, the organization fits into the Neutral Model.

An example organization that falls into the publishing model might be the new drug division of a pharmaceutical company. There are many people involved in gathering data and documenting clinical trials. There are a fair number of people involved in reviewing, approving and assembling the information. There is only one point of distribution, the Food and Drug Administration (FDA). A diagram showing this model is in Figure 11-2.

Figure 11-2
Publishing
Model

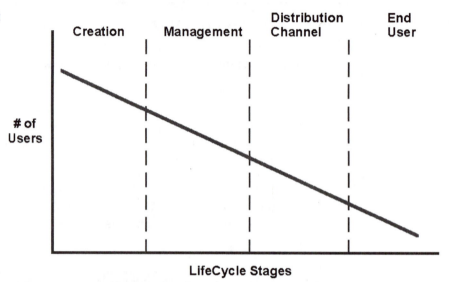

Another organization with this profile might be the group that puts together the user documentation for a product in a manufacturing organization. A wide number of people work to put together a user's manual, yet it gets delivered to one person, the purchaser of the product.

The second model is the neutral one. A common example of this may be the design organization of a manufacturing company. A group of engineers may be involved in creating the original design drawings and specifications. There are often just as many people involved in reviewing, approving, and controlling the flow of these documents. At the end of the document lifecycle, these documents may be used by engineers in manufacturing and production planning. This model is diagrammed in Figure 11-3.

The last and perhaps the most common model is the Consumption model, a model where a small number of people are involved in creating and reviewing the documents, but where a very large group uses the documents. This is leveraging, where a small investment in creating information can be used by a large number of people, adding lots of value (and return on investment) in the process. This model is illustrated in Figure 11-4.

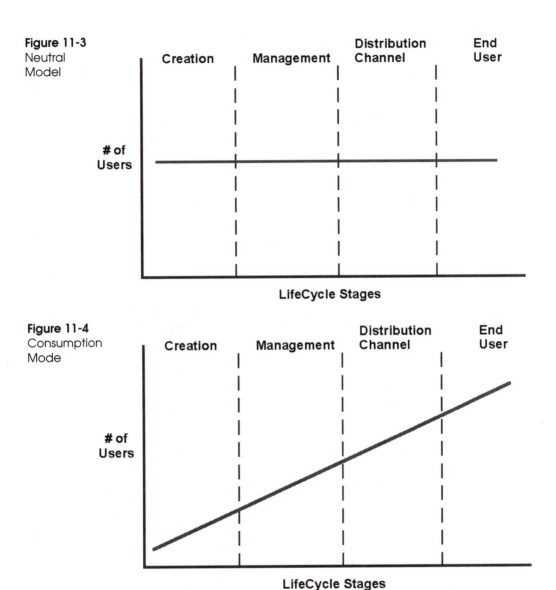

Figure 11-3
Neutral
Model

Figure 11-4
Consumption
Mode

One example of this model is the operating procedures in a processing plant or refinery. Only a small group of people is involved in
producing the documents, but they are used by hundreds or even
thousands of people in running the plant, hopefully more efficiently
and safely because of them. This model also fits the typical administrative departments of large companies, one where creating a corporate
policy may involve a dozen users, but it is read by tens of thousands of
employees.

By looking at how the various organizations fit these models it is possible to quickly get a high level of understanding of what parts of the document lifecycle, and therefore the EDMS will need to be addressed. While it is always dangerous to stereotype, there are often common goals within organizations that fit each model. For example, a publishing model group is often looking to reduce the cycle time to produce the document thereby reducing costs or getting things to market more quickly. In a design organization, often the goal is to leverage the investment made in previous designs by re-using existing materials. In the consumption model, the focus is on reducing paper, keeping documents current, and ultimately making it quicker to find the right information.

Choosing an Organization for the Pilot

There are many considerations when looking to choose an organization for the first pilot of an EDMS, but there are a few key issues. These considerations are important to ensure that the first pilot is successful, for if the pilot effort fails, even for legitimate and justifiable reasons, it will be difficult to resurrect the project and do a second pilot. This makes the pilot decision very important.

The first and most important consideration is management commitment. This usually means they have determined, usually on their own, a compelling need for an EDMS solution. This translates directly into interest, commitment of people (both managers and workers), and a willingness to change the way the business is run, should that ever come to pass. All other reasons will pale in comparison to this last one; in fact, without this last consideration, the rest are irrelevant.

Another key consideration is the particular model the organization wishes to conform to. Because of the leverage involved with the consumption model, this is often the best choice. An organization with this structure will generally require a smaller investment to build the pilot, which is easier to sell. Also, the potential payoff is much larger, since it can be leveraged across many information consumers, showing a very good return on investment.

Finally the third big consideration is the size and complexity of the organization. The solution must address a reasonable size group with something more than a simple document set. Otherwise, the pilot runs the risk of being trivialized as "too simple" a demonstration. On the other end of the spectrum, if the organization is too large or the system too complex, the time required to implement it and the risk that it will fail will be considerably larger.

Again it cannot be overstated that the right organization be selected, and realistic goals for the pilot established. If the pilot fails, it will be an enormous effort to get buy-in to try an EDMS solution a second time. Only with the support of management of both the EDMS team and the pilot organization can the business problem be defined and a set of goals and objectives developed. These must be jointly agreed to and documented clearly in the project plan.

Choosing a Project Team

The formation of the project team is very important to any project and is equally true for developing an EDMS solution. In choosing the correct team, it is important to understand the basic elements of EDMS, and the technology part of this text has provided this basic understanding. Developers should be able to define the types of technology used and the people and/or organizations which understand these items best. The team should be drawn from these groups.

It is also important to recognize that the project team is a "core" team. People will be added and removed from the team as the project moves through various phases, and through different lines of business where specific expertise is required. The core team needs to have some of the skills listed below but can develop them over time and become the expert which is needed.

However, it should be recognized up-front that the core project team put in place today will need to become the document management support group of the future. Even as recently as two years ago, it was not uncommon to find EDMS teams being replaced with clerical type people once the implementation phase had been reached. This was often done because the EDMS was considered a "back room" function. If an EDMS is fully developed, it will be as mission-critical an application as any accounting or manufacturing planning system a company has.

Another of the most common mistakes is to view EDMS as "just another software system" and therefore turn over the system to the IS organization to develop and implement. Earlier we compared and EDMS to a typical RDBMS application. In the case of an RDBMS, once the user interface and data transaction rules are adequately defined, the "users" can be left out of the development and to some degree, implementation processes without a major problem. However, in an EDMS the requirements are not so easily defined, nor are they the same from one line of business or department to another. Therefore, turning the project over to the IS organization entirely is a mistake.

Now this is not to say that the IS organization will not play a major part in this effort. The unique nature of an EDMS system demands an equally unique team. To develop this team presents a significant challenge because a wide variety of skills from a diverse set of disciplines is required. To gather the entire skill inventory would require a rather large team in most organizations, and this large team presents its own set of problems. In large team settings, individuals often look for defined roles with clear responsibilities. In the diverse world of EDMS, these clearly-defined roles are very difficult to establish.

If a team could be brought together with all the requisite skills, it is likely to be so large that the project would, in fact, be a part-time job for most members of the team. This results in the sense of purpose and orientation towards a common goal being lost. Another way a large team would complicate the effort is by allowing one "expert" to constantly look over the work of another. Significant rework would be likely and precious time and resources will be lost.

OK, so how, then, do we solve this problem? First we begin with a recognition of the skills required for the project. Then individuals can be chosen that best meet the overall criteria. Where expertise is lacking, either training must be provided or the experts must be "borrowed" and put into the project. All of this leads to the conclusion that the Project Manager is an absolutely critical choice to the success of the effort. The wrong choice will lead to outright failure or failure by default in that the project will simply go round in circles and never move forward.

Let's look at what is required of the project manager for this type of EDMS project. The project manager will be expected to:

- Build a cohesive team from a disparate group of individuals. This includes getting them trained on the technologies to be used as a part of this effort.
- Develop a detailed project plan that addresses the effort, budget, and schedule for the overall project including the initial analysis, installation of an EDMS infrastructure, and development of the tailored versions for each organization, or line of business.
- Define and manage the effort required from the project team, "customer" organizations, and supporting groups within the company.
- Oversee the refinement and customization of the methodology used to guide the EDMS and balance technical issues with business implementation concerns to keep the process productive and efficient.
- Manage the day to day activities of the project team and plan the overall, "big picture" schedule.
- Establish a solid communication channel between the client and the project team so information can flow freely in both directions.

If these are the tasks of the project manager, then what are the skills required of this individual? Some of the more important skills are:

- A good communicator, both verbally and in writing
- An individual adept at team building
- A person with a strong IS background coupled with some business management experience; preferably with EDMS technology
- A person with exposure to the field of knowledge acquisition
- A good decision maker, even in light of incomplete information
- A person with an aggressive, get-the-job-done attitude
- A structured individual who can develop a plan and stick to it
- A person with spheres of influence in many areas of the organization, and, perhaps, most important of all
- Someone who is comfortable with change and who can work with others to manage it.

An EDMS implementation is as much about changing the way the organization works as it is about developing and implementing complex systems. These systems, if properly developed and implemented, will by their very nature change the way work is done in the organization. They will re-engineer the organization, but from the bottom up rather than the top down. Often this leads to conflict not at the so-called working level, but rather at the first and second level supervisory positions. This is where project managers will have to pull from all their skills in communicating, negotiating, and managing change in order to make the system a success. One thing can not be overstated: the choice of the right project manager will spell the success or failure of a project.

As we look past the project manager's position, how do we choose and build the rest of the team? This question is not so easily answered. Each and every company or organization is different and therefore the right team cannot be dictated from a distance. However, there are two things that can be said about the team. First, as mentioned above, it should be kept small, at least in the early stages. A team of 3-4 people total is usually a good place to start. The second is that the team must possess a variety of skills that fall into two general categories: technology and business process. The more overlap between the disciplines that can be brought to the team the better, and it will help keep the team at the desired size. Let's review each of the types of skills, capabilities, and experiences required for each of these two areas.

First, the technology side or developer:

- A thorough understanding of the basic EDMS technologies including current tools available on the market in the areas of:
  - Document Viewing, in both page and pageless layouts
  - Indexing and Searching, full text, keyword, semantic
  - Conversion, content and format converters
  - Document Management, including library services, versioning and configuration
  - Authoring Tools, including graphics, word processing, desktop publishing, CAD
  - Workflow
  - Imaging, including OCR
- Networking and System Architecture
- Software Development Methods and Processes
- Relational or Object-Oriented Database Management
- Skills in Operating Systems such as UNIX, or NT
- An understanding of document construction including markup languages such as HTML or SGML

Remember that while it is important to get as strong a team as possible, in many circumstances it is better to get someone who is "good" in many areas and an expert in none, than to get several experts in each area. There are two primary reasons for this. First is that generalists will generally work better in a team environment where they must perform a number of different tasks and fulfill several roles. The second is that since these solutions will use off-the-shelf components, experts will quickly identify the "limitations" of a particular tool and want to search for a more perfect tool or build a custom solution. In general, this effort adds little value, consumes a significant amount of time, and usually ends up delaying progress.

It is important to remember that the team is generally not going to be "building" a system from the ground up, but rather assembling one from off-the-shelf technologies. This results in more of a need to understand the concepts of the EDMS problem and learn how the tool chosen meets this need. It often requires learning how to configure the tool to meet the needs of the customers, not developing custom solutions. This type of work may not demand the expertise required to build an information system from scratch. Often, it has been found that experts in a particular field or technology are bored by the task of configuring tools for a particular job and would prefer to be developing custom systems.

Shifting to the analysis side of the team from the technical, we find that a different set of skills and capabilities is required. These are generally softer skills, but no less important. In fact, if the analysis effort is wrong, no amount of technical expertise will be able to construct a system that meets the user's requirements. It is the role of the analyst to transform the needs of business organization and users, stated in relation to their jobs and performance, into the functional specifications for an EDMS. The analyst phase requires the following skills set:

- A thorough understanding of knowledge acquisition techniques
- Excellent communication skills, both oral and written
- A basic understanding of Document Conversion, and Management
- A basic understanding of Document Viewing, Workflow and Authoring
- A detailed understanding of Instructional System Design
- The ability to estimate the impact resulting from implementing an EDMS
- A general IS background, including system and network exposure
- Creative thinking with structured thought.

As discussed earlier, the more overlap the team has in the roles of technical developers and analysts, the stronger the team will be. This overlap will also help to reduce the number of people on the team. Remember, it is important that the team be broad in the scope of skills, perhaps giving up some depth, in order to form a solid working team. This will put some pressure on the project manager to be able to borrow or leverage the available expertise outside the team when needed, but will reward him with a team that will grow in skills and capabilities as the project moves forward. It also lays a very solid foundation for the transformation of this team to the role of a supporting infrastructure once the majority of business organizations reach the implementation stage.

Analysis

Armed with a team, an approach, a plan, and a target organization, developers can turn to the next phase: analysis. This phase is focused on determining exactly what the system must do to meet the business objectives. This requires a detailed understanding of the organization, the people, the systems and the environment. The critical question now is *how* to do this.

Overview

Previously, a performance based approach was presented with the analysis starting at the end point and working its way back through to the stage where information is delivered. This process model is presented in Figure 11-5.

Figure 11-5
Performance
Based
Analysis
Process

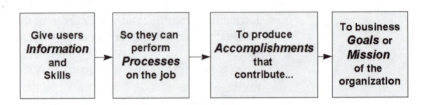

If we can determine what the business is trying to do, and what accomplishments are expected to achieve those goals, then we will know what is expected of the individuals in the organization. Once it is clearly determined what the individuals must do, then it is not a difficult task to determine what information (i.e., documents) are needed to properly perform those duties. Similar to the analysis process for performance, the analysis process for an EDMS must start at the end user and work its way back. This process is illustrated in Figure 11-6.

Figure 11-6
User
Centered
EDMS
 Analysis

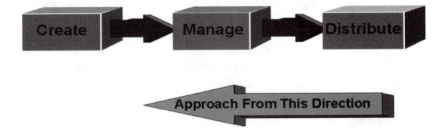

Knowledge Acquisition

A successful EDMS is one which will deliver the correct information to the right person, at the proper place and time. The analysis process will determine, for each user or class of users, the correct information and what the proper place and time are. This means finding out what the successful performers do and how they do it, and building a system that will enable all the performers to do it. Ideally, all performers, including the current top performers, will improve by repeatedly using the EDMS.

Therefore, the key to successful analysis is the right overall approach (i.e., user-centered), along with the right tools for the job. In this case, the right tools are those used in knowledge acquisition techniques, for what is really occurring is the acquisition of knowledge about proper performance from those who know it best. Then this information can be transformed into requirements and ultimately into a system design.

Knowledge acquisition, as a discipline, has its roots in expert systems. The concept of knowledge acquisition is to extract, transform, and transfer the domain knowledge of a human being into a computer system. The concept is still quite valid, but the discipline is now used for a variety of things beyond expert systems. Some other common uses for knowledge acquisition are:

- Software Requirement Analysis
- Instructional Systems Design
- Job Task Analysis

In short, the knowledge acquisition process can be used anywhere it is important to extract and understand how people do what they do in order to affect others in some meaningful way.

Knowledge acquisition has been developed as a formal discipline because it is often very difficult to get people to articulate what it is that they do. Looking at training is always a good way to understand the issue of knowledge acquisition. Why is it that the people who are the best at some particular task are often the worst trainers? They often explain things with many intuitive (to them, not the trainee) steps left out. It is like trying to teach children to ride a bike; we all know how to do it, so why is it so hard for them? We leave out lots and lots of little but important details. This is the same reason why knowledge acquisition requires a formal process. There are four methods of knowledge acquisition frequently used in the analysis phase of an EDMS. They are:

- Interviews
- Process Mapping
- Focus Groups
- Observations

A brief overview of each one is provided below in the context of how they might be used.

NOTE: It is not the intention of this text to detail all the elements and issues of knowledge acquisition. There are several texts on the subject, and one particularly good one is *Knowledge Acquisition: Principles and*

Guidelines by Karen L. McGraw and Karan Harbison-Briggs, (Prentice Hall, 1989).

Interviewing is exactly what one would expect. The analyst prepares a set of questions to establish a framework, and then uses those questions to begin an interactive, two-way dialogue with the user. Questions are asked and answered and the conversation may take many side paths around a basic topic. The reason for prepared questions is to try to keep the session focused and gain the most information in the least amount of time. It is a very popular and effective technique. This is very useful in a number of places in the analysis process.

Process mapping is geared toward documenting how a particular task or function is carried out. This is meant to be much more of a one-way communication. Here the analyst will attempt to get subjects to explain the process in great detail and attempt to restrict their part of the conversation to asking probing questions. The intent is to prevent the analyst from "contaminating" the results by steering the session. This technique often requires practice and a strong degree of self discipline. It is particularly effective in extracting the actual tasks in a job or steps in a document's workflow.

Focus Groups are very similar to interviews, except tha two or more workers are interviewed at the same time. This can be helpful as the individuals play off one another to arrive at consensus answers. Places where people disagree may indicate confusion and warrant further investigation in individual sessions. Sometimes after several sets of interviews, a focus group is conducted to review the results. This allows several people to resolve individual differences. These sessions are widely used throughout the analysis. They do require more effort and practice because handling a group of people and keeping the conversation focused can be difficult.

Observation is the process of going to the actual work place with individuals and watching them perform. This is often more difficult and time consuming than an interview, but can be far more revealing. Many of us, taken to a conference room and asked what we do, will recite what we are supposed to do, not what we actually do. Also, many visual clues of what we do and how we do it are not available in the sterile environment of the interview. This task is very effective at finding out *exactly* how people accomplish their tasks. Often, this approach is used in conjunction with an interview afterwards, where many of the actions taken may be questioned and discussed.

These techniques are used at many of the points in the analysis process. The better the team is trained and skilled in the art of knowledge acquisition, the more effective the analysis process will be. Formal training for the team, or at least the analysts, should be strongly considered before embarking on the first analysis project.

Analysis Process

The actual analysis and knowledge acquisition process is divided into six stages, some of which can be performed in parallel, others in series. These stages are:

1. Alignment and Organizational Profile
2. Initial Document List
3. User Profile(s)
4. Document Profiles & Survey
5. Environmental Profile
6. Capacity Data Sheet

The flow and relationships between these stages are shown in Figure 11-7.

Figure 11-7
Analysis
Process

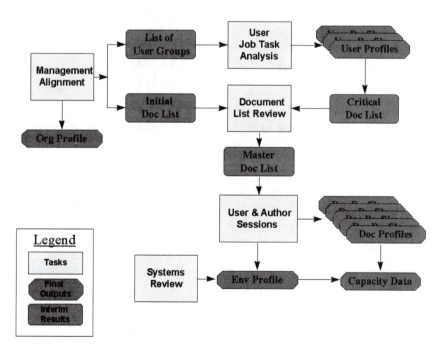

For each of these stages, the results can often be documented on a prepared form. This ensures the proper information is collected and presented in a consistent format from analyst to analyst and from organization to organization. The following sections provide a detailed overview and major issues to be addressed in each stage.

Alignment and Organizational Profile

The analysis process begins with the alignment and organizational profile. The alignment refers to ensuring that the project manager from the client organization is thinking about the effort in the same way as the project team. The alignment process is really an in-depth review and discussion of the project plan with this project manager. If there are any issues or differences of opinion on the approach, schedule or resources, this is the time to address them. The project plan should be modified to include any items discussed and then agreed to by both parties.

The second part of this first stage is the organizational profile. It aims to capture all the necessary information about the organization to support the requirement specification and the other pieces of the analysis process. It begins by capturing the mission of the organization, what it is that they do at the highest level. Next, this is brought down a level to ask what are the top few functions or processes performed by this organization. Who are the customers or focus of those functions?

Next, the process looks at the success criteria, and performance is measured for the group engaged in these activities. How do the people know they are doing things correctly? Examples might be measured output per-person per-day, call handling times, revenue generated per week, etc. There should be clear goals and feedback as to the current measure of performance. This will be important because this is how an EDMS or any other system should pay for itself. The system in its final form should be able to impact these numbers. But there are, of course, exceptions to every rule.

In many organizations the sole driver may be safety or regulatory compliance, where the system is being instituted because it is needed, regardless of its impact on performance. However, if an objective is clear, often some measure of performance can be found, where the driver of the system may also be the gauge which measures improvements to the system itself. It becomes the monitor for internal continuous improvement.

Rounding out the organizational profile should be an organizational chart and a list of users and locations. For each user group, there should be a related primary function. This element will determine how many classes or groups of users exist within the organization. This will be important later in determining the user groups to meet with.

In summary, the organization profile is looking to collect the following information:

- Mission Statement
- Top Functions or Processes
- Success Criteria and Performance Goals
- Primary Customers for the Organization
- Organization Chart
- User Groups by Function and Location

Initial Document List

The second stage of the analysis process is the initial document list. Often many organizations, when hearing they are going to undertake an EDMS, create a list of "all" the documents they use. This would be consistent with a document-centered approach. While this is not used to drive the process, it can be very helpful to cross check the other parts of the analysis process. Very simply, it is a list of all the documents used by the organization, which may be subdivided by the user groups who actually use the documents.

Often this list is created by asking a number of people, looking over desks and bookshelves, and recording every document that appears. The problem is that often many of these documents go unused, either correctly or incorrectly, but are nonetheless unused and therefore add no value to the organization. The goal in the next several parts of the analysis process is to get a true list of what is used and needed. This initial list is then used to cross check that list and see if anything was missed or forgotten.

User Profiles

The third stage of the analysis process involves user profiles. Here is where many knowledge acquisition techniques come into play. Actually, what occurs in the user profile is effectively a job-task analysis. This stage focuses on keeping users away from questions about documents until their entire job functions have been fully explored. Then very specific questions can be asked to identify the documents used and perhaps the information they need but don't have. The analyst gets to pick and choose the knowledge acquisition techniques which will work best to extract and collect this information

The first step is to define the user's job title and description. It is important that all users in a particular group agree upon the job description. It is possible that users may actually be performing different jobs and require that the group be sub-divided. This division may be different than the way the organization groups them, but as long as the job description is the same, that is all that matters. Next, the top few tasks for that job are identified; this is the list of tasks the person performs to meet the job description.

The next step is to understand each task: how often is it performed, how important is it, what are the consequences of improper performance, how the tasks are measured, and what bottlenecks or obstacles have to be overcome to perform the task? It is often the case that performance measures or goals are not directed at the task level; whether this is appropriate or not is of no consequence here. Also, for each user group, it is important to get their level of computer expertise (novice, comfortable, super user) and what their expectations of the EDMS are.

The final step in the job task analysis is to identify what documents are used to assist in performing the tasks. For each document, it is important to know the following information:

- Exactly what information in the document is used?
- How is the document used?
- How important to that task is this document?
- How frequently is the document used?
- Where is the document located and how is it accessed?
- How helpful is the document (does it contain what you need)?
- How long does it take to find what you are looking for?
- What information do you need but do not have access to?

Also it can be helpful to know what mechanisms the users have to provide feedback on the documents either to their supervisors or to the authors. It is always amazing to note how far out of contact the creators (authors) and the consumers (users) of a document can be. It is not uncommon to find that the author and end-users of a document have never met or even discussed the document. Many times authors write what they feel the user needs to know, only to discover that the users never use the document because it does not have what they really need. Simply taking all the documents on the list and putting them into an EDMS would never help in this situation.

A user profile is developed for each group of users within the organization, and while sometimes this can be one group, other times it may mean ten or more. Understanding what the different end-users need allows the system to be tailored, adjusted, or configured to meet each user group's individual needs. This will make training, deployment, and use of the EDMS much easier.

In a review of the user profile stage, the following information must be obtained and documented for *each* group of users:

- Job Title and Description
- Major Tasks, Performance Measures, and Obstacles
- Task frequency, Importance and Consequences of Deviation

- Computer Experience, and Expectations of EDMS
- Documents and Information Used for Each Task

This may seem to be a lot of information to simply get the list of used documents, but it the list of documents that will *improve* the performance of the users. This gives the EDMS its ability to impact the bottom-line performance of the organization. In closing, it also is what enables the EDMS to be a system which delivers the correct information to the right person at the proper place and time, rather than an electronic library which serves as an end unto itself.

Document Profiles

Finally, the focus shifts to documents. By reviewing all the user profiles created, a complete set of mission-critical documents can be assembled. These documents are the ones that are necessary to the proper performance of a job. This list is then compared to the initial document list created earlier. All documents not on the list should be carefully reviewed as to why they are not there. In some cases people may have forgotten something and a quick re-interview will clear it up. In other cases, documents that may be on the initial list, but not on the user profiles, simply aren't critical.

Earlier, the idea of business-critical and non-critical documents was raised. Critical documents are valuable corporate assets and deserve to be controlled within an EDMS. The other documents, while they may have value and be used in various places in the organization, are not mission-critical and, therefore, generally do not warrant the attention of time and resources to manage them. The documents the users put on the user profiles are, however, critical. The ones on the initial list and not on the profiles may or may not be critical. It is important to recognize that the documents not considered critical in one organization may be critical in another. The analysis of another organization will reveal this fact, if true.

Document profiles are focused on gathering information about the critical documents. This process may involve further interaction with the end users, will certainly involve the author, and likely involve coordinators, such as reviewers and approvers. A document profile is generated for each document the users deemed critical, but here a document can mean an entire manual consisting of ten chapters and numerous figures. The profile is organized in a logical perspective, as only the user would see it, and not the author.

The document profile begins by recording the title and purpose of the document. It follows that with the structure of the document, for example ten chapters that comprise a given manual, each document type within the profile would be detailed. A manual might contain sections on theory, descriptions, procedures and forms, and within each section there may be a number of documents. Or a document profile may be generated for a particular type of document such as policies. There may be hundreds of policies; so the goal is not to document each individual policy, but rather the information relevant to the class of documents called "policies."

The information to be gathered for each document type can include, but is not limited to, the following:

- Type or Class
- Quantity (within the organization)
- Average number of files per document
- Average number of pages per document or per file
- Average storage space per document or per file
- Format(s) for documents (what software was used to create it)
- Contain Graphics? Pasted, linked or embedded?
- Format(s) for graphics (what software used to create it)
- Physical Size (layout) and storage space for graphics

Another piece of information needed is the metadata or attributes required for each document. This information can often be gathered by asking "If one were to search for this document, what key terms would be used?"

The next major part of the document profile is really focused on the creator and contributors. The first task is to identify who owns the document, usually the individual responsible for creating it. Sometimes, they may not be the same, or because people move around, the document should be tied to a job function, not a person. However, the person is necessary to help fill out the profile. Questions around the revision process are next. They can involve how often change occurs, how revision numbering is achieved, what types and triggers for changes are used, and how many revisions are kept and for how long. On the people side of the review process, is it formal or informal and is the review on paper or electronic, and if electronic what format? Last is the issue of comment collection, management, and retention.

As the document profile discussion moves into the review process, the entire issue of workflow is raised. The workflow for a document must be carefully defined. It must include the Routes, the Roles and the Responsibilities for the document. This is where the process mapping technique for knowledge acquisition is valuable. For each step in the process the same issues as review and revision must be addressed. This workflow should show all known critical users for the document. The analysis process may be driven by one user group indicating the importance of the document, but there may be other critical users in another organization. Sometimes the author can provide that information.

This is a most crucial step in the entire process - defining the business process. Often creators, coordinators and consumers can tell you what is done, not what should be done. It is this thinking that has to change - get people to think outside the "box", not about what is organizational or politically doable, but rather how it *ought* to be. It is often said that Henry Ford had this type of vision, because if he simply tried to make a wagon go faster he would have invented a way to put more horses in front of it, instead of the automobile. These sessions must get people focused at not shaving one or two days off a one month process, but how to get the entire process to one or two days. This is where the BPR really comes into play and significant gains can had. It is important to allow enough time for this critical step.

The final part of the document profile is security. From the workflow developed above should come the security information for the document in terms of who can edit, review, approve, etc. In addition, general security decisions need to be made about who can see, view, and even copy the document.

In some situations the audience for a document is so large or dispersed that to conduct interviews or even focus groups is not practical. In this case, document surveys can be used. A general questionnaire is created with multiple-choice answers for each item. The survey is then sent to a wide variety of users to obtain the necessary information. It is important to recognize that returns on a survey are typical less than 10%, so the sample must be large enough to ensure that sufficient forms will be returned.

The document profile can be summarized as addressing the following items:

- Document Title and Purpose
- Structure and Organization
- Document Data (size, pages, formats, text, graphics)
- Attributes
- Revision & Review Process
- Workflow
- Key Users
- Security

Environmental Profile

The environmental profile is the systems configuration profile. It is designed to capture all the information about the existing systems, and any standards to be adhered to. The profile documents the standard configuration for the desktop machines (clients), including hardware, operating systems, and application software. It also covers the servers and networks for the organization. It must capture any standards that are being enforced or major changes to the systems coming anytime soon. The goal is to record the information necessary to assist in selecting a compatible EDMS and what limitations may be faced by having to address the lowest common denominator in terms of hardware, software, operating systems, and networks.

Capacity Sheet

With the data contained in the document profiles, approximate numbers can be developed for local and server based storage for this system. This may include the imaging of many paper documents. Consideration must be given to mirroring for no system downtime, or redundant non-mirrored storage for reliability. Also the issues of near-line, off-line, back-up, and archiving storage must be considered. Cost and life of media are important elements in this decision. This requirement must be compared to the existing and planned environment to determine if any major issues exist.

Functional Requirement Specification

The functional requirement specification (FRS), sometimes referred to as the software requirement specification (SRS), is a listing of all the things the system must do. Its purpose is not to specify how to do these functions, but simply to show that these functions are required to meet the user's needs. This requires going through the profiles and interview notes and other documents provided by the client organization and extracting the requirement statements.

Often the requirement specs can be organized by EDMS functions, such as:

- Creation
- Conversion
- Management
- Workflow

- Searching
- Viewing
- Security
- Systems

The systems section refers to the standard operating environment of the organization. For example, in one group the server standard may be Windows NT, and in another it may Sun Solaris. This type of information is critical to selecting and implementing a system.

However, there are no absolute rules on how to organize or prepare a requirements specification. In many organizations, the IS department may have a standard outline or template. This format should be considered, but with some careful review before committing. Often, an FRS or SRS from an IS department is focused on a system to be built from the ground up, and therefore the outline provided may be much broader and generic and not fit well with an EDMS. On the other hand, it may be just fine to work the EDMS elements into one of the sections, and simply label N/A those sections that do not apply.

Generally, when writing a functional specification nearly every line begins with "The system must be able to . . ." The requirements are often kept to short statements. Sometimes examples can be very helpful. In essence, this list of requirements will become the evaluation matrix for the tool evaluation and selection task of the prototyping phase.

A functional specification is often fairly technical in detail and its intended audience are people with IS backgrounds, so this is not usually a problem. The profiles are generally attached as an appendix and will often provide a less technical document that is understandable to an interested user. The next phase is prototyping, which will bring a majority of these requirements to life, allowing the users to see, feel, and touch these requirements.

12

Prototyping

Prototyping is the act of building a scaled-down version of the EDMS that has the look, feel, and functionality of the ultimate system. It is used as a way to present the results of the analysis process. Simply put, it is bringing the system requirements to life in a way that users can see, touch, and interact with in order to verify that the requirements have been properly captured.

A prototype often serves a variety of functions. Among the most important ones are:

- Provides a visual representation of critical requirements
- Promotes more detailed discussion of end users' needs
- Establishes end user buy-in for the system
- Enables all users and developers to establish a common vision
- Gains support and funding for full scale EDMS project.

Many times the development team believes, through a very thorough analysis, that they fully understand the users' requirements and are ready to begin design and development of the EDMS and therefore no prototype is required. This can be a fatal mistake.

Even if the development team does, in fact, exactly understand the users' needs and knows exactly what to build, a prototype should be built so that the users have the opportunity to make changes. This shows the users that they are, in fact, the focus of the system, and it enables them to see it as "their" EDMS application, not the development team's. Do not underestimate the value of having end users who support, talk-up, and even promote the use of the EDMS. This "championing" process can be very powerful in getting funding or helping with the implementation phase later on.

The Prototyping Process

The prototyping process can be divided into three major activities. They are:

- Selecting a Tool
- Building a Prototype
- Performing a Gap Analysis

These activities are not sequential; rather, they are interwoven to get the job accomplished most effectively. Figure 12-1 shows the detailed steps in the prototyping process. Each of these elements is explored in the sections that follow. Also, it is common to run through several iterations of these steps to get the prototype to an acceptable product.

Figure 12-1
Prototyping
Process

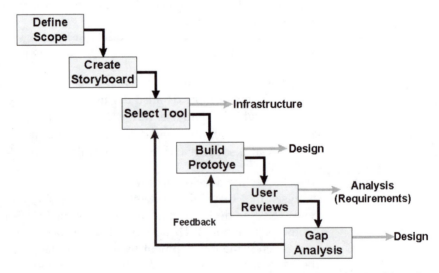

In some cases the input gathered in this process, usually from the end users, may require going back and reanalyzing some of the requirements. It is expected that some requirements will change, but these changes should be relatively small and will not have a major impact on the system. If they do, then some rework of the analysis and requirements gathering is necessary. This is part of the reason the prototype is so critical. It allows all players to reach a very tight consensus before a tool is selected or purchased and before a significant investment is made in design, configuration, or development. All of these tasks are time consuming and expensive propositions; it is important not to have to revisit these activities.

Defining Scope

Establishing the scope of the prototype is the first step in the prototyping process. A prototype for an EDMS generally consists of four elements: User Interface, Creation, Management, and Distribution. The goal of this task is to determine which of these elements will be addressed in the prototype. It can be as simple as addressing only one of these elements or as elaborate as encompassing all four.

Earlier, in the planning stage of analysis, the organization was profiled to determine which elements (create, manage, distribute) of the document management system were likely to be most critical. At a minimum, whichever of these elements is the most critical should be included in the prototype. This particular element will likely be the focal point of the prototype. But there are at least three different roles in the organization, and to some degree each of these should be addressed by the prototype.

In many organizations the profile is one of few authors and many consumers. Here the prototype will focus on what content to present and how best to present it. For the authors and coordinators, a few simple screens or even demonstrations of products may be sufficient to serve as "their" prototype. The key to a successful prototype is to hit the target for the most dominating group of users.

One exception to this rule is when some reasonably hard cost-benefit data analysis is available. Even if the consumer is the focal point, it may be possible to show that by streamlining the authoring process, significant dollars can be saved. In this case, the prototype must include, and more than in a cursory way, the authoring community. This could hold the key to obtaining the necessary funding.

Another influencing factor in defining the scope of the prototype is the clarity and consensus on the requirements established from the analysis phase. If there are areas where the requirements were not clear or many users still disagree on the differences between needs and wants, then the prototype should address these areas. One of the major goals of the prototype should be to validate the requirements and establish a common vision for the system.

Choosing what elements to include in the prototype is important, but there are two other significant considerations that need to be weighed in the prototype definition. The first is user interface and the second is the breadth and depth. In considering the user interface, the first question to answer is whether or not the tools will be used "out of the box." Often this choice is driven by budget. Using something right out of the box will cost less. It does cost less to *develop*, but it may cost considerably more to *implement*. This is a very important issue and should not be summarily dismissed.

If the system will only be rolled out to a limited number of people, it may be less expensive to train them and get them proficient with the system than developing a custom application. However, if the audience is large, custom development can reduce the overall cost. The amount of training, and support costs incurred will be dramatically reduced if the system can adapt to the users' terminology and the way they work. Even in a 500-person implementation, if training could be completed in two days instead of five, that saves six person-years of labor just from sitting in the training class.

For the purposes of the prototype, it is best if the new interface can be put over the existing EDMS client to demonstrate how it will work. A less expensive and quicker way is to build a "visual presentation" of the interface with a 4GL tool in order to demonstrate the look, feel, and layout of the screen. The proprietary tools from a vendor can be used to demonstrate the functional part of the prototype. It is important to remember that this is a prototype, a limited content, limited functionality, scaled down version of the final system. It is not intended to show every user, every function, and every screen in the final system.

The last consideration in defining the prototype scope is the breadth and depth. The analysis process, even for the pilot, was likely to have identified several user groups all with somewhat different needs. The objective is to show the breadth of the final system with the prototype. This is meant to show how much content, how many types of functions, or how many different users will be supported in the final system. Then for one user, a subset of the full content or functionality will be flushed out in this prototype. This is its depth, where the focus will be on the most critical users.

The scope of the prototype must then include which phases of the EDMS problem will be demonstrated: creation, management, and distribution. It must decide if a custom user interface will be developed and for which phase. Finally, it must establish a broad brush outline for how much will be portrayed in the prototype, and how much detail will be presented in the heart of the prototype.

Storyboarding

Once the scope of the prototype is defined, the next step is to begin to bring the prototype to life. It is expected that each of the individuals involved in the analysis phase thus far all have an idea of what the final application will look like. This concept is referred to as a mental model--the visual representation inside one's head of what something looks like. This might be what the screens in the EDMS look like or the image of how documents are organized in some sort of "virtual bookshelf." These images are very powerful constructs to make an EDMS meet the user's needs.

The goal of this task is to elicit these ideas, get consensus among the users, and then document them. Storyboarding is the act of sketching out, often on paper or whiteboards, what the EDMS will look like. It can range from ideas on how to organize and present content to rough screen layouts. It should also include task and function-oriented navigation, or how to get from one place to another in the system. Finally, it must include use of the proper terminology for each task, function, and document. Common terminology is an important by-product of a successful analysis and prototyping process. It helps establish a standard for all users.

Storyboarding is usually done in sessions with a mix of users. For example, if it is the distribution phase being storyboarded, the consumers will dominate, but the authors and coordinators should be present and participate. After a variety of focus groups have been through the process, the storyboards are then built into a cohesive map of how to get work done in the EDMS system.

The storyboards are shaped into logical navigation and functionality--all focused on user tasks, not features. They must also reflect the documents to be included in the system and the logical organization of them. This set is then shown to a large audience of users, those in the primary groups and those outside it. Feedback, both positive and negative, is then gathered. Several iterations are usually required to get the storyboards into their final form. Sometimes the storyboards can be numbered, and simple scenario maps made to list the tasks to be performed and the storyboards that correspond. This can then be distributed, reaching a larger audience for feedback without having to give individual presentations.

Depending upon the nature of the project, storyboards can be left as hand drawn, rough sketches, or polished into electronic format using presentation packages such as PowerPoint, Visual Basic, or anything in between. While polishing the storyboards is nice, it is far more important to make certain that the mental models of the participants have been accurately extracted and captured. This is what will spell success or failure of the system.

Tool Evaluation and Selection

The storyboards often provide a pictorial representation of the most important requirements from the users. Often though, these storyboards skip over critical requirements because those requirements are background tasks, things that occur behind the scenes. Versioning models might be one example: the storyboards might indicate that a document is versioned, but not concern itself with when the revision occurred, perhaps during check-in or check-out. However, this is a very important issue.

Tool selection is the process of comparing the tools on the market to the requirements captured in both the storyboarding and analysis process. This evaluation process can be very formal or rather informal; that decision is left to the project team. There are some good techniques to use for performing this evaluation.

The first step is to gather information on what tools are available in the market. The World Wide Web offers an excellent starting place. Most major vendors have Web sites that provide a substantial bit of information on their products, both capabilities and specifications. This text has a corresponding site that has cataloged and organized a number of vendors and other useful sites for gathering information on the EDMS market. It can be found at the following location:

http://www.goucher.edu/~docman/

Trade journals, industry associations, and conferences are also good sources for finding potential suppliers, and some of these are cataloged at this Website.

In a formal evaluation, a comparison matrix may be developed, putting requirements down the left and tools across the top. Then each tool can be reviewed and evaluated against each requirement. A simple or elaborate point system can be devised to help weigh the most important criteria. In many cases there are a few key criteria that may eliminate many tools, thereby reducing the effort in evaluating tools. This is useful in evaluating the technical aspects of a set of products.

Price and a stable supplier are also important factors to consider. This is an emerging market and new vendors are arriving constantly. One should carefully consider the stability and financial health of the vendor as well as the technical product they are offering. Price should be considered once the technical evaluations are complete. It does not make sense to choose a product which is less expensive but that does not meet the organization's needs. Alternatively, paying for features or capabilities one is not likely to use is not prudent either.

One way to reduce the effort and shorten the time in evaluating products is to ask the vendors to do it for you. Often a requirements package can be quickly turned into a request for information or request for proposal. It is highly recommended that several scenarios be developed and vendors be asked to respond to these as well as the requirements. As we have seen earlier, all vendors provide some type of attributes. But how many? Can they be customized? Are they document-class specific, or are they revision specific? Using a few scenarios can go a long way to flushing out all these "little" details.

If a custom interface or integration with other systems is an important consideration there a few other factors to look at. Consider how open the system really is and what API's are provided by the vendor. Support for the emerging industry standards of ODMA, DMA and the Workflow Management Coalition (WFMC) should be carefully reviewed. Vendors are very often willing to provide demonstrations, evaluation copies, and even visits to similar clients. Take advantage of these items to help evaluate and select the right tool.

For the purposes of the very first prototype (i.e., the pilot), the tools reviewed and selected should be only those required to complete the defined scope of the prototype. The rest of the tool selection process can be completed after the initial pilot has been accepted. This keeps the time and effort to a minimum at this early stage. It is also possible that later in the pilot prototype the selected tool may have to be reconsidered if it can not stand up to the users' requirements. The tool selection and evaluation process is actually part of the infrastructure process, but was presented here to make the work process easier to follow. The infrastructure phase is designed to make sure the right tools, architecture, and standards are put into place to build a proper foundation for a robust EDMS.

Building a Prototype

The analysis process of asking users what they need and want in a system was the first step in establishing a working relationship with these key players. At the end of the analysis process they were asked to review a list of requirements. Most of them had never seen a requirements document before, and it is doubtful that many of them actually read it. The next step was the storyboarding process, where they got to talk about and sketch out a bit what this new system, and the resulting EDMS, might look like. That phase got them a little more interested.

Many of these users are likely to never have been asked, "What do you need and what do you want in a system?" So soliciting good input is often difficult. Many of them can tell you want they don't want, often citing examples of current systems, but they can't tell what they do want. The prototype is the mechanism to give them that opportunity.

The prototyping process is generally one where the EDMS team goes off and builds something to look at. Doing so may require that skills with specific tools and packages be available. These skills can be acquired in several ways. The first is to send part of the team to a particular vendor's training class. Another is to involve the vendor or systems integrator in assisting with the prototype. This will certainly cost more but can really help get the prototype moving. Developing skills in-house or going outside is dependent upon budget, schedule, and likelihood that the tool selected will be the one put into production.

The EDMS team will need to gather sample documents as well as the storyboards and requirements for use in development of the prototype. The prototype may also require putting in some demo systems and configuring several machines in the users' work environment for them to be able to see, feel and touch the prototype when it is complete. Often one or two users are targeted to become part of the prototyping team. Regardless of how accurate the storyboards are, there are always questions on this or that. Having someone that can answer them quickly, and with the right perspective really helps to keep things moving.

At about the halfway point of the prototype, there should be sufficient progress to do a first cut review. Often this involves a limited set of users, but helps validate that the prototyping efforts are on the right track. Any major issues raised by these individuals are resolved, and the minor ones are documented. Then the first real review is scheduled with the users. There will be bugs, incomplete screens, and missing functionality - but it is important to get user input at this time.

The user reviews are covered in the following section. However, the feedback from these review sessions is documented and incorporated into the prototype. The prototype is then reviewed again. Typically, two reviews are sufficient, but it is not uncommon to have three or four. If the number of reviews goes beyond that it is likely the team has hit one of two problems. First, the group is trying to design the final system, and not just a prototype. This is where the breadth and depth issue comes into play, defining the size of the prototype and keeping to that size.

The second issue is that the analysis process did not adequately capture the requirements. This might be the result of inadequate analysis or changing requirements. If it is the former, some rework is required. If it is the latter, the project manager, and user's sponsor must work to keep the requirements reasonably stable. Until the cause is identified, addressed, and resolved, going forward is a futile effort.

The prototype, as discussed in the scope definition, may have as many as four parts:

- User Interface
- Creation
- Management
- Distribution

While it is impossible to define from a distance what these prototypes might consist of, there are some common elements to these pieces. The table below outlines the three major elements and shows where the interface may come into play and what components typically comprise each of them.

Table 12-1: Components of Prototype

Prototype	Key Components
Creation	<ul><li>Electronic templates for primary authoring tool(s)</li><li>Interface for these templates, including styles, formatting, presentation</li><li>Document layouts</li><li>Table of contents or organization of document(s)</li><li>Sample content for document showing level of detail</li><li>May demonstrate document conversion</li></ul>
Management	<ul><li>Repository client application, with - Commercial interface, or - Modified interface, or - Complete custom interface</li><li>Or, integration of repository functions to existing apps</li><li>Demonstrate the following (as applicable): - Check-in/Check-out, security, versioning - Customized attributes and queries - Custom workflow including review, approval, etc. - Adding comments to documents in review</li><li>Show how this customization can be accomplished (i.e., through an interface or through coding)</li><li>May show document conversion facilities, if any</li></ul>

Table 12-1: Components of Prototype (Continued)

Prototype	Key Components
Distribution	• How to produce paper and electronic outputs • Presentation and organization of content, usually this *is* the interface • Electronic viewing application or Browser • Demonstrate the following (as applicable): - Viewing, zooming, panning - Full text and attribute searching - Printing, single / sets of pages and documents - Feedback (Notes, Redline, Email) • Hyperlinks to locate information and move among related content • May include document conversion

User Reviews

The prototype, built on the storyboards and analysis results, is the place where the requirements are brought to life. The users can then see what the system might be like and how it might operate. They can, informally, test out their own scenarios to see if the system can deliver what they need.

Once the prototype reaches the halfway point it is usually in good enough shape to be shown to the users. The first few sessions should be done with users whose needs are similar. These sessions should start out as a presentation, then evolve into a working session. From the development team there should be at least one presenter, one recorder and one observer. The observer can watch the audience for non-verbal clues and reactions that may not be easily captured in other ways.

The review sessions often begin with a project recap. Then the prototype is displayed. The presenter should walk through the general screen layouts, then the basic features and functions. Next should be a walk through each screen in the system in some logical fashion. Following that several pre-planned scenarios should be presented to walk the users through the system navigation, functions, and features. Then the floor should be open for discussion.

It is important to be as honest as possible. Users will often ask for things that are either technically impossible or extremely expensive. If this is the case, tell them. Most knowledge workers in today's organizations understand cost justification and competitive pressures. If possible offer alternative ways to accomplish similar tasks. A two-way dialogue with the users can be very beneficial. Frequently it is the same users asking for the impossible who come up with the most ingenious work-arounds.

When holding these sessions there are some expectations the development team should have going in. A few are outlined here. First, most of the feedback will be on the negative side; remember users often can't tell what they want, just what they *don't*. The development staff has to be careful not to take these comments personally, despite all the hard work that went into the prototype. Most of the feedback is likely to be genuine and sincere.

Some feedback may not be quite so sincere, as it is sometimes a test. Will they really change it to give me what I want or are they just blowing smoke? If the agreement is made to change something, do it, for your credibility is at stake. If it is discovered that it can't be done, then go back and tell them that. Also go into a review session with attachment to nothing that has been done so far, for it is all likely to change, and honestly it will be for the better. After all, the users have to live with the system everyday, and their acceptance will make it a success.

In every group there will be one or two vocal individuals with positive and negative feedback on the prototype. Get those individuals into separate, individualized meetings and capture that feedback. Try to capture what excites one individual and upsets the other. Find a way to play up and play down these items. Address or resolve them if possible. The staunch supporter may now become the champion needed for implementation, but only if that individual is so inclined.

There will be lots of comments and feedback in good review sessions. There are three key phrases one should be prepared for when trying to capture the most important issues. They may begin something like:

"That's not what I meant, ..."
"Oh, you know what I forgot, ..."
"If you can do that, can you do this? . . ."

Each of these comments has the potential to dramatically change the requirements established in the analysis phase. Some of these ideas will be the ones that enable reengineering of the process and offer significant improvement in performance and productivity. On the other side of the coin, these issues can require revisiting the analysis process, redefining the scope of the prototype, or choosing another tool. Having to go back and rethink or look at what has already been done is OK, and it is certainly less expensive to do it now than discovering this at implementation time.

One example of this redefining of requirements will be taken from part of an actual project. In building a custom interface for document delivery one interview with users indicated a strong desire to have a notes capability. This was *interpreted* to mean the ability to put annotations or "electronic yellow post-it notes," similar to those found today in Adobe's Acrobat Exchange, right on a document. During the first prototype review, when the notes feature was demonstrated, the audience was not particularly impressed. During the discussion that followed, it was revealed that "the sticky notes are neat, but we want *shift* notes," meaning a logbook to record the events during the shift in a running chronological fashion. By exploring this further with users during interviews after the review session, another requirement emerged: they wanted to be able to search those notes by text, author, topic, and date.

Technically, these shift notes were far easier to implement than the yellow sticky notes. The prototype and review session allowed the team to catch this interpretation error, resulting in a system that better met the user's needs and easier to build. A simple requirement change at this stage, but an expensive architecture change if it had been caught later. Involving the user in the process is vital.

Gap Analysis

At this stage the requirements have been defined and the prototype built and agreed upon. The users and the EDMS team have a clear and common vision for the final system. There is, however, one more step to complete the prototype and close the loop between requirements and the system to be delivered. This step is gap analysis--the process of looking at the gaps between the requirements and what the tools and technology can deliver.

This step enters the process because many off-the-shelf tools are used to construct an EDMS. If the EDMS was going to be built entirely from scratch, there would be no need for this step, as the system could be constructed to exactly match the requirements. When using off-the-shelf tools, many times there are gaps between what the users want and what the tools can provide.

A first draft of this gap analysis may actually be produced during the tool evaluation and selection process. The goal of the evaluation process is to determine which tool most closely matches the stated requirements. In other words, to pick the tool with the least significant gaps. Since not all requirements are created equally, those deemed most critical must be met. Ideally, the evaluation can form the starting point for the gap analysis.

The gap analysis process actually has two phases: identifying the gaps and deciding how to fill them. Let's begin with identifying the gaps. Often the best way to perform this task is to create a matrix, similar to the one created in the evaluation process with requirements running down the left hand side. The list of requirements must be complete. Many of the requirements are of the type that may not be evident or could not be demonstrated in the prototype. These requirements must be carefully reviewed against the capability of the selected tools. This task requires a careful review of the product literature, short segments of visual or technical prototypes, or involvement of the vendor's staff to match these requirements to the tool.

Generally, the first two columns across the top of this matrix are the names of the products that address this requirement and the second indicates if this requirement is met with existing functionality. This provides the first list of gaps.

Deciding how these gaps might be filled and what level of effort and/or cost of that effort are the next steps. There are several ways to fill each of these gaps. Some of the most common ways are listed below:

- Customizing the tool (custom coded extensions)
- Future enhancements from vendor (next version of product)
- Third party products that can be integrated or used with the tool
- Other tools that might have this functionality built in
- Procedural - the work process can be used to address this item

Each of these is a potentially viable method of filling the gap. For each project some or all of these approaches should be considered and to some extent an estimate of the cost or level of effort should be assigned. This will allow for cost-effective decisions on how to deal with the gaps.

Briefly let's make sure the intent of each of these approaches is understood. The first, customization, means custom developed applications or functionality. This usually requires either an application programming interface (API) or some other way to open up the tool. Sometimes vendors or systems integrators have developed similar capabilities for other projects/clients and these can be leveraged into a less expensive solution. Of course, the downside is that this custom code must be supported. Some thought must be given to how it will work as tools are upgraded from one version to the next.

Depending upon the criticality of the requirement, it may be possible to see if and when a vendor may add that functionality to the product. If the timing is right, this can be a very good approach. However, it is important to get details from the vendor or ask to see the alpha/beta releases or even prototypes to ensure that what they are building is what is needed. Generic features lists can leave a lot of uncovered functionality; providing specific requirements and asking for comments back is not an unreasonable request. Often, this will require non-disclosure agreements with the vendor.

Sometimes functionality can be had by purchasing a third party product. This product may work as a standalone tool, such as a conversion package, or it may be integrated, such as a different indexing and search engine. Vendors often have lists of third party add-ons if the integration is critical. If some customization is going to be done anyway, it may be possible to get a product that meets the organization's requirements and integrate it into the overall EDMS application.

In some cases, it may be possible to change a work process to add an additional step rather than have to integrate several packages or tools. In the ideal situation, this may not be the best approach, but it may be a cost effective solution. It also offers a way to keep the process flexible; it may be easier to change tools or even business processes if the only integration is human and procedural. One word of warning here: do not overlook the burden being added to the performers and the training that will be required. The costs for this may far outweigh the expense of integration.

Finally, if there are enough gaps with a particular tool or if critical ones can't be filled, it may be time to select another tool. While this effort is not trivial, developing and implementing a system that doesn't do a good job of meeting requirements will not likely succeed. If a new tool must be selected, some important considerations must be reviewed. The most important one will be how does this new tool match up against the prototype built with the first tool. If it is identical, there is little concern, but the likelihood of that is small. Often a new tool requires at least mocking up a part of the prototype and going back through the user reviews. This can result in several new iterations of prototypes, user reviews, and even another shot at the gap analysis.

13

Infrastructure

Infrastructure is the foundation on which the EDMS is built. It consists of standards, hardware, software, and networks--both new and existing used to provide the basic layer of the EDMS. In many organizations a significant portion of the EDMS infrastructure already exists, so this aspect of development often focuses on verification of many elements and development of only a few new system pieces. In some situations, this task may require significant upgrades or installations of PCs and networks, as well as some new EDMS components.

The IS organization is well acquainted with the process to get new systems up-and-running. However, most business applications are comprised of client and server applications as well as a database that runs over a LAN. An EDMS, on the other hand, often involves several different technologies, networking and multiple servers. It is unlikely that an organization is as familiar with these technologies as it is with, say, PowerBuilder and Oracle for a custom application.

When the term infrastructure is used, it almost always associated with the tangible elements of a system: hardware, networks, applications, etc. Less tangible forms of infrastructure are equally or perhaps more important, but because they do not impact the systems operations on day one, they are often overlooked. This chapter is dedicated to ensuring that all the infrastructure issues get addressed properly and do not slip through the cracks.

Same but Different

The infrastructure effort follows the same basic process that the content and system development does. The major phases of this process are shown in Figure 13-1. The relationship of the elements within the infrastructure as compared to those in the system/content part of the process is the same. Figure 13-1 shows the infrastructure elements shaded and running down the left side of the page.

Figure 13-1
Overall
Methodology

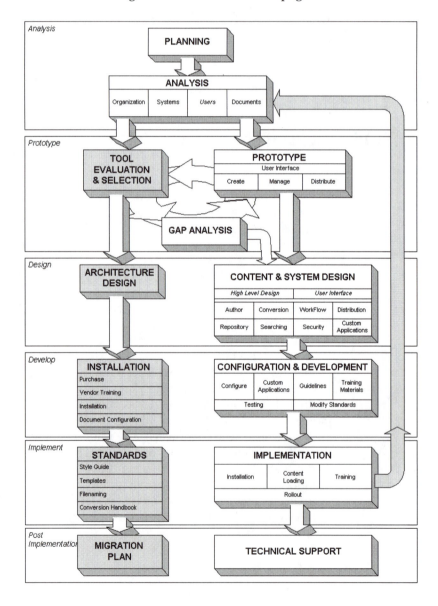

What is different here is that there is no return arrow for these tasks. While they follow the overall phased methodology, in most instances this process is only executed *once*. With the infrastructure in place, there is no need to rework it for each line of business or organization. Note, however, that there is a block in the system and content side of the process in the Develop Phase labeled "Modify Standards." Certainly, some elements will change with time, but there should be little difference in the infrastructure from one internal organization to the next. This common foundation is, after all, a critical element in leveraging information across the organization.

The methodology shows the infrastructure beginning in the prototype phase, with tool selection and evaluation. In actuality, it starts back in the analysis phase, most notably, with the Environmental Profile. That document is used to record the existing and future plans for hardware, software, and networking within the organization. The capacity sheet from the analysis phase also provides important information about the infrastructure needs and requirements. As illustrated above, the infrastructure process is comprised of five major tasks:

- Tool Selection and Evaluation
- Architecture Design
- Installation
- Standards
- Migration Plan

The infrastructure tasks are presented here, in one chapter, because it is easier to discuss them that way, but it is expected that these tasks be executed as a part of each phase of the overall process, as outlined in Figure 13-1. Each of these tasks are outlined below, except for the Tool Selection and Evaluation processes, that were already discussed in Chapter 12 dealing with Prototyping.

Architecture Design

This architecture design task is probably the one most commonly associated with the term "infrastructure." It is a design activity focused on laying out the physical system. This comes from having an understanding of the basic concept of operations or high level design.

This step outlines which servers will be used for what functions and defines the specifications for those machines. Each server must be properly configured based upon the anticipated use of that machine. Also, any special hardware, such as optical or CD-ROM jukeboxes and scanners, must be considered in the design.

Beyond determining the server configuration, it is necessary to specifically plan the client system configuration as well. Specific testing may be required to verify the various EDMS client software packages will operate properly along with the "normal" software for each group of users. This can be a difficult task, but establishing a standard configuration will make installation, performance and support significantly easier. Also, determining the requirements for system memory and monitor size are common issues.

Network topology is the next topic to consider. For example, many of the EDMS technologies require TCP/IP in order to communicate between client and server. This is true for Web-based delivery systems as well. This can have a profound impact on the network design, layout, and configuration. It may require only a few changes or a complete overhaul of the network. Understanding which users will be performing which tasks can greatly assist with network planning. For example, generally speaking the imaging process of capture, conversion, storage is a high bandwidth activity. It often deserves its own "zone" on the network. Furthermore, if one group of users will be the highest-incident users for imaging search and retrieval, it is often best to store the images on a server in the same zone to minimize the overall network load. Careful consideration of all the functionality required, by whom and where they are located, can pay handsome dividends in ease of system implementation and overall performance. It is important the architecture design reflect the anticipated needs of the different user communities.

There are typically two outputs from this task: an architecture diagram and a list of system specifications. The architecture diagram defines which hardware elements will go where and what they perform. The list of system specifications can be used to develop what new systems or upgrades to existing systems are required for the infrastructure.

Finally, it is important to remember that an EDMS application will grow over time, usually exponentially, so developers must plan ahead in terms of expandability and scalability. It is often less expensive to buy additional memory on a box when it is purchased, rather than buying enough to get by and then needing the IS or EDMS team to perform an upgrade in the near future.

Installation

This task is exactly what one would expect and consists of four elements:

- Purchasing

- Training
- Installation
- Documentation

The first step is to transform the tool selection and architecture design outputs into purchase orders. What is often needed here is a way of acquiring new machines or upgrade existing ones. This must also include the entire suite of software, both on the client and server sides. For some EDMS systems, this may also require additional RDBMS licenses, depending upon organization or site license agreements the company may already have in place.

The next step, while purchasing is in progress, is to acquire training by the EDMS vendors. This can comprise hardware and systems-level training, such as that for specialized scanner or a Unix-based operating system. This must also include the software training on the EDMS tools themselves. The software level training is often divided into three categories, which must be chosen appropriately. What most vendors provide are 1) user-level training, 2) developer-level training and 3) systems-administration training.

Embarking on the first EDMS project for your organization is not the time to cut corners; rather, we suggest getting all the right people properly trained at the outset. On the user side, it is not uncommon, and in fact is a good idea, to send a couple of users and trainers to a class. This puts the organization in the position of having the ability to do its own training when the time comes. More about this later in the discussion of EDMS Implementation.

Once the training is accomplished, at least for the EDMS team, it is time to install and setup the EDMS system. Since most systems have base-level functionality right out the box, it should be possible to test the system even though the custom solution is not yet complete. Finally, if changes are made during installation, remember to document them so there is a record of "as-built" components and not just those that are "as designed." Remember that a lot of this technology is new to the organization and clear records will pay handsome dividends in later troubleshooting of any problems that may arise.

Standards

As we have seen countless times throughout this text, an EDMS is a flexible collection of tools and technologies brought together to best fit the defined needs of the organization. It is not simply a database application front-ended with some tool that restricts input for each field to X bytes of a particular type; EDMS applications are far more flexible. But this flexibility is often double-edge sword making the system easier or more difficult to use. For example, two groups may use different authoring packages, say Word and WordPerfect. Each can create documents and check them into the repository. So far, so good. But the conversion routine was only designed to deal with Word documents. Now what? There is no easy answer to this kind of problem. The real answer is to establish a set of standards (Word, for example) and then stick to them.

But there can be countless standards, and it is impossible to dictate what they should be from a distance. The following table lists some common standards, their intended audiences, and what they contain.

Table 13-1: Typical Standards

Standard (Audience)	Description
Style Guide (Creators)	This document outlines how a document is to be presented/developed. It focuses most of its attention on the presentation and layout of each type of document in the organization. For example, it might specify that all section headings will be centered, 14pt. Times and use the style name "Section Title." This document also covers accepted conventions such as "all headers will contain the document title and all footers will contain revision, date and page number." It is designed to give authors a common set of rules to follow in order to get consistent looking paper and electronically constructed documents.
Templates (Creators)	Templates are set of pre-defined styles that embody most of the elements specified in the styleguide. As organizations grow and become more sophisticated with respect to structured electronic document creation, more templates will be developed for each type of document the organization creates. Templates should be managed in the EDMS itself. Templates often include standard or boiler plate entries for consistency and ease of production. It is another way to help standardize the creation process.
Writer's Guide (Creators)	This document comprises a set of instructions for how to put together documents for each document "class." There may be sections on procedures, job aids, proposals, narratives, etc. This document is concerned more with the content, than the presentation and layout. For each document type or class it provides a sample Table of Contents, a discussion of what each section should contain and the level of detail. It may also provide samples, or guidance on how to phrase certain types of statements. This document is often part of the Style Guide - giving the creators only one source document to use to address content, layout and presentation.

Table 13-1: Typical Standards (Continued)

Standard (Audience)	Description
File Naming Convention (All)	These conventions define a departmental, divisional, or corporate-wide standard for how to name files and directories. They must be logical so that advanced users will be able to recognize most files by their names. It should be targeted at the lowest common denominator, usually the DOS/Windows limitation of filenames. The goal is to try to reach unique filenames across the entire organization. For Web-based delivery, directory names are critically important for the WebServer. These must be also be included.
Management of Change -or- Change Control Plan (All)	This is the document which outlines the company's approach to controlling documents and for how those documents are routed for review and approval. This can then be used as guidelines for electronic workflow and version control in the EDMS. It doesn't dictate the workflow for any specific document or class, but provides general guidance which allows people to understand why the workflow is the way it is.
Conversion Handbook (Coordinator)	This document offers the sum total of the corporate wisdom on how to convert documents from one format to another. It may simply be a list of the best tools for specific conversions or as complex as step by step instructions for using a particular tool to convert between two specified formats.
Acceptable Software Tools (All)	A list of acceptable software products that are the endorsed corporate standards. These are usually specified for each platform and perhaps type of user. Often there is a primary and alternative application in each category.

It may appear that some of these so-called "standards" are really policy or procedural documents. For example, the line between whether a Management of Change document is a standard or a policy is actually unimportant. What is important is that these guiding principals are documented and followed. A uniform approach that requires every document of a class to be developed with the same tools, templates, and styles, and which holds similar content, is a good strategy for sharing these valuable corporate assets across the entire organization. Imagine how much easier it is for a knowledge worker to transfer divisions in the company and see that the new procedures, look, feel and function like the ones she was used to. No downtime to learn an new format. These standards help the organization to be able to better leverage these knowledge resources.

Migration Plan

When dealing with custom developed applications, there is often not a formal migration or enhancement path. Planning the next release is something done only when the situation really demands it. However, for commercially available software, vendors frequently release new software upgrades that require migration. An example might be Netscape's Navigator browser. Netscape began in 1996 with version 1.X as the official release. In the spring version 2.0 came out, and 3.0 followed quickly. Finally, the company planned to get version 4.0 out to better define its market share. Each version had, of course, new capability and was not downward compatible. This presented a confounding situation to corporate users: Do I stay with what I have or upgrade to the new release? Do I upgrade now or skip a software release entirely? This type of decision-making calls for a migration plan.

A migration plan requires an organization to set down a policy as to if-and-when upgrades will be handled. If the only cost of implementing a new version of software was its purchase, the answer would be simple. But the costs go far beyond the tool itself - which changes the decision entirely. And unfortunately, an EDMS solution is often an integration of multiple products. That means upgrading to the next version of any one package will require, at a minimum, some software testing. On the other end of the spectrum, new scripts or integration code must be written to support the new tool.

Again, there is no simple answer, only the guidance to make sure each organization has a clear migration plan. It should address all the aspects of an upgrade. Will each new version be reviewed and what criteria will be used to determine whether or not to upgrade? Are there specific features that are desired and the organization will upgrade when the new functionality is available? How will it be tested? Will it be piloted to a limited group of users before full scale implementation?

Generally, towards the end of the first pilot system rollout, the EDMS team should sit down and develop an migration path or plan. It is often helpful to involve the tool vendors to understand what new functionality is coming and when it will arrive. Upgrading simply because the vendor released a new version of its tool is often not a compelling enough reason to change. The reasons that do count, from the user's perspective, should be well documented.

14

Design and Development

The Design and Development phases can be presented together because they are inexplicably linked to one another. They are, however, executed as distinct tasks for two key reasons: to ensure that the design is complete, or at least most of it, is complete before development; to provide a good management checkpoint for project control.

The goal of the design process is to transform the functional requirements and prototype, the *what* of the system, into the *how*. The development process is intended to take the design and turn it into a living, breathing system. In this sense the designers and developers are knowledge workers acting as consumers, taking the information captured in the requirements and then design document and adding value for organization by using that information to produce, respectively - a design then a system. Ideally, it will be a system that meets the business objectives of the organization.

This chapter provides a basic, high-level process for the design and development of an EDMS. It must, however, be recognized that the choice of tools and the scope of work outlined by the requirement specifications will have a significant impact on the execution of this step. The tools selected can force a change in the process; a given tool may have capabilities or limitations that may require a slightly different process. It may even be that a specific vendor has a preferred and more-detailed process when designing and developing with its tool. As we have stressed before, this methodology is to be a guideline for the process, not an absolute.

Issues in Design and Development

Upon first look at the design and development process, there are a number of issues that face the EDMS team. These issues, if properly recognized and addressed, will turn pitfalls into opportunities. The first is to look at the design process as "optional." If there is a working prototype and it is getting rave reviews, why waste time doing a design when the team can move directly into development, or better yet into production? With today's software development methodologies moving more toward Rapid Application Development (RAD), this idea is not uncommon. In fact, if all you had was one group of user types, not three, and one set of documents, instead of dozens, and all the tools were already completely integrated, it would probably make sense. Given that the situation is rarely that simple, time spent designing the system and considering the issues of how one user or document set leverages off another is time well spent.

Furthermore, ignoring the technology issues of multiple systems integration efforts, we might consider the project management aspects of the situation. How long will it take to build the system? When will it be done and how will we know when it is? Has it been properly tested? Is this is likely to become a mission-critical system? What are the risks involved with using these tools, vendors, or architecture? Is it even feasible to integrate the various tools together?

All of this leaves far too many unknowns for the typical business pragmatist who is paying for the system. Thus, our approach here is to take advantage of many of the concepts and ideas founded in some of the newer software development approaches, but keep the basic framework of a proven, staged development model.

One way to help implement this type of approach is to do the complete design, but phase in the development process. This must be planned into the design. The analysis and prototyping stages have gotten users excited and interested, so they can't wait forever to see a working system. You must captivate them by delivering something more quickly. Find a way to design the system into modules and then deliver the modules in a phased approach, perhaps every couple of months until all the functionality is in place. This keeps the users involved and can actually make the development team more successful, suggesting that an end is in site. They will get their spirits lifted each time the users embrace a new portion of the system.

In this phased approach, it is important to consider the issue of configuration versus customization. Let's define these each before going forward. *Configuration* is the process of taking tools and simply setting them up for a particular situation; it generally requires no software coding. An example may be creating a document class and the associated attributes. *Customization*, on the other hand, is the development of custom software applications. In some systems, the line between these two is less than clear, but by looking at the tools selected, one can usually draw a line, even if only for planning.

Generally speaking, it is best to get the system up and running with minimal customization, resulting in it being more efficient, less complex, and easier to manage. Then, in a later phase, add in the customization. This gives the users a chance to get familiar with the system and its capabilities while the customization is being done. There is one exception to this rule, it concerns the user interface. If a custom interface is to be developed, then this rule won't normally apply. The reason is that the users will spend time and resources to learn the existing interface and then have to relearn a new one. Of course, if the new interface is only a bit different, then this may not be quite so true. No process can dictate what only common sense on the project manager's behalf would recognize.

Finally, it is important to recognize how an EDMS differs from a typical business application. In many systems, the development team builds a new application over a database, but much of the data is transferred from a legacy system. The users receive a system with functionality and content. In an EDMS, the team builds the system architecture, a framework of sorts, but the content is placed into that framework by the end users. The system generally won't arrive pre-populated because in large part the information needed (attributes about a document) don't yet exist. They must be created by the individuals who understand the domain of the documents: the creators, coordinators, and consumers. So the EDMS team builds a framework and some processes, but the content is left to the end users.

Design

The design of a system focuses on how the system will deliver the agreed-upon functionality. It draws on the requirements specifications, the tools selected, and the prototype--now focusing on the *how*. This design process can be divided into three distinct elements:

- Architecture
- High Level Design
- Low Level Design

The architecture or overall design, already addressed in Chapter 13, will be touched upon here along with the High Level Design. A discussion of the Low Level Design then follows.

High Level Design

The high level design is best thought of as an "operations document." It is intended to be shared with the client project manager and interested users; it offers a vision for how the entire system will work. It combines the roles and responsibilities of the users, along with the architecture and system functionality, to paint a picture of how system will deliver the desired outcome.

The high level design must be written in an understandable language, for its intended audience, and not in technical details. It should clearly communicate who will perform which functions, where, when, and how. It generally includes the architecture diagram to indicate system layout and specifications. The goal is to make sure that the intended users understand what they will be required to do, what the system will do, and how this interaction will occur.

Often, flowcharts or process maps are very good tools for illustrating the concept of operations. This phase of the design gets one level below system requirements, but not in any great detail. For example, it may outline that someone will have to organize the existing procedural documents and fill out a data table with attributes so they may be checked in automatically. It may indicate that this will be a batch process to be set up during the day, and then run over night. But it does not outline how the system will process the documents and their attributes. The goal of this stage is to ensure that users agree with what they will have to do and how there respective jobs might change. Again, this is as much about human change and business process reengineering as it is about EDMS functionality.

As this concept of operations begins to take shape, it will illustrate how some applications may interact or be integrated. It is at this point where the EDMS team may decide to do some technical prototyping. These prototypes are really for the team's own use and not for end users. They are designed to ascertain whether or not a particular function of the proposed system is technically feasible. Often these prototypes are not full working applications.

Another critical aspect of the high level design is its phased-in approach. In delivering the system, a phased approach refers to the development of a definable set of modules or functional EDMS units, which are then tested before delivery to end users. Often, the high level design and system architecture design are put into one report to the client project manager. This document serves as further guidance for the low-level design that follows.

Low Level Design

The low level design, sometimes referred to as the "detailed design specification," is a technically oriented, detailed-laden document that outlines exactly how the system will accomplish its stated objectives. In this model there are two pieces, the user interface design (if applicable) and the EDMS design itself. These components are presented in more detail below.

User Interface

The user interface design is only applicable if a custom interface is to be developed. The work in the Analysis and Prototyping phases will clearly indicate whether or not one is required. If one is to be built, it will be generally be driven by the prototype. The prototype, in most cases, shows only a small model or slice of the overall system. It may offer a few screens, while the final system might have several times that number. The number of screens in the final system will depend upon the scope of work, but more directly on the functionality outlined in the high level design.

The high level design, along with the requirements and the prototype, will be the primary inputs to the user interface design. The user interface design must outline each and every screen in the system. It must illustrate the layout, color scheme, terminology, and functionality for each screen. These screens must be reviewed by the users to determine their clarity, functionality, and acceptability. This ensures, once again, that the users have signed off on exactly what they will be getting.

The first pass of the user interface design is focused on the graphical nature of the screens and how they map to the user's jobs. The next pass requires a detailed object map for each element on each screen. This map covers how the object will react graphically, to what stimulus and exactly what functions must be executed when the object event is initiated. This is a common task in any 4GL system design and software development environment, and the details are left to more traditional software methodologies.

EDMS Design

The design of an EDMS at this level is dependent upon a number of critical factors. The most important ones are the tools selected, the functionality to be delivered, and the knowledge level of the development team. Each has a different impact on the overall system.

The EDMS tools selected have a considerable impact on how the system will be designed. Some tools may have limitations that require workarounds or customization to resolve. Some tool vendors have standard design documents or forms that can be used to ensure that all the correct information required to configure and/or customize the tool is captured.

The functionality required will also determine the amount of configuration and customization required. It is important to have a clear picture of what is to be delivered, and to the degree outlined in the high level design - how it must be accomplished.

Finally, the development team's technical capability will impact the level of effort and detail in the low level design. If the team members are very experienced with the tools selected, then less detail is required to get them to build the system the way it was intended. On the other hand, if the team is rather inexperienced, it may be best served by outlining the design in minute detail.

The problem with stipulating a design from a distance is the lack of knowledge of the specifics of the case at hand. There are, however, some basic elements that should be addressed in any EDMS design. These are usually the technology elements covered in Part II of this book. A typical design might include sections on the following topics as outlined below.

Authoring: Detailed functionality required by creators in the typical word processing or other creation tools. It may include detailed template outlines, macros or applications that operate inside the authoring tools to facilitate proper, structured electronic documents. May be generic to many document classes or specific for each one.

Conversion: Exactly how documents of a particular type, in a particular format, are to be converted. It may outline the specific enhancements to an available filter, the configuration settings for a filter set, or the need to clean up a document after conversion. This may be specific for all documents in a organization, specific to a format or specific to a class, or a combination of all three. It must also address the details of an imaging subsystem, if one is required.

Workflow: Generally outlined for each document class. Includes roles, responsibilities and routes. It covers the type of workflow, and any attributes required by the workflow process. It must clearly indicate what triggers the workflow (persons or processes) and why. It must also clearly state how this workflow interacts with the versioning process. Generally this is done graphically.

Repository: The most comprehensive part of the design in a typical EDMS. It must include, but is not limited to, the following items:

- Users
- Document Classes
- Versioning
- Messaging
- Relationships
- Archiving
- Renditions

- Groups
- Attributes
- Access
- Notifications
- Storage Location
- Formats
- Architecture Model

Security: Covers access to the EDMS for overall viewing, editing, etc. This refers to system-level access (such as passwords, etc.) and not document-level access, that is handled by the repository design.

Searching & Indexing: What types of indexing and retrieval will be available and to whom? What is required to coexist with the repository and what is required as a separate entity--for example with a Website. It must outline how many indexes are to be created, along with the purpose and content of each.

Distribution: Includes which model is chosen for distribution: Publish, Repository Viewing, Access or Hybrid. Defines how paper documents will be handled, what features are required, and how they will be used for viewing, including:

- Hyperlinking
- Indexes
- Zooming
- Printing

- Tables of Contents
- Viewing
- Redlining / Annotations
- Searching

Custom Applications: States the purpose and goal of each application. Details the inputs, outputs and exact steps for each application. Defines error trapping and management, as well as likely problem points, especially if the input is a document and is incorrect in content, presentation, formatting, or filenaming.

The goal of the low level design document is three fold: first, to ensure the EDMS team that it has considered all the issues. By putting these issues down on paper and conducting reviews, the team can be confident that there are no incompatibilities in the resulting system. Second is to enable the development team to build a system without constantly having to ask someone "what do you want to happen here." Finally, since the design is documented, a test plan can be developed from this low level design to ensure the system meets the users' requirements.

Development

The development tasks for an EDMS can be divided into five elements as defined below.

- Development
- Testing
- Guidelines
- Training Materials
- Standards Modifications

Development and Testing

In some respects, the term "development" here is a misnomer. In the context of software, development usually means coding, while in an EDMS it usually means configuration. But configuration can, in some instances, mean both coding or customization. It all depends upon the requirements and design.

In either case the tasks here very much follow those in a traditional software development process. Once the design is complete, the developers either configure the system or code custom applications. In this type of system, the configuration is usually an early phase with custom development in a later phase.

Testing is required for both configuration and customization work. It begins with the development of a test plan, built from the details of the low level design. Testing is built up, starting with the unit level, moving to the module level, and up to the application testing stage. And it culminates with integration testing.

For simple configuration work, the most expedient tests are scenario-driven but follow the same build-up process. For example, can the user enter in the right attributes when checking in a report? After that function has been tested, the conversion of the report can be checked for accuracy and repeatability. Finally, can a document be properly distributed, passing it from the repository to perhaps an HTML converter, and can links be created that are made available on the Web? This ensures that each EDMS component works individually and that the individual elements don't add any surprises to the entire process.

Since the configuration and custom development aspects, including testing, do follow a standard systems development process, they will not be discussed further here. There are numerous other texts available that outline detailed software development methodologies, but it is also quite likely that the IS organization has adopted or developed a preferred process, and that it be used for this phase. Involving the IS team at this phase of the project is a prudent idea.

Guidelines and Training Materials

While developing the actual system is of paramount importance, it is also important to recall that creating a successful system is about striking a balance between people and technology. This part of the development process is about putting materials together that accomplish this objective. These items are focused on the users of the system: the creators, consumers, and coordinators. Once again, the system must be looked at from those individuals' perspectives. What will they need to be proficient with the system? How will it impact their job performance? How long will it take them to become comfortable with the applications and the process? What type of training will be required? All of these questions are among those that must be answered in order to properly develop accurate and useful materials.

Consistent with the overall methodology presented in this book, the approach to any training problems is to begin with the consumers and then work back to the creators of the material. In this case it means answering the questions above, considering the impact of the system on the users, and then developing the right set of instructive materials. This means going out and understanding these users and what they will need for proper training. Once that is defined, the training task is simply more focused.

The next chapter on implementation will shed some light on how to analyze these users in the context of training them on a system. Chapter 15 also provides the necessary insight on exactly what materials to develop. This task then indicates the stage at which to build the materials required to support an EDMS product rollout. More often than not, however, the entire project focuses on the system development and delivery, and the users become an afterthought. But as our readers should know by now, this runs contrary to the central theme of this book. Therefore, it comes as no surprise that this text demands that user training be placed on par with the system development process, and not something to be done only if there is enough time or funds available at the end of an EDMS project.

To complete this subject, it is good to define in high level terms what is meant by "training materials" or "guidelines." Training materials are very much focused on how to complete a task. That task might be to check-out, revise, and then check-in a document, or it might be how to image, archive, and retrieve an entire manual. The guidelines are the background reference documents that provide the corporate knowledge of why some EDMS task is accomplished in a specified way. The guidelines provide additional information for those so inclined, but for the typical job performer, the training materials, often in the form of job aids, are directly aimed at getting something done better or more efficiently.

Standards Modification

In the infrastructure discussion, we discussed the development of standards for the organization. These are typically developed once so they can provide a common framework for all groups within the company. They are not expected to change often, but they will change at times. The most likely reason for this change is the result of learning something new from a particular organization, perhaps a new requirement. When this new issue arises we are left with the problem of now having to have everyone learn from it. This element of the development process is geared for this exact occasion. The intention is to allow the established standards to be modified when new information or requirements come to light.

This is not to say that every minor change would require a modification to the standard. If the standard were to change constantly, it would offer little value to the organization as a whole. However, to be truly useful standards must evolve with the organization. As the organization becomes more comfortable with EDMS technologies, these standards will become widely known and accepted. Having them up-to-date and accurately reflecting the corporation's best practices can go a long way toward standardizing the organization's EDMS activities.

15

Implementation and Support

Few people who work in software development will deny that implementation is place where a project can become a success or failure. As we have said before, if the system isn't properly focused or designed it will fail. However, even well targeted and constructed systems can fail at the implementation phase. One of the problems with implementation is that it presents a different and somewhat unique view of itself depending upon one's point of view.

Typically there are three vantage points from which to look at the issues surrounding implementation:

- EDMS Team (developer)
- Organizational Unit (owner)
- Users (Creators, Consumers, Coordinators)

Each of these view points is valid. The problem arises when implementation is planned with only one view point in mind. Another key factor in the implementation stage is timing. Unfortunately implementation is the last stage before the system goes live. As with any task or element at the end of a process, it becomes the point where all the prior sins and bad acts culminate: gaps in the analysis which slowed the prototype; lack of timely prototype reviews by users; technical issues in design; and extra time required in testing. All of these items contribute to cost overruns and schedule slips. However, budgets are often not revised or final "Live Dates" are not slipped; rather, the implementation phase simply gets fewer resources and a shortened schedule. This is often a fatal mistake.

By recognizing early on what is required in the implementation phase, some of the planning activities can occur in parallel with the design and development efforts to ensure that the implementation phase is really ready to go and does not become a scapegoating activity for the rest of the project. In systems where the impact is on hundreds or even thousands of users, this can be dramatic.

Many times, with only weeks to go before the "Live Date," the project team finally begins to look at implementation. If there are a thousand users, how long will it take to install all the client software and test it? If it is one hour per user, that equals 125 effort days! Where is that amount of time allotted in the schedule? It is often too late at the end of testing phase to begin to deal with this aspect; critical planning, therefore, must be moved up earlier in the process. Often a pilot system with limited users can be used to gauge the magnitude of the implementation efforts and become a planning model for all the organizations which follow.

Planning

Perhaps the most effective way to plan for implementation is to take a look at implementation through different users' eyes. Informed by these different facets of implementation, developers will be able to know what needs to be accomplished in the task of implementation. Then it is simply a matter of figuring out how and when to best address these elements.

The first group of people with a vested interest is the EDMS is, of course, the team itself or the developers. They are the ones who have built the system for the organization. From their vantage point the major issue in implementation is how to install and test the system for all users. This task is then seen as one of software installation, possibly some configuration, and then testing. Of course if there are a large number of users, this task can be very time consuming.

The second set of players in this EDMS development phase is the organization receiving the system. Recall that users should have been told that the EDMS team is building a framework or shell of the system, and that *they* must populate it with the content. Their focus is now on how to get the content into the system so that they will have something to use. They must allocate resources to accomplish this task and generically expect some training on what is required. They should recognize that unless specific applications have been developed, it is essentially a manual process to load the repository. Also, the task of defines the attribute information for each individual document is required.

Finally, the end users (all three of them--creators, coordinators, and consumers) need to learn how to use the system. This task is often focused on the features and functions of the system. However, what is often overlooked here is that the system changes the way these people work and what is desired for training, in fact, is task-driven training. In either case, training must be developed and delivered to these users. This task can be extremely expensive when you consider that training often takes people away from productive, revenue-generating activities. The execution of this training endeavor is, therefore, of paramount importance.

In all three of these approaches, one thing should be clear: it is not possible for any sizable organization to accomplish all three implementation tasks over night. Installation of and training on the system for hundreds or thousands of end users takes a significant amount of time. Also, populating the system with sufficient content so that it is useful and functional takes time as well. Because of these factors, a detailed "rollout plan" is often required. In essence, this plan lays out a phased time line within the organization for how each of these elements will come together at the right time so that the system can go *live* and be useful and effective.

Finally, once the system is in place and running, users will require one-on-one assistance. There are many ways to provide this assistance, and again this can be phased along with the rollout. It may start with training, move to coaching, on to interactions with super users, where ultimately the EDMS becomes more mainstream and moves toward traditional help desk type support. Of course the help desk team must be trained as well. In summary, then, the implementation of any system requires at least these four elements:

- Installation
- Content Loading
- Training
- Rollout Plan

Each of these is covered in more detail in the following sections.

Installation

Technically speaking, installation is not a difficult task. Once the installation routine has been developed, it is simply a matter of execution. However, *execution* is the issue when it must occur hundreds of times. The EDMS technology is not alone on this front, however. The IS organization faces this situation nearly every week with other software applications. No doubt this group has a method by which to accomplish this task in the least painful way possible. In fact, it is important to involve the IS organization early on in order to learn from their experiences on large-scale software deployment. Second, it is important to ensure that IS understands and agrees with what is being installed, along with the where and how of this implementation. If the company or organization as a whole has established a "standard system configuration," the EDMS application should not be a renegade system, but rather a part of this standard.

If the significance of this step is recognized early on, then the IS organization can be involved back in the Design and Develop phases. If the IS team was involved, as they should have been, in the infrastructure design and initial installation, many of these issues should have been addressed earlier. It may be possible to work with the IS team to include the client application in the next round of upgrades being rolled out. Even if the software won't be used for a while, it can be installed awaiting use.

Putting the software out early also enables the EDMS team to test the setup on a wide variety of systems across the enterprise. This can be useful when determining the performance of the application at the stage of integration testing. Also, it allows the configuration to be tested in a number of real-world settings. One of the most time consuming tasks in installation is not the actual loading and configuration; it is troubleshooting the system when it doesn't work. If done early enough, it may even be possible to develop a simple set of guidelines for dealing with non-standard configurations or for troubleshooting.

Content Loading

The key to this stage is to get the sponsoring organization to understand what this entails early on. Telling them that they will have to load their own system usually doesn't sink in on the first pass. Using the data from the analysis, particularly the document profiles and capacity sheets, should help point out just exactly how many documents will need to be loaded.

Often it is useful for an organization to develop a prioritization plan. The top priority documents can be used for testing by the development team so that the system will have some, albeit small, content when first delivered. It is important to recognize that content-loading can be divided into three pieces, two of which can be accomplished in advance to shorten the time in implementation, which is always a critical issue. These three elements are 1) to gather and organize the document sets, 2) to determine and record all the required attribute information for *each* document, and 3) to load the documents into the EDMS. Developers should not underestimate the time required for the first two tasks. With most of the files scattered across individual machines and file servers, and unclearly named, it can take hours to locate a single document. Then the document must be verified to be the latest copy, offering another potentially substantial and time-consuming effort.

The next task is to determine the correct attribute values for each document. This requires someone who truly understands the document content along with the list of attributes gathered in the profiles and formalized in the design stage. It is often best to develop a simple form, whose order reflects that of the interface to facilitate data entry during loading/check-in. One possible alternative is to use operating system capabilities to record attributes for a document, then use this data to load the repository. This requirement must be addressed in the system requirements phase in order to ensure that some type of "automatic" loading application is available.

Once these two elements are complete, the document loading task is essentially one of data entry and file transfer. This means the task can be handed off to someone with less skills and experience than the critical EDMS content specialist in order to get the system populated. It may even be possible to use temporary clerical staff to accomplish this task, which of course requires some training on their part. Regardless of who executes this task when it involves thousands of files the time can be considerable.

Training

Training for a new information system, EDMS or otherwise, is a significant undertaking if done properly, but the rewards can be dramatic. The key to unlocking the potential of the system is to properly assess the type and depth of training required. This, coupled with the right method of training delivery, can really take an EDMS from being "just another application" to one that becomes a useful tool for accomplishing document-related work.

The first task in developing and delivering usable training is to recognize how the users will use the system, and for what purposes. In the case of the EDMS, this information has already been captured. It was captured in the user profiles during the analysis process. These documents indicate which tasks users would perform in the course of their normal jobs. These can be used to determine what training is required for each user community. This allows the training to be task and job-driven, rather than feature and function-driven.

This distinction is not often understood, so to clarify it, let's look at the example of word processing. A person may be handed the task of writing a manual for some given topic in the organization. Since the corporate standard is, say, Word, these users might be sent to a training class on this product. There they would learn, for example, how to bold and italicize words, create tables, etc. However, they are no better off towards writing the manual in terms of structured content; they also need training on a process for that task. Perhaps, developing a set of objectives, drafting a table of contents, writing sample sections, etc. The first type of training was based on word processing *features and functions*; the latter was *task-based*. The right training answer, then, is provide task-based help and incorporate feature-based knowledge right into that training when and where it is needed.

The same holds true for an EDMS applications; the user must be provided training on what the buttons are and what they do, but this is only useful when presented in the context of doing real work with the EDMS. Users will ask: How can I find an existing document on a particular topic, make changes, and put it out for review? This requires task or domain-specific knowledge and some feature-based training. Another way to address this is to create simple training scenarios around features, such as search and retrieval for a document; check-out, editing, and check-in of a document, etc. Then these scenarios can be embedded into a sequence of steps that comprise individual tasks. The key is to know what tasks each user needs to be proficient at and make sure the training addresses that task.

The second element in developing training is to choose the right training intervention along with the proper delivery format or mechanism. For example, will the training be classroom or computer based? Will it be offered in one-on-one sessions or simply be a handing out of training materials? Each method has merit, but understanding the users' capabilities and the amount of change required of these individuals can help drive the right training solution.

Too often, though, training is simply relegated to the classroom, which can be a mistake. Let's take a look at why. In most instances, when people speak of training, they think of going to a classroom and being given a presentation--classic stand-up training. While this can be effective, there is one key point to recognize with this approach. For adult learners who already have some understanding of the job and tasks before them, classroom training is not very effective because it is often seen as a waste of time by the trainees. Also, many organizational studies have shown that knowledge retention in such circumstances is often only half what it should be after leaving the classroom, and drops dramatically over the next month or two.

Why does this retention drop? One reason is that most adults are accustomed to just-in-time knowledge transfer situations; they don't have a need to learn everything right now. They will learn things when they have a compelling need to use that knowledge. Hence, they learn best on the job when a real situation is at hand. What is needed, then, is the typical college training model. We don't teach engineers in college how to build a bridge; we teach them engineering basics and then teach them how to use available resources where they can then learn the specifics of bridge building at the time and point of need.

What this really means is that classroom training needs to focus on the big picture concepts of the new system and perhaps how it works relative to the old system. It must outline the tasks to be accomplished by each user group and the changes to their jobs, tasks, and functions - specifically at the day to day level. Then the class can be directed at exercises that focus on *using* the training materials provided to accomplish the task.

These materials then should be task-oriented with accompanying step-by-step instructions. Incorporated into these materials are all the features and functions information. What this offers the trainee is an overview of the system and a chance to learn how to use the training materials and other learning resources provided. These step-by-step documents are often referred to as "procedures" or more commonly "job aids," which are designed to aid the user in the accomplishment of their jobs. If a job aid is created for each task in the system, then the trainee is not being asked to memorize how to accomplish lots of tasks, but simply know how to use and where to find these job aids when needed. This facilitates just-in-time learning.

In structuring this type of training it is often best to follow these simple guidelines: TELL them, SHOW them, HELP them, WATCH them. *Tell* the users what they need to know about a task and how to use a procedure or job aid. Next *show* them how to use the EDMS applications and let them watch you go through steps as an exercise. Then let them do it while you *assist* them with details. Finally, let them do it alone and be *available* just for questions. This type of training generally produces the best results.

One advantage to this type of approach is that it minimizes the time in the classroom, which reduces costs. Second, it gets users away from the habit of memorizing things, and instead gets them referring to the documentation. That makes it easier to implement changes by simply replacing the job aids and not having to retrain an entire user community. Another way to sharpen the training approach is to offer very focused classes. This way you don't put an entire class of people through basic or overall training sessions, only half of which may be relevant to their jobs. Rather, they should be taught what they need to know, when they need to know it.

In the EDMS context, this might mean developing separate materials for creators, coordinators, and consumers. Then pieces of this material are mixed and matched for end users. Some users will only be consumers, others will be all three. By focusing on exactly what the users need, the training can be shorter and more targeted.

Finally, after the initial training is completed, there are other interventions that can be used to make sure the users are learning what they need to know and are performing as expected. One approach is to adapt the old Management By Walking Around technique to Teaching By Walking Around. For the first few days or even a week or two have a knowledgeable person roam the halls or cubicles looking in on users to make sure they don't have any unanswered questions or nagging unresolved issues. These overseers, depending upon their skill set, may also be able to ensure that people are not trying to go back to the old ways of doing business--handling documents by hand. This can really help the users and demonstrate a commitment to making the user comfortable with the new EDMS technology.

Remember that putting in new EDMS systems and making them successful from the business perspective requires striking a balance between the human being in the process and the technology itself. In this book we set out to address this with our user-centered analysis and prototyping. Training is the final place to make sure that this balance is maintained when deploying the new EDMS out into the workplace.

Rollout

Having users trained on an EDMS that has no content is of little value. Equally poor is having trained users on the EDMS with all the content loaded, but not having the system available to them. The goal of the rollout activity is to coordinate these tasks.

The rollout process involves making sure that all three elements discussed so far--installation, content loading, and training--occur in the proper sequence. Because of the retention issues associated with training, it is important to recognize that the training must precede, as closely as possible, the system going "live." Beyond the high level sequencing of the tasks is the recognition that while content loading may be able to be accomplished centrally, the other two tasks cannot be.

Since these two tasks involve large numbers of users, a phased plan may be appropriate. A joint team may be dispatched to a location in order to get the installation completed, while the users are being trained. At the end of the training one individual may remain behind to provide support. It should be obvious that everyone from the user to the sponsoring organization's management be involved in the development and acceptance of the rollout plan.

Support

On-going support is a necessary task for almost any information system, and EDMS is no different. What is different, though, is that during the first few EDMS implementations additional support is almost always required. There are two ways to approach this situation.

One solution to additional or on-going technical support is for the EDMS team to provide telephone support to the first user communities. This puts the organization's most knowledgeable people on the other end of the phone with the users, often resulting in quick problem resolution. This is important as the first couple of EDMS rollouts will set the tone for the success of the rest.

There are additional benefits from this approach. First, the EDMS team will get first-hand feedback on the system. It may be possible to identify areas for improvement, rather than solving the same problem dozens of times over. These improvements can take the form of software upgrades, improved classroom and on-the-job training, or more precise or informative job aids.

A longer range goal for the EDMS team should be to get the corporate help desk knowledgeable enough to take tech-support calls. This means training them on both the features and functions and the tasks at hand. If the EDMS team has worked the help desk before, they will be in a better position to guide the corporate help desk staff over those places where there are known problems.

One additional approach to the on-going support issue is the concept of the "super user." A super user is someone in the business organization that understands the system very well and can answer lots of typical user questions instantly. There will always be a super user for any major system. Whether or not these positions are recognized and accepted, they will exist and should be used effectively. The key here is to try to identify the super user and provide them with additional training to allow them to help with the training and knowledge transfer tasks.

In embracing the super user concept, it must be recognized that some percentage of this person's time will be spent helping others with the system. Consequently they will not be able to handle their former workload. This can be an important issue for EDMS productivity. In typical IS applications, the users' capabilities are often very limited to data entry, data review, and generating reports, where there is not a lot of room to deviate from the basic work processes. Yet an EDMS is open to be used in many different and varying ways by all. This often requires someone in the client organization who can guide or at least channel all the new ideas to the right players or decision-makers.

In the end, support will be a critical issue for an EDMS. Ultimately that support should come from existing and pre-established channels. In the meantime, the issue the EDMS team faces is how to provide sufficient support while balancing the act of getting the next organization analyzed, prototyped, designed, developed, and finally implemented.

EDMS Marketplace

This part of the book provides information about select vendors and their tools, technologies, products and philosophies of EDMS. The electronic document management market is just beginning to move out of its infancy and into the mainstream. During its infancy and these early adopter days, it has been the vendors that have really defined the market. They had the vision to look to the future and develop a solution to a problem often unrecognized.

This part of the book is divided into three sections. The first allows four of the leading vendors to share their views and products with the reader. The second is a comprehensive list of document management vendors. Finally, not actually included in this text but rather accompanying it, is a World Wide Web site that contains a virtual library of information on document management.

Chapters 16 and 17 focus on the repository component, as this is the heart and soul of the any electronic document management system. The Web site has broader focus looking at searching/indexing, workflow, conversion, creation, and viewing tools, as well as the repositories.

The Website established for this book is located at **http://www.goucher.edu/~docman** and is designed to provide accurate and up to date information on EDMS technology vendors. It also includes a variety of other document management related information such as other EDMS Websites, conferences, seminars, trade journals and professional associations. It will also be used to keep the book's methodology current as it evolves over time.

16

Select Vendor Profiles

This chapter contains a set of so-called "white papers" or technology "backgrounders" from four leading EDMS vendors who are considered major players in the document management marketplace. They are:

- Documentum, Inc.
- Interleaf, Inc.
- Open Text Corporation
- PC DOCS, Inc.

When looked at collectively, we believe that their diverse views, which are ultimately reflected in the products they deliver, will help to further define and shape the EDMS market. Moreover, each of the vendors has come to the EDMS market from a different perspective and has evolved a product set from that unique starting point.

At the 10,000 foot level, the vendors each started in different places with the document management problem. For example, Interleaf came to the EDMS arena from the publishing perspective, leveraging their strong customer base in using Interleaf tools for professional and technical publishing. The volume of documents created by their users begged for an EDMS solution.

PC DOCS came into the market from the legal perspective, helping law firms control important case files. Their initial focus on document management, therefore, stemmed from the desktop point of view.

Documentum set out into the EDMS market aiming at the enterprise-wide solution for document management. Their first foothold in the market was in the pharmaceuticals industry.

And Open Text evolved its document management strategy from a strategic merger with Odesta. Open Text was also the first vendor to substantially move away from the traditional client-server based EDMS approach to a total Web-based architecture.

Each of these vendors provides a very capable set of tools that can address document management problems faced by many organizations today. For this section each vendor was asked to cover two basic points: 1) its point of view concerning the document management marketplace (basically its philosophy towards document management), and 2) a basic overview of its system's architecture and products. Thus, the papers that were solicited for inclusion in this book were not meant to cover in detail the technical underpinnings of each product, which is a task left to more lengthy vendor-supplied documents on their own World Wide Web sites. Rather, we hope that by providing diverse viewpoints on EDMS technology that complement our own approach, our readers will walk from this book with a much deeper understanding of document management in general.

Document Management for Accelerating Business Processes

Document Management

A good idea, but everyone knows the solutions are costly and take forever to implement, right? Think again:

- Like its competitors, a worldwide pharmaceuticals company has an 18-year window to earn a profit from a new drug before it goes generic. A large portion of that time is consumed by research and development, efficacy testing, and the extremely document-intensive new drug submission process (which varies from country to country). The more the company can automate and streamline all the document processes involved in producing the submission, the faster the drug can be sped out to the market. In fact, the company estimates that every week it can shave off the time to deliver a new drug to market which means an additional $5 million to $10 million in profits! With stakes like that, it's no wonder that this company has re-engineered itself around enterprise-critical document management technology.

- A large aerospace manufacturing company faces a different set of document challenges -- as do its airline customers. A jet aircraft is "re-invented" many times during its life -- throughout the manufacturing process, and every time the plane receives maintenance and repairs or is re-configured for a specialized purpose. Supporting documentation and maintenance manuals have to be kept in synch with the plane's exact configuration at any point in time. It's easy to see why this company has bet on document management technology to leverage re-usable information and produce accurate, up-to-date documents.

- A state legislature had a twofold challenge: to streamline its document processes, and to rightsize off the mainframe. Every day, legislative personnel have to bring up to date more than 50 key documents pertaining to bills, committee hearings, and other legislative activities. In many cases, different documents contain duplicate information. Using advanced document management to re-engineer the processes involved in creating these documents has avoided untold hours of duplicated effort and re-keying, resulting in greater accuracy. Another bonus -- the result of moving document functions off the mainframe and into a client/server architecture -- is improved accessibility to documents for legislators as well as their constituents.

These real-life examples come from vastly different industries, and the business processes vary widely. But regardless of the business they're in, these organizations all share a common goal: to automate, accelerate, and simplify enterprise-critical business processes. They've learned that re-engineering document-intensive processes is the path to more accurate information, shortened time to market, a better-served customer base, and sharper competitive edge. They've also learned that developing and deploying a tailored document management application need not be difficult or time-consuming. Finally, these organizations have one more thing in common: the Documentum Enterprise Document Management System (EDMS)™.

The true power behind the Documentum EDMS is the *virtual document*, a unique combination of information objects that can come from any source and from anywhere in the enterprise. As determined by a company's own business rules, a virtual document can be assembled on demand. Information has to be saved only once to be re-used many times, and users can retrieve all the information they need through one simple query. Put another way, the virtual document is the re-usable output of a business-critical process. Through re-usable document components called DocObjects™, Documentum provides the enabling technology for the virtual document.

This paper describes the challenges companies are facing with their document-intensive, business-critical processes and the reasons why document management technologies have not offered a viable, practical solution for building virtual documents -- until now. It will describe the Documentum EDMS, based on such foundation technologies as object-oriented programming, client/server computing, and open standards. It will then describe Documentum EDMS's key functionality and object/relational architecture, and the ways in which the Documentum EDMS can be deployed as the foundation for automating all of an organization's business-critical processes.

Taming the Information Beast

Information -- on paper or stored electronically in a dizzying array of formats -- is driving virtually every industry today. In fact, an organization's ability to work efficiently, make knowledgeable decisions, deliver on time, and meet customer expectations requires on-demand access to accurate and timely information, as well as the timely distribution of that information.

Thanks to the information systems technology revolutions of the 1980s and 1990s, desktop users are empowered as never before to do individual tasks. A proliferation of productivity tools such as word processors and spreadsheets have further strengthened individual productivity. But productivity breaks down in processes that require a number of individuals to collaborate and contribute information, across organizational and geographic barriers.

Re-Defining the Document

The mechanism for encapsulating and distributing information is a document. In today's enterprise, a document has come to represent much more than simply a paper or papers containing text. Whether it exists in hard copy or electronic format, a document can be whatever data type that conveys information most effectively to the reader: a text file, a spreadsheet, a graphic or image, or even a video clip or sound bite. Any of these elements can stand alone as individual documents, or they can be put together in different combinations to compose a compound document.

Whatever their format and wherever their location, documents represent the culmination of knowledge workers' work -- and they can be essential to the business-critical processes of a company. Processes related to the capture, production, and dissemination of documents are especially important in information-intensive industries such as pharmaceuticals, manufacturing (especially build-to-order manufacturing in which highly-customized products are delivered to meet specialized, individual needs), highly-regulated industries such as telecommunications, and the biggest document producer of all, government.

Barriers to Document Productivity

Regardless of the industry, companies are increasingly challenged by inefficiencies and lack of organizational control over their document-intensive processes. In fact, these inefficiencies in managing document-encapsulated information have mission-critical impact, because they strike at the heart of a company's ability to be competitive by delivering quality products on time.

The challenges that companies face in effectively managing document-controlled processes center around the following issues:

Protecting intellectual capital

Knowledge workers -- and the products of their knowledge -- are among a company's most strategic assets. In the case of a pharmaceutical company, these assets consists of the base of accumulated information resulting from decades of experimentation, data gathering and clinical trials, performed during the research and development phase for various drug products. The knowledge base also consists of the training and expertise of the knowledge workers themselves -- the researchers and physicians involved in the new drug application (NDA) process. Such corporate knowledge has invaluable worth to this company -- it's the intellectual capital on which the company values its very existence.

The difficulty for companies lies not only in keeping this intellectual capital protected and organized, but in making it easy to access and re-use.

Maximizing knowledge workers' productivity

If knowledge workers are among a company's most strategic assets, they're also one of the most expensive -- representing one of the highest cost areas for a company in proportion to their productivity. This is primarily due to the lack of tools that automate group collaboration and assist knowledge workers in performing their jobs more quickly and efficiently. Companies need better systems for making information accessible to the people who can turn it into competitive advantage.

Breaking down information barriers

The Gartner Group estimates that 80% of data stored in a PC-networked environment resides on local, disconnected hard drives, rather than a LAN-based file server.[1] Further, this data is scattered across autonomous and geographically dispersed business units of a company and runs in a wide range of hardware and software configurations, with little compatibility or data sharing capability between systems. It's easy to imagine the difficulties this presents to a company whose product is tied to the capture, production, and dissemination of information.

---

1.   *"Integrated Document Management: Controlling a Rising Tide,"* Gartner Group, September 3, 1993.

Consider, for example, the process manufacturing companies go through to bring a new product to market. In most environments, this process is sequential -- it probably begins with the marketing department, whose task is to come up with a business plan and marketing requirements for the product. Then, engineering develops an initial product design. Finally, the specifications are passed on to the manufacturing organization. The entire process takes place with little, if any, interaction among the various departments, and no collaboration -- resulting in repeat effort, duplicated information, and wasted time.

Managing the work processes involved in information creation and dissemination.

Companies also need better tools for tracking and managing individual work processes, to ensure that the overall process unfolds smoothly and on time.

An example is the assembly of a sales proposal -- a process that companies in any industry can identify with. A sales manager has 10 days to respond to a customer with a proposal for a new product that meets that customer's specialized needs. First, the sales manager needs to pull together any "boilerplate" information from past proposals that can be re-used (typically, this information comprises 70% to 80% of the final document). Then, responsibilities are divided among various departments to pull together the remaining information that will tailor the proposal to the customer: the marketing department has to write a business plan and statement of direction for the product, the engineering department has to provide timetables and feasibility information, the support department has to provide a plan for the product's support and service, and so on. Without a system for tracking the progress of each different player and ensuring that the different pieces are pulled together into a single proposal as quickly as possible, the manager may miss his deadline -- and the company loses an opportunity for a sale.

Maximizing the re-usability and accuracy of data

Another result of the departmental and geographical information barriers that exist in companies is the duplication of data in various formats. Without an effective means for re-using the data when necessary, it must be re-keyed -- resulting in lost productivity and a greater margin for error. In the state legislature, for instance, different groups were responsible for producing 50 documents a day -- many of which contain duplicate information.

Providing tailored products for specific needs

Companies are also struggling with the information challenges of providing "build to order" products that are tailored specifically to certain customers or individual markets. This challenge takes on even greater dimensions for a company who must deliver a customized version of an extremely complex product with many discrete parts, such as a jet aircraft or a telephone switch. The aerospace manufacturer, for instance, must begin assembling supporting documentation for the jet as soon as the initial bill of materials (BOM) is produced -- and the documentation must be kept in line with the specifications in the BOM as it undergoes changes during the manufacturing cycle. In another example, the regulatory requirements for submittal and approval of a new drug vary widely from country to country. Pharmaceutical companies face even further delays in the release of a drug if they cannot easily customize the information to meet the requirements of every country in which the drug is to be approved for use.

The Document Management Landscape

By definition, document management systems are designed to capture, assemble, and disseminate information that is encapsulated as documents. Over the past decade, companies have become increasingly networked -- opening up new possibilities for electronic information sharing and suggesting the potential for such newer technology concepts as workgroup computing. As a result, the software industry has offered numerous products under the banner of "document management systems" that propose solutions to companies' multi-dimensional document information management issues. In many cases, these products are "point" solutions that only address certain aspects of document management, such as imaging or text retrieval, and they have difficulty handling a mixture of information formats. And, besides being difficult to implement and use, most solutions are not easily customized to adapt to changes in the business.

But the most important shortcoming of most of today's document management products is that they don't address the fundamental processes that are causing information bottlenecks in the first place. By simply overlaying new technology onto old processes, companies often end up with a costly software system that still doesn't meet their information needs.

As a result, many companies have been reluctant to make any new large-scale investments in document management technology. They recognize (often from the hard lessons of experience) that most of today's solutions just don't meet their key requirements. These requirements include:

- *Access to documents without barriers.* These include not only physical barriers such as coordinated access across departments or geographical locations, but barriers resulting from incompatible hardware, software, and data types.
- *Rapid application development.* The ability to rapidly develop and deploy applications is vital in any environment where time is of the essence.
- *Scalability.* Companies need a solution that can be easily implemented for any-sized environment -- from the workgroup to the enterprise.
- *A fully customizable, extensible solution.* Companies need to be able to easily tailor information to meet the needs of different customers and markets, and systems that can easily be extended to adapt to changes in the business.
- *Ability to leverage re-usable information.* To solve duplication and inaccuracy problems, document management should be able to treat documents as interchangeable objects that can be combined and re-combined to meet different needs.
- *Ability to re-engineer document processes.* To be effective, document management should facilitate world-class re-engineering. In other words, document technologies should help bring about changes in the fundamental capabilities of an organization. The focus becomes enhancing, extending, and re-using information, regardless of its format or location.

The Emergence of Intranets

Almost overnight, the World Wide Web has become a serious business communications vehicle. As easy-to-use and economical tools, Web browsers are becoming standard equipment on more and more business desktops. Companies are setting their sights on the Web to provide a single, transparent interface to all information—from external Web content to internal, business-critical documents. However, Web browsers and other Web technologies lack the basic document management functionality required to turn this dream into reality.

Many companies are moving quickly to deploy "Intranet" applications, using Web technologies to provide employees with controlled access to internal documents and other information, inside the company's firewall. An example of an Intranet application is a large investment banker that delivers a 100-page daily update over the World

Wide Web to more than 100 of its foreign traders. The payoff is two-fold: the traders can immediately access needed information using their familiar Web browsers, and the company has cut time and costs by replacing a manual cut/paste/fax process with a completely auto-mated one.

By itself, however, the Web presents some roadblocks to these efforts. Most of the information on the Web is static, with updates occurring infrequently and unpredictably. As such, Web documents neither reflect nor effectively support key business processes. Search and retrieval tools for the Web are still fairly limited, as are security mechanisms. Document integrity cannot be assured since documents typically reside in more than one location—the Web server and the cor-porate document repository. And, with hypertext, document integrity takes on an even more complex dimension with the large number of links that must be continually maintained and updated.

Documentum Functionality: Delivering the Virtual Document

The Documentum EDMS is a family of open, object-oriented soft-ware products specifically designed to address the challenges of deliv-ering Intranet and client/server-based document management applications. The Documentum EDMS has been built from the ground up to dramatically improve the productivity of any organization -- whether it's a workgroup or department that needs an immediate pro-ductivity payback from the new technology, or a company who is implementing document management as part of a more long-range vision to re-engineer its most business-critical processes across the enterprise.

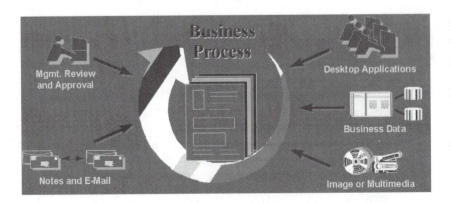

Documentum is the first company to deliver the virtual document - a mechanism for automating and accelerating all the processes involved in gathering knowledge, encapsulating it into a re-usable form, and disseminating it throughout the enterprise. The virtual document is enabled through seven key document processes: creation, editing, reviewing, assembly, storage, retrieval, and distribution.

Core Functionality

The Documentum EDMS fully exploits today's most powerful information technologies. Documentum's core technologies and functionality include:

DocObjects

Written in C++, Documentum's true power stems from its object-oriented approach to automating document processes. By representing documents as DocObjects, Documentum creates the ability to re-use and re-combine information in new ways that add even greater value to the business process -- promoting ease of application deployment and helping to avoiding costly errors and duplication of effort.

DocObjects are self-describing document components that can be accessed and processed independently of any particular application. DocObjects can be defined to represent documents or components of documents at any level of granularity (i.e. paragraphs, sections, images, tables) and can be easily combined and re-used in an almost infinite variety of ways.

Shown below, a DocObject encapsulates *attributes* that describe a particular document object, the actual *content* of a document object, and *operations* (also called *methods*) which are commonly used document management functions such as *check-in/check-out* or *print*. Methods are invoked by sending a message to the document object via an application programming interface (API). Methods are self-contained in the DocObject and may use the object attributes to inform their behavior. For example, the *print* method uses the *format* attribute information to figure out how to correctly print the document content.

Library Services

The Documentum EDMS automates all storage and management functions such as checking documents in and out, cataloging and organizing documents, and implementing filing schemes based on user-friendly metaphors such as folders and cabinets. These services enable the user to retrieve all needed information based on a single query, and to transfer document information automatically between formats.

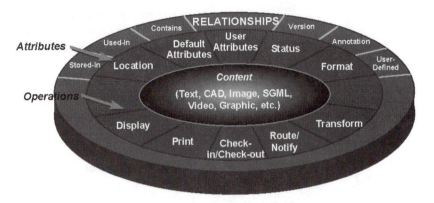

Workflow

The Documentum EDMS implements powerful workflow features for documenting, organizing, and monitoring all of the functions and people involved in a business process. The software is based on a work process model, which enables easy development of document management applications that are both process- and event-oriented. In other words, the Documentum EDMS supports workflows for production applications as well as those that are more ad hoc and project-oriented.

The Documentum EDMS's workflow is managed by an object called a router, which defines simple or complex task sequences (including those with dependencies) that can be easily saved and re-used. The user can define routes for individual documents, folders containing a group of documents, and composite documents. Further, these routes can be defined according to the necessary sequence of reviewers. For instance, in some cases a document must be reviewed by one person only after it has been reviewed by another. In other cases, the document can be reviewed by multiple people at once.

Routing and event notifications are automatically issued through standard electronic mail systems while all documents remain under the secure control of the server.

Dynamic Document Assembly

Dynamic Document Assembly™ (DDA) is one of the most powerful features of the Documentum EDMS's object-oriented technology. DDA allows the user to automatically pull together individual document objects into a larger object called a composite. An individual object can belong to more than one composite, which makes updating simple -- every time the object is changed, the changes appear in every composite that contains the object. Further, DDA works independently of specific publishing applications, meaning that composites can be assembled transparently from objects created in both SGML and non-SGML publishing environments. DDA also allows the configuration of new workflow processes "on the fly."

Document Interchange

Document interchange automatically invokes filters for easy, seamless exchange of documents from one user environment to another. Documentum's viewing features allow documents to be viewed as files of the publishing environment in which they were originally created.

Scalability

Documentum EDMS applications are highly scalable with regard to numbers of users supported by a server platform, as well as the number and size of document objects. The Documentum EDMS can easily scale from workgroups to departmental and multi-departmental applications. In addition, the Documentum server architecture consists of multiple server processes which utilize common, shared memory for communication and caching -- making effective use of a variety symmetric multi-processor (SMP) hardware architectures.

Application Tailoring/Extensibility

The Documentum EDMS is highly extensible, designed to be easily tailored by users and application developers without requiring them to do C++ programming. Instead, the system allows user customization through the high-level APIs, as well as standard rapid prototyping and development tools such as Microsoft Visual Basic, and PowerSoft's PowerBuilder. Documentum also offers Quickbuilder and Docbasic to rapidly customize the Documentum environment. Unlike many other document management systems, extending a Documentum application does not require programming relational database tables, and all operations can be executed on-line while the system is in production.

SQL Compatibility

Documentum's Document Query Language (DQL) provides easy compatibility with SQL data residing in a relational database management system (RDBMS), as well as any database the RDBMS can connect to. DQL is a superset of ANSI SQL that provides a single query mechanism for all objects in the system. With a single DQL query, users can retrieve all desired objects -- saving them from having to do multiple queries for different types of objects.

Documentum's Enterprise Client/Server Architecture

The Documentum EDMS is designed to take advantage of all the benefits of client/server architecture, including lowered computing costs, higher performance, and more flexible user access to data. For instance, Documentum's client/server implementation actually minimizes network traffic by storing documents on one server -- keeping users from having to query multiple servers to retrieve a document.

The Documentum EDMS is able to deliver the benefits of the virtual document because it has an architecture that is fundamentally object-oriented. At the same time, the architecture is based on an *object-relational* model that combines the richness and depth of object technology with industry-standard SQL relational databases for storing and managing document relationships and attributes.

The Documentum EDMS client/server architecture is shown below:

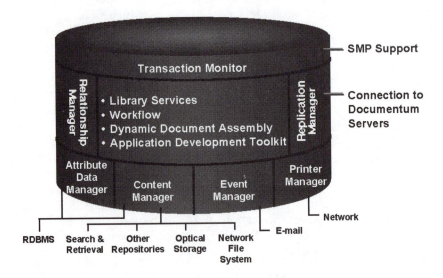

The Documentum Server

The *Documentum Server* is the nerve center of the Documentum architecture. The Documentum Server provides a distributed *Docbase*™, an object-oriented document repository that stores and manages all system objects and the mapping of their attributes into relational database tables. The Docbase is able to manage all types of document objects -- ranging from text, images, voice and graphics to multimedia and workflow. The DocBase also provides a set of pre-defined objects and operations tailored specifically to document management applications.

Because of its highly portable, POSIX-compliant code, the Documentum Server supports a range of UNIX Server platforms including those from Sun Microsystems, Hewlett-Packard, and IBM. In addition, the Documentum Server provides a rich set of document information management services to support the visual, WYSIWIG environments of today's desktop windowing systems -- including the Apple Macintosh, UNIX platforms under Motif, and MS Windows.

Documentum Workspace™

Documentum Workspace is a graphical, drag-and-drop user environment that lets users transparently access any distributed document or business database and perform all document-related functions. Documentum Workspace is available for MS Windows, Apple Macintosh, and UNIX/MOTIF clients, and it integrates with popular desktop applications to present all the services of the Documentum Server. With Documentum Workspace, DocObjects are represented by familiar visual metaphors such as cabinets and folders, which users can drag and click on to execute such basic functions as browsing and check in/out.

Documentum Accelera™

Documentum Accelera is a product that integrates popular Web browsers and servers with the Documentum Server™—providing secure access to business-critical documents stored in a Docbase™. Accelera transforms the World Wide Web and Intranets into platforms for companies to securely distribute business-critical information and for business users to easily locate and access information on a global basis. Through standard Web browsers, users can navigate and query a Docbase, view business-critical documents, participate in pre-defined workflows, and receive notifications of document and workflow changes—all within the context of a company's own business rules and processes.

Documentum UnaLink™

UnaLink is a integration of powerful enterprise document management with the groupware capabilities of Lotus Notes. By extending Documentum's functionality to Notes users, Documentum UnaLink provides a bridge between group collaboration and the critical information processes that drive a business.

Documentum LeafConnect™

Documentum LeafConnect is an integration of the Documentum EDMS with Interleaf 5. LeafConnect enables Interleaf users to take full advantage of Documentum's flexibility and power while working with the familiar Interleaf application on Windows PCs and UNIX/Motif desktops. The integration of the two products is designed to help organizations streamline processes involved in a document's entire life cycle, by facilitating document creation, approval, and publishing.

Tools and APIs for Tailorability

The Documentum EDMS is highly extensible, with a range of tools and APIs for tailoring document management applications to specific business requirements and classes of users.

The Documentum Server API is a high-level, object-oriented interface that can be accessed by professional programming languages such as C, C++, or Java and from rapid application development tools such as Microsoft Visual Basic, VBA, and PowerSoft's PowerBuilder. Documentum Workspace includes an API for integrating other desktop applications, and tools for tailoring and extending the user environment and for defining custom document attributes and workflows.

The Documentum Application Developer's Toolkit™(ADT) includes the following:

Docbasic. Docbasic is a standards-based implementation of Basic which enables developers to customize the Workspace user environment and embed business rules directly within the Documentum Server.

Quickbuilder. Quickbuilder™ is a screenpainter tool which enables developers to customize screen elements such as toolbars and buttons. Quickbuilder is completely compatible with Docbasic and the Server and Workspace APIs, and screen objects created with Quickbuilder can be easily integrated with Docbasic routines.

Java API. The ADT includes a Java API which enables users to build custom applications for the World Wide Web based on the Java programming language.

Conclusion

Enterprise wide document management technology is an idea whose time has finally come. The technologies are finally in place to support document management applications that truly automate and simplify a company's most enterprise-critical business processes. But so far, only Documentum is offering these organizations a simple way to exploit this technology, through rapid development and deployment of tailored document management applications.

As many organizations are discovering, the Documentum Enterprise Document Management System is today's most effective weapon for leveraging the intellectual capital that comprises an enterprise's true value. Perhaps for the first time, a true opportunity exists for companies to exploit document technology as a weapon for greater productivity, accelerated business processes, and re-usability of information -- for building competitive advantage.

Interleaf

Transforming Information Into Knowledge

Introduction

There is a quiet revolution occurring in information technology today. It's called "document management."

What is driving the enormous appetite for document management? There are two factors.

The first is the development of the technologies that enable document management. Among the most important are open systems and client/server computing.

The second is a business factor. Organizations are under more competitive pressure today than ever before. Over the last decade, many leading businesses have honed their product offerings, improved quality and service and cut costs to their limits. Today, the focus is on finding non-traditional sources of competitive advantage.

Competitive advantage in the marketplace is usually realized when a company can leverage its available assets. These have typically been products, price, promotion and place. And while these are still extremely important, companies must now find non-traditional means of leveraging marketplace advantage. Information - particularly the most valuable business-critical information - is now seen as a corporate asset that can be leveraged and used to stay ahead of the competition.

Alarmingly, the most valuable, business-critical information is often the least managed in organizations today. Document Management is the enabling technology to control this information.

It is this aspect of document management that makes the technology so compelling to organizations. It is becoming clear that document management software literally enables competitive advantage, by giving organizations control of their most important information - business-critical information.

Solutions that Transform Information into Knowledge

Successful businesses are distinguished by their ability to access, enhance, share and leverage business-critical information. This knowledge is ultimately captured in documents, both printed and increasingly, in electronic form. Interleaf's document management technologies ensure that the right information is delivered to the right person in the right location at the right time in the right format. The result: corporate competitive advantage through just-in-time information distribution, shortened product time-to-market, decreased costs, and enterprise-wide sharing of intellectual capital. Specifically, Interleaf's systems operate freely in an open systems environment to:

- Manage business critical information developed by word processors, PCs, graphic packages, spreadsheets, database managers and virtually any other application.
- Assemble what may be highly complex multimedia documents automatically and dynamically from data generated from geographically dispersed sources throughout a user's network
- Create and deliver easy-to-use online documents, formatted for optimal on-screen readability, with powerful tools for finding customized information tailored to the needs of each individual user.
- Deliver a complete publishing and production environment on the World Wide Web, including the capacity for hyperlinking between and among various file types, and for managing and updating multiple webs.

Documents

Definition

Until very recently, a document was generally agreed to be a piece of paper - for instance, a memo, a letter, a mission statement, an RFP, a marketing plan, a bill of materials or a customer invoice. The paper presented information - usually text, or text and graphics - laid out on physical pages, for the purpose of communicating.

But computer technology has changed all that.

Today, a document is increasingly being seen as electronic and containing numerous types of information - text and graphics as well as data, spreadsheets, CAD, images, video and voice. Documents are the vessels of information - they contain it and they give it shape and structure. A document makes information understandable.

Today's digital document is the composite of information coming from multiple sources, brought together for the purpose of communication.

Use

People use documents in two very specific ways.

Documents are a way of *communicating* complex information. Documents are vital information interfaces and there is no better way to ensure understanding and gain agreement than by "putting it in writing." Because of this, it is critical that the documents you use always have accurate, up-to-date information.

Second, documents are a way to *develop* information. For example, a sales manager writes a proposal, a marketing manager reviews it and adds information, the head of the finance department puts some numbers into it and the personnel department uses it to evaluate staffing.

Documents play these important roles because everyone understands them and knows how to use them. They are rich ways of communicating. Documents structure information in a way that is familiar to most people - making the information communicated by them usable.

Importance

Documents are important - in fact, essential - to organizations, again for two simple reasons.

First, documents are the means through which *information* is captured, managed and controlled. And those documents that capture business-critical information - the information of the highest value to the organization - are the most important of all. They are the means by which essential information gets developed and communicated throughout the organization.

Second, documents are at the heart of every important *business process*. They are the way one process "hands off" to another. They are the means through which people interact to accomplish an organization's goals and objectives. The more important the process is to the organization, the more essential the document reflecting it becomes.

Together, these two characteristics of documents make them the means by which organizations maintain and even gain competitive advantage in their marketplace.

Document Management

What is it?

It depends on who you ask. The definition is evolving along with the technology.

Interleaf defines document management as not only the technology that manages documents, but more important, that manages the information within documents. Interleaf regards document management as a set of software and services through which business-critical information is managed by enabling the creation, assembly, control and distribution of this information. Document management is about more than documents - it's about information and strategic business processes.

The benefits of document management

When employed to gain control over an organization's most important and valuable information -the third kind of information - the major benefit of document management is competitive advantage: it permits that organization to compete more effectively in its marketplace. It does so by improving the access, accuracy and velocity of important information flowing through that organization, which in turn has several benefits.

- It shortens time to market because of increased productivity in each of the supporting departments - from marketing, engineering and manufacturing to training, maintenance and customer service.
- It improves quality by allowing greater control of quality system documents - simply because related documents are controlled and distributed at the right time to the right people. It also allows better access to critical information that drives the process the quality system documents rely on - MRP, CAD, spreadsheet, word processing, database and other applications.
- It improves customer satisfaction by making sure the right information gets to customers when and where they need it.
- It increases worker productivity by enabling business teams to access, share and act on accurate information.
- It lowers costs, because shared access to information eliminates redundant efforts. Duplication is kept to a minimum, and no costly mistakes are made for lack of information.

To better illustrate these benefits some short case studies are presented in the Knowledge Management Award section at the end.

The Business Process

When viewed from the business process perspective document management becomes an enabler - a solver of problems - real business problems.

- It unclogs the arteries of business, permitting the free flow of important information across platforms and applications. In doing so, it enhances response time significantly.
- It improves the quality of information by ensuring that information is always accurate and up-to-date.
- It guarantees adherence to standards, whether they be industry standards such as SGML or an organization's own standards (the way you present yourself to your customers).
- It addresses workgroup inefficiency by giving workgroups a simple way to create, access and reuse information, then communicate that information across the enterprise.
- It gives companies an effective way to address regulatory standards by capturing and documenting essential business information and processes.

Documents are Unique

When you stop to think about it, documents are a unique kind of information.

- They can be unpredictable, created on an as-needed basis in virtually any form.
- They are dynamic. They can be changed, modified and enhanced within very short time periods, or over long life cycles.
- They are complex. Documents can be structured in many different ways.
- They may contain different qualities of information - some business-critical and of vital importance to the organization, some relatively unimportant and having a short life.
- They may contain information in almost any format - text, spreadsheets, CAD, data, graphics or images.
- They may contain volatile source information from CAD, spreadsheets or MRP that needs to be updated frequently.

But no matter how they differ, documents have one thing in common: they are the circulatory system of an organization. And they must be managed to be effective.

The lifecycle

To improve the flow of this information throughout the organization it is incumbent to look at the document lifecycle. However, there is really no such thing as a typical life cycle, because documents are so dynamic and different people use them in different ways. But there are often four steps, or stages, that many documents go through.

The first step is **creating** documents. Users create documents in a variety of ways. They use a pencil and paper, a word processor, a CAD system, a spreadsheet or some other means to originate information in documents.

The second step is usually **reviewing** documents. Users - sometimes the creator of the information - review the information contained in documents, sometimes commenting on it, sometimes changing it.

Often there is interaction between step one and step two, as the information in the document undergoes significant change. During this stage, the document is often stored in a "work-in-process" repository, where it stays until the third step.

The third step is **assembling** documents. At this point, all information objects have been created and reviewed (and approved up to some level of authority), and they are assembled into a completed document.

When step three is complete - after its round of reviews and sometimes additional creation - the documents are stored in a released document repository.

The fourth and final step is **distributing** documents for others to use and comment on. This can be done either electronically or on paper.

Often, as one version is released, a new cycle starts all over again, with the information contained in these documents constantly being changed, improved and updated.

The more important the document is to an organization - the more it captures business-critical information - the more dynamic and long is its life cycle.

Over the long haul

The lengthy and complicated life cycle of an important document can rapidly lead to deterioration of the information it contains because it becomes old and outdated.

A document management system is essential in preventing this by managing the information.

Document management means making sure that the right people review the information at the right time.

Management means keeping track of the interdependencies of information in the documents, so that as changes are made, everyone who depends on or uses the information is kept informed.

Management means streamlining the overall cycle by making information easy to find and easy to use.

Management means ensuring that you can access any previous version of a document and view it exactly as it appeared at that time.

Management means giving you more value for your investment in documents by making it easy to find and reuse the same information in many places.

Interleaf's Product Philosophy

Many vendors offer pieces of the total document management solution, however that makes you the integrator. Interleaf is the one vendor that provides a complete integrated set of tools to address the complete document lifecycle. Interleaf provides open, standards compliant, scalabe, industrial strength products to meet the need for creating, reviewing, assembling, and distributing document based knowledge through the department, enterprise or even over the World Wide Web.

As open systems architecture continues to drive user networks around the world, Interleaf has integrated its products and designed them for compatibility with all major applications, allowing users to plug and play to meet any document management challenge. We provide our customers with product solutions designed to meet their customized needs. In some cases, this may mean a specific member of the Intellecte product family. Increasingly, however, the marketplace is demanding complete business solutions. To meet this need, Interleaf offers integrated solutions composed of various applications, products and services, which are marketed under the Intellecte brand name.

The introduction of Interleaf's Web-based products extend these Intellecte solutions to the Internet. Using the World Wide Web as a publishing platform allows Interleaf to offer its customers additional and unprecedented flexibility to their business processes.

Interleaf Intellecte Product Family

Intellecte/Access

The Intellecte family of knowledge management products is advanced, open software for the electronic management, assembly, retrieval, distribution and publishing of business-critical information.

With the implementation of Intellecte/Access, customers have an integrated, enterprise-wide solution for leveraging their document resources. With the openness of the bundled products, users will be able to draw from document resources, regardless of original authoring systems, and deliver the relevant information to the appropriate users in a consistent, targeted format. Intellecte/Access consists of the latest, enhanced versions of RDM document manager, Production Manager automation software, WorldView System for online distribution, Liaison API, and optionally, Interleaf 6 for workgroup publishing plus implementation services.

Intellecte/BusinessWeb

Intellecte/BusinessWeb is a web-based solution that provides instant and transparent access to multiple instances of your knowledge repositories. These repositories can be managed by Interleaf' s document manager RDM, Interleaf WorldView distribution system and other webs. Intellecte/BusinessWeb is a software and services solution that leverages Interleaf document management and delivery systems by adding Internet access to the information you want your work force to see and use. The Intellecte/Business web consists of the latest versions of RDM, the BusinessWeb application template, Liaison API runtime, and optionally, the WorldView System.

PRODUCTS

RDM Document Management System

Interleaf RDM is the most complete document management system available. It is an open, scaleable, integrated solution to locate, control, re view, revise and distribute up-to-the-minute information that is critical to your business success. From assembly and operating manuals to policy/procedure guides, to regulatory submissions and quality initiatives, RDM is the ideal document management tool. It mirrors your business processes, enabling you to streamline the tasks of accessing, creating, and revising document objects wherever they are used across your organization.

The RDM Server is available on SunOS4, Solaris, HP-UX, IBM RS-6000, and Digital UNIX operating systems. The RDM Client is available on Windows 3.1, Windows NT, Macintosh, Sun Solaris, HP-UX, IBM RS-6000, and Digital UNIX operating systems.

Production Manager

Production Manager leverages the functionality of RDM and WorldView Press. It automates the process of creating online document collections that can be viewed and navigated with WorldView Viewer.

Production Manager is available on SunOS4, Sun Solaris, HP-UX, IBM RS-6000, and Digital UNIX operating systems.

Liaison API and Integration Infrastructure

Liaison is an object-oriented framework that provides a single object model that uniquely spans document authoring, document management and document delivery functions. Liaison's high-level interface eases integration and customization across the network. Liaison is available on SunOS4, Solaris, HP-UX, Windows NT, and Windows 95 operating systems.

WorldView System

Interleaf's WorldView System is the only electronic distribution system designed especially for long, complex documents. It s powerful production engine allows you to assemble many different types of data and transform them into meaningful collections that can be distributed electronically and viewed by end users on a wide range of standard computing environments, including Windows, Windows NT, Macintosh and UNIX. With WorldView, you can build custom electronic distribution applications that provide instant access to business-critical information.

The WorldView System includes:

WorldView Press, which collects, processes, and links all the information within the source documents. It adds consistent and compelling presentation or formatting across potentially huge document collections.

WorldView Viewer, the users' window into information, enables them to easily access, navigate, and print documents. Through the viewer, users can control their access to the specific information they need to do their jobs.

The WorldView Viewer is available on Microsoft Windows 3.1, Microsoft Windows NT, Macintosh, SunOS4, Solaris, HP-UX, AIX, Digital UNIX operating systems. The WorldView Press is available on Windows NT, SunOS4, Solaris, HP- UX, AIX and Digital UNIX

Interleaf Workgroup Authoring

Interleaf 6.1 offers a comprehensive feature set for document creation, composition, and assembly on Windows NT, Windows 95 and UNIX platforms. A powerful workgroup application, Interleaf 6 enables local or global collaboration, making it easier and more efficient to share information and manage document projects. Interleaf 6 delivers all the functionality of desktop publishing and word processing plus more - large- volume publishing and workgroup support in one easy-to-use package. With its powerful information management features, your workgroups can create, assemble, revise and manage documents throughout their lifecycle. And support for multiple languages means you can strengthen your position worldwide. Interleaf 6 is available on SunOS4, Solaris, HP-UX, IBM AIX, Digital UNIX, Windows NT, and Windows 95 operating systems.

Interleaf 6 SGML

Interleaf 6 SGML is an integrated solution for assembling and publishing SGML and non-SGML documents. Powerful workgroup and graphics capabilities combined with complete SGML support provide a robust system for high-quality publishing while complying with standards. This extended version of Interleaf's premier publishing system provides full access to the advanced features of Interleaf 6 while creating documents to conform to an SGML Document Type Definition (DTD). Only Interleaf 6 SGML lets you manage SGML and non-SGML documents throughout their lifecycle in one integrated system. The current release of Interleaf 6 SGML is available on SunOS4, Solaris, HP- UX, IBM AIX, and Digital UNIX operating systems.

Cyberleaf

Cyberleaf is a powerful, comprehensive Internet publishing application that allows you to create and maintain high-quality text and graphic Internet document webs, using standard authoring tools, including Microsoft Word, WordPerfect, and FrameMaker in addition to Interleaf's own authoring tools. Cyberleaf combines HTML and GIF data conversion and hyperlinking with complete web production and management capabilities in one easy-to-use, push-button application. Cyberleaf is available on SunOS4, Solaris, HP-UX, IBM RS-6000, and Digital UNIX operating systems.

FastTAG

FastTAG is a powerful, comprehensive tool for translating unstructured documents into pre-defined style sheets to facilitate reuse. It then converts documents into other applications or standards, including SGML. FastTAG's openness and support for the widest range of source document types, including ASCII files, WordPerfect, and Microsoft Word, make FastTAG one of the most complete conversion tools available. FastTAG is available on SunOS4, Solaris, HP-UX, and Microsoft Windows 3.1 operating systems.

SGML Hammer

SGML Hammer is an essential tool for converting SGML information to other electronic formats, including word processing, publishing, HTML, SGML, and markup for CD-ROM and typesetting. As a result, information becomes an accessible and reusable resource for non-SGML users. SGML Hammer is available on SunOS4, Solaris, HP-UX, and Microsoft Windows 3.1 operating systems.

Knowledge Management Awards

In the fall of 1995, as part of an effort to encourage recent customers to evaluate their business applications from an ROI perspective, Interleaf launched the first annual Knowledge Management Awards (KMA). The competition was open to their customers who have applied Interleaf products towards solving a business-critical problem through an integrated document management application. The specific criteria included:

- Measurable benefits realized by implementing Interleaf products (ROI and/or competitive analysis);
- Innovative applications of Interleaf products;
- Proven end-user acceptance of the system; and
- Applications implemented in multiple departments, sites or enterprise-wide.

Additional consideration was given to business solutions that integrated multiple products and technologies, including Interleaf and non-Interleaf. Finally, the winning application had to be fully deployed.

Entrants were asked the following questions:

- What was the initial business problem you were trying to solve?
- What is the Interleaf solution?
- What Interleaf products were used?
- Why did you select this solution?
- How has your Interleaf solution made a significant difference to your organization?
- How did the end users accept the solution?
- Were there measurable benefits?
- Do you have plans to extend your solution?

THE 1996 KNOWLEDGE MANAGEMENT AWARD FINALISTS More than twenty businesses were selected as finalists in the first annual Knowledge Management Award competition. Recurring themes throughout the applications were:

1. Ease of integration of Interleaf technology across multiple

platforms and operating systems, and with legacy systems and software applications,

2. Mission-critical business applications, and
3. End user acceptance.

The finalists represented many industries including: pharmaceutical, aerospace, discrete and process manufacturing, utilities, high-tech software, telecommunications, financial services, transportation, and education. Intellecte/BusinessWeb shipped after the submission deadline for the KMA. Interleaf expects to see Web-based document management in next year's Knowledge Management Award solutions. Below are brief summaries of a few of the 1996 finalists:

AEROSPACE: Northrop Grumman Corporation

All of the policies and procedures at the Commercial Aircraft Division's Hawthorne Center were originally hard copy. The aerospace company's division of 900 employees wanted to solve the following problems: reduce maintenance time demanded by the voluminous manuals; reduce the several-months approval cycle resulting from each document; track and control hard copies; and update their antiquated on-line document viewing system. As a solution, Northrop Grumman selected Interleaf's Intellecte/Access integrated system. WorldView provided easy access to all procedures, permitting full-text search and quick navigation for all employees. RDM routes approvals, accepts annotations, and archives the entire review cycle of a document. Employees especially like the ability to add unique reviewers to their workflow process when required. Northrop Grumman's management systems analysts claim that Interleaf 6 is "a perfect fit," integrating well with the other Intellecte tools, and meeting all their authoring needs. They conclude, "No one else could offer what we found in WorldView, RDM, and Interleaf 6. And we are still discovering new features every day!"

MANUFACTURING: Integrated Device Technology, Inc.

How do you make a clean room cleaner? Integrated Device Technology (IDT) produces cutting edge semiconductor devices, and requires the component assembly area to be clean at the sub-micron level. Accessing policies and procedures documents in the clean room was a definite hindrance. In addition to improving sub- microscopic cleanliness, IDT wanted to improve manufacturing efficiency along with their policies and procedures document distribution. Since selecting RDM, WorldView, and Interleaf authoring tools, IDT has purified their clean room from all paper and related contaminants, experienced a substantial reduction in manual maintenance and revision man-hours, and enjoyed a high quality of integration with other computer resources. Best of all, according to the project team, "it' s fun!!"

FINANCE & INSURANCE: Standard & Poor's

Standard & Poor's (S&P) initial business need was to streamline the publishing cycle and create a central repository of all analytical information. This notable leader in financial industry analysis was also interested in improving the productivity and value of the editorial and production departments by minimizing manual administrative duties. Interleaf's Intellecte/Access system including RDM, WorldView and Interleaf publishing tools was selected by S&P because of its flexibility in integrating with other standard products such as Microsoft Office, and in-house solutions such as Core and custom 4 GL modules. The use of Interleaf's API has allowed S&P to build a customized solution that provides an intuitive and easy interface for users, while incorporating a document management repository. This customized solution, named the LinX System, had an extensive impact on S&P's business process, including: improved productivity of analysts, editors and production staff by minimizing the time devoted towards the administration, formatting, and rewriting of articles; provision of a publishing repository and process to create large volumes of documents from multiple electronic sources (input) to multiple electronic and paper delivery mechanisms (output); improved ability to distribute to a wider audience, faster and cheaper; and connected "islands of production" -- areas with discrete document management and publishing responsibilities, under a single technology umbrella. It accomplished this transparently without disruption to the way individual analysts and editors like to work.

PETRO CHEMICAL: Hibernia

Safety and environmental responsibility are at the heart of the construction of the $5 billion offshore drilling project in the North Atlantic ocean. The project is owned by a consortium of Mobil Oil Canada Properties, Chevron Canada Properties, Petro-Canada Hibernia Partnership, Canada Hibernia Holding Corporation, and Murphy Atlantic Offshore Oil Company. Construction and commissioning will be complete by the spring of 1997, and the first oil is expected to flow at the rate of 135,000 barrels a day for about 20 years, representing an $11 billion revenue base. Construction is complex, complicated by harsh North Atlantic weather. After locating the site, selecting the best software to manage the myriad important construction details was considered critical to the success and timely completion of the project.

Interleaf's Intellecte/Access was chosen for the task. RWD Technologies of Columbia, MD, was selected to consult with project engineers, offshore operators, technicians, and managers to customize the integrate d solution. Among the complex factors demanded of Interleaf products: manage more than 100,000 electronic documents in a wide variety of formats; incorporate 200,000 scanned pages; provide hyperlinks of technical drawings between 90 different platform systems and make these available to users both onshore and offshore; allow for high speed updating and 7x24 access; and ensure absolute security of documents without impeding a reliable revision, routing, and approval process. As an example of the successful implementation, the project team cites that even seasoned North Sea offshore operators, expecting the usual 8 to 10 minutes retrieval time for a single CAD diagram, were delighted with WorldView's drawing delivery rate to a rural Newfoundland site of four seconds each, and resulting 11 x 17-inch output in less than a minute.

PHARMACEUTICAL: Apotex, Inc. Ontario, Canada

Because the pharmaceutical industry is strictly regulated, Apotex views document management as a necessity, as well as an opportunity to improve efficiency. Interleaf's products were first deployed five years ago, and the systems analysts have found numerous applications beyond their original intent. Standard Operating Procedures are documents which detail the procedures of every task within the manufacturing, testing labs, and maintenance of the company -- from how to repair technical equipment to how and when to wash the walls. These documents currently total 52,800 pages of constantly changing, and frequently critical information. The Intellecte family of products solved the problems of: how to find what you need when you need it, fast; how to access the information at the point of need (i.e. shop floor); how to ensure up-to-date SOP books; and how to do all this cost-effectively. Authoring in Interleaf had many advantages, including easy creation of hyperlinks. RDM allowed an easy, accurate, customizable yet automatic, approval process. WorldView gave easy enterprise access to the nightly updated WorldView collection of SOPs.

TELECOMMUNICATIONS: Northern Telecom

This large telecommunications company wanted to publish and deliver "just-in-time" documentation to their customers. The technical manuals required multiple authors to produce the text in "chunks" that allow each customer to order customized books, dealing only with the subjects they specifically need. Interleaf's authoring option that prevents multiple authors from altering a format, coupled with the Developers ToolKit, allowed Northern Telecom to generate the "SooperBook" tool to perform checks on multiple information chunks, and generate accurate customized manuals of an average 1200 pages. Multiple authors can input text in complete confidence that their individual input styles will be automatically formatted to generate customized books exhibiting the highest degree of consistency and quality. These books are currently produced and distributed to Northern Telecom customers throughout the World.

UTILITIES: Boston Edison Company - Boston, MA

To address a voluminous and increasingly unmanageable Standards and Procedures manual, Boston Edison needed a relational database, a workflow management tool, and an electronic document library. The Intellecte/Access product was selected by this large northeastern utility company because, according to the project manager, Interleaf's EDMS solution "contained a comprehensive set of tools that met all of our functional needs, was very competitive in cost and was compatible with the system architecture of the Boston Edison computer network." In the first year of operation, Intellecte/Access allowed Boston Edison to achieve its EDMS objectives. Review cycles were exponentially shortened, and half of the 2,000 policies and procedures were updated. The dramatic change in accessibility and reliability led to a significant increase in the use of these business-critical documents.

Summary

A document management system can benefit your organization in many ways.

When it is implemented to manage your most important, business-critical information, document management can help your organization achieve competitive advantage.

It does this by ensuring that your organization's most vital information is accurate and easy to access.

By improving the accuracy and velocity of business-critical information, document management technology can improve time to market, increase product quality and improve customer satisfaction, while lowering costs. It does all this simply by enhancing the productivity of workers in your organization.

There are many types of document management systems available today. Some manage office-level information. Others address information in specific vertical industries. A few are open, capable of implementation across multiple applications, hardware platforms and networks.

But only one, from Interleaf, integrates the full range of document management technology, allowing users to control documents, assemble them in diverse formats from multiple sources and distribute them with intelligence that aids those trying to use the technology. And only Interleaf's is sufficiently robust that it can manage document management applications no matter how complex they may grow.

Open Text Corporation

The Death (and Rebirth) of Document Management

Document management can only achieve its dream if it wakes up first. (Is that Zen-like or what!)

So long as document management thinks of itself as a type of database application, it will remain a niche tool for documentation specialists. If, however, it wakes up to the reality of the World Wide Web, it can become the most ubiquitous of applications, next to word processing, file management, and Windows solitaire.

Of course, it will become an application everyone uses only when no one has to know that he or she is using it. Universally used, universally unrecognized Ö therein lies the fate of document management.

The failure of document management

Here's a syllogism.

Everyone uses documents.
Documents are the lifeblood of an organization.

Therefore, everyone uses document management.

This is the basic argument the document management vendors have made for ten years. Yet, it is very hard to find any corporation that actually has more than 5% of its employees using document management.

Likewise, for over five years, the document management vendors have been saying, correctly, that only 5% of an organization's data is in relational databases. Most of the rest of it is in documents. (Sound familiar?) What the document management vendors have *not* pointed

---

Reprinted with permission from Open Text.

out is that of that 95% of data outside of relational databases, typically far less than 5% is under the control of a document management system.

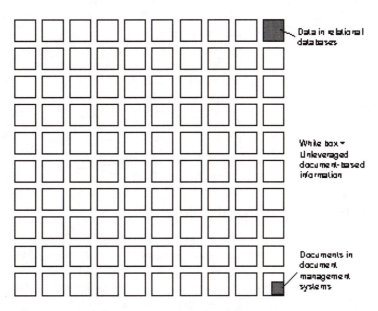

Only 5% of corporate data is in relational databases. Although most of the rest is in documents, less than 5% of the documents are in a document management database.

By the industry's own standard — the percentage of desktops with document management systems or the percentage of documents in a document management system — document management has failed.

It hasn't even come close.

The causes of failure

Why has document management failed? The answers are obvious to any organization that has contemplated installing a system. Document management is:

- <u>Hard to install</u>. Document management usually requires integrating several different technologies. This is hard and risky work.
- <u>Hard to use</u>. Users have to learn a new piece of software that interrupts their accustomed way of working. Further, usually the

users don't see any benefit — document management's benefits tend to be at the organizational, not individual, level.

- Proprietary. Document management has demanded organizations make serious commitments to proprietary software and architectures. This raises the cost of potential failure without increasing the value of success.
- Expensive. The per seat cost of document management systems has been very high, sometimes more than the cost of the hardware itself. Besides increasing the startup costs, this also makes it a full-brainer (the opposite of a no-brainer) to add more people to the circle of users.

These are some of the more important reasons why, according to CAPV, a leading consulting firm, more document management projects fail than succeed.

The consequence of failure

The result of these causes of failure is that document management systems typically reach only the full-time document professionals in an organization. And they only use document management systems for the most complex, high-value documents they can find.

This is the problem that document management currently solves. It solves it adequately.

But it makes document management into a niche application.

People don't love documents

Document management currently is architected, spec'ed, designed and priced to meet the needs of the high priests of documents in an organization.

It uses a conceptual model that is familiar to the high priests.

It uses an interface designed for the high priests.

But the brutal fact is that most people don't love documents as much as document management vendors and document specialists do.

Most people don't want document management. They don't know what it is, and they don't see why they should care.

They don't want document management. They want to get their work done better. And faster.

Oddly, that's *exactly* what their managers, and their managers' managers, want them to do.

And that is why document management as it is currently construed will never achieve the vendor's dream of ubiquity.

But — surprise, surprise — there is hope.

Enter the Web

"The Web changes everything." This is the motto that will be emblazoned over the portal of the mid-90s.

Unfortunately, at first sight, the Web changes everything for the worse when it comes to documents. (Don't worry, we'll show you how it makes it all better, too.)

Thanks to the Web, we now have —

- Unfathomably more documents
- More people than ever who want to connect to those documents
- More complex relationships among the documents (via hyperlinks)
- More locations at which there are documents and people who want to connect
- Less control

This is a potent mix of factors. But it is life and so we must bravely pick ourselves up and move forward.

Yes, it's another paradigm shift

When in doubt, check your paradigms.

The root of the problems traditional document management faces is the paradigm on which it is built.

Traditional document management came out of the database world. They treat documents as data and thus do what any self-respecting data manager does — it shoves them into a repository. It manages some of the relationships among the documents. And you enable users to perform transactions (check in, check out) against that data. It is essentially a hub-and-spoke view of the world with data at its center.

The jury will rule that the demise of document management was a case of Death by Paradigm —

- The repository-based view is not a natural one for people working collaboratively.
- It is too tightly controlling except for high-value document "jewels."
- It adds layers of work to people using documents to get their work done.
- It is a complex, troublesome system that only document specialists are motivated to use.

Pair of Paradigms

This stands in sharp contrast to the Web paradigm.

Where repository-based document management is centralized, the Web is decentralized.

Where repositories are only for the highest value documents, the Web handles the full gamut of documents.

Where repositories require a hub-and-spoke process that mediates between people, the Web provides direct connections among all people and all information.

Where repository-based document management is only for document specialists, the Web is for everyone.

The Web, in short, changes everything.

The Internet and Intranets

The Web by itself is a publishing medium. It is a set of global pipes through which people access documents.

But it's read-only.

You find what you want (using an incredible free tool such as the Open Text Index at *http://www.opentext.com*), you read it, and then you're done.

The Internet is for publishing.

Intranets, on the other hand, are for getting connected work done.

An Intranet is a private web that uses the protocols and the standards of the Internet but adds some level of security.

You <u>can</u> use an Intranet as a publishing medium. That is the approach of the repository-based document management vendors. They add a Web-page user interface that allows you to locate and view documents in their repository. And that's it.

<u>Or</u>, you can use an Intranet as an <u>application platform</u> like a PC or a LAN. It is an infrastructure on which you run programs.

The difference is enormous.

If you treat an Intranet as an application platform, you can fundamentally change the way people work together.

Read that sentence again. It's important.

What's so good about Intranets?

Imagine you woke up one day and discovered that someone — elves, perhaps, or an unexpectedly benevolent federal government — had created a global infrastructure.

Suppose it supported international standards such as TCP/IP, HTTP and HTML.

Suppose it supported a cross platform "universal" user interface and desktop.

Suppose it was really easy to use.

Suppose all anyone needed to participate was a Web browser and a password.

Suppose it was secure.

Suppose it was really low cost.

Congratulations. You've just imagined Intranets.

Intranet applications

Intranets are the new platform for applications.

The distinctive feature of this new platform is that it's *connective*. It connects people to people and people to information.

What then are the applications that are particularly suited to this new platform?

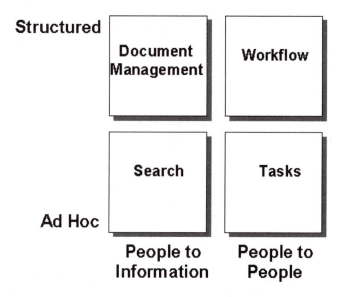

- *Searching* — With access to unimaginable quantities of data, enabling people to find information assumes new importance.
- *Document management* — The documents worth managing — the ones containing strategic information — are usually worked on over time by several people.
- *Tasks* — People organize themselves around tasks with shared goals.

- *Workflow* — Where the steps required to bring a project to completion are predictable, software can help make the process both more creative and more efficient.

The project metaphor

Any one of those four capabilities could serve as the basis for an Intranet application. But they are particularly powerful if they are integrated.

Once they are integrated, they feel different than a collection of their parts. To express this, we need a new metaphor. The one that works best, perhaps, is that of a *project*.

What is a project? It's a group of people with a shared objective and a deadline.

What do people need to accomplish their shared objectives — to work together better?

- Intranets — a global infrastructure that allows people to work together, defying the laws of <u>space</u> in order to get their job done in <u>time</u>.
- Intranet application software — tools that let them work well together, now that they are all in the same "project space."

A project space is a virtual work room that enables people to communicate and to share tools and information.

Unfortunately, to explain "project space" with the phrase "virtual work room" is just to substitute one buzz word for another.

Beyond the buzz words, a project space is, in effect, an Intranet home page. Every project gets its own page. For example, you might have pages for:

- A product
- A task force
- A workgroup or department
- An event

Some pages will be permanent, others long-lived, others evanescent. What they have in common is they help a set of people to get something done together.

The elements of a project

A project typically has the following elements:

- Members
- An objective
- Tasks — the steps to be accomplished
- Workflows — the process by which the steps are accomplished
- A shared library of resources (documents, spreadsheets, URLs, etc.)
- Searching — a way to find more materials for the library or just for immediate use
- Discussions — a way of conversing that is both freeform and organized
- Accountability and management tools — aids so the project members, or the managers, can see the current status and measure performance

The project space should provide tools for each of these.

A day in the life

What is it like to use an Intranet-based project system such as this? Let's imagine a day in the life of Sal, world-class team member.

Sal is on the road today. She wakes up at 5:00AM (7:30AM New Foundland time) and does what she does whether she's in her office or otherwise located: she connects to the Internet (this morning through her laptop and modem), fires up her Web browser, and uses a bookmark to reach the WristIO 2000 Intranet home page. (The WristIO 2000 is a new telecommunications product.)

The Intranet software asks her to log in and authenticates her password. This is handled by the SQL database that's underneath the system.

Now that she's in, she sees a Web page that lets her go straight to a project area. But she decides first to check her in-box to see what tasks are on her plate. The system can automatically assemble an in-box because it tracks all workflows, task lists and processes for the multiple projects in which Sal participates.

One task is flagged in red because it's overdue — Sal is supposed to be certifying the WristIO 2000 as safe. To do this, she has to read engineering trial reports and write a Safety Declaration which will be submitted to the federal regulatory agency as part of the required paperwork. (The engineer trial reports are themselves the results of processes that have their own work flow.)

There's a comment attached to the task saying that her team has just discovered that the WristIO leaks in the shower, delivering a mild shock to its owner. Not good, although some people apparently enjoy it.

In fact, a quick look at the visual workflow status shows that she is in fact right in the critical path. Everyone else has finished on time. She alone is the hold up.

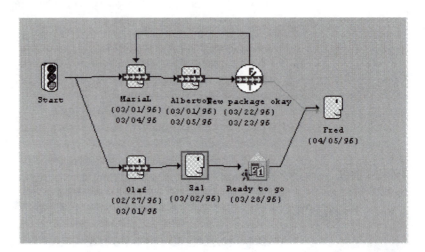

So Sal decides to check a project in which she participates — product safety. On its Intranet home page she finds a library of relevant materials, including documents, URLs, and saved queries. She browses among these and finds that the answer may be to change the type of adhesive used to seal the unit.

So, she decides to visit the project discussion area. Sure enough, one of the topics is "polymer bonding." She reads the messages engineers have exchanged on this topic. Wendy and Xavier have had particular perceptive comments.

With this as background, she decides to search for more information on polymers. With a single query, she searches the corporate library as well as a set of servers containing documents not entered into the library. She finds some information, reads it within the Web browser (because the system translates office formats into HTML on the fly), and feels ready to make her recommendation.

Back she goes to the task at hand. She clicks on the link to the Safety Declaration, which now gets downloaded into her word processor. She writes her report and then presses the "Done" button on her system. This uploads the altered document back into system.

Sal now goes back to her in-box. The step she's just completed no longer is listed because the system has moved it to the next step in the process.

Her work is done, the process is under control, and she's been able to do it all with nothing but a Web browser.

But where's the document management?

Very nice, but where's the document management?

Right under Sal's nose. And that's the point. She has gotten all of the benefits of document management without any of the work.

For example, when she clicked on the link to the Safety Declaration and it loaded into her word processor, the system automatically checked her permissions, performed a "check out" from the corporate library and reserved the document from being simultaneously edited. When she uploaded it back into the system, all of the document management tasks were silently accomplished for her: checking the document in, updating the version number, un-reserving the document, updating the audit trail, and handling all the details of configuration management if the document was a part of one or more compound documents.

But all Sal saw of this was clicking on a hyperlink and clicking on a "Done" button.

Likewise, Sal has also been using a complete workflow system, but may not know it. All she sees of it are her in-box and the visual status maps that give her tasks some context. She does not know or have to know about conditional routing, parallel and serial flows, milestones, rendezvous steps, etc.

Likewise, the "electronic document distribution" component of the system is presented to her as a friendly tool, not as an alien environment into which she must enter. To Sal, it's apparent as a search tool — one quite similar to the ones she's used to using on the World Wide Web. The fact that the search engine can search across multiple servers and multiple file types only means to her that she doesn't have to know or care where documents are or what format they're in. Once again, the complexities of a document management are hidden from her.

In short, she can be a document management system <u>user</u> without having to be a document management <u>expert</u>.

What's happened to document management?

In the Intranet system we've been describing, document management is still there. But it's changed —

- It's become invisible. Users don't know they're using it.
- It's become more flexible, handling documents that are outside of the vault as well as inside of it — for example, not constraining searching to within the repository boundaries.
- It's become process-centric rather than document-centric, fo-

cusing on helping people get their word done rather than on their data.

- It's become a pervasive application, rather than a tool for document specialists.

Assumptions old and new

Along the way, some old assumptions have been overturned.

First, the traditional document management vendors have insisted that "Document management isn't about managing documents. It's about managing information." That contains an important insight about what is of value in a document. But, it is overturned by the fact that document management isn't even primarily about managing information. It's about enabling people to succeed at their jobs. It's about helping processes and interactions, not about managing a particular type of data.

Second, the industry has patted itself on the back because "Documents are the most complex data type." Well, yes, documents are far more complex than relational data. But they pale next to the complexity of people and projects.

Third, we have heard for ten years that "SGML is the real answer to your document woes." There certainly are problems for which SGML is the only answer. But, SGML has been permanently "niched" by HTML. So many people use HTML and so many documents are in HTML that HTML will evolve upwards to do much of what SGML does; there is little chance that SGML will manage to migrate "down" to expand its market share very significantly by displacing HTML. (In fact, of course, HTML *is* the way SGML migrated "down.")

Fourth, the industry has looked at documents as containers of information. Advanced systems can even handle compound documents that act as a meta-container for documents. While there is much continuing utility in such an approach, it obscures the fact that documents are becoming *applications*, not containers. Documents increasingly do things. We *use* them as much as we *read* them. It's time to wake up and smell the Java about this.

Achieving the dream

In light of how Intranets change the playing field, let's revisit the reasons document management has failed at becoming a mainstream application:

- "Hard to install." Since most of the pain has had to do with integrating the required pieces, a system that already integrates what's required — because it's focused on projects rather than documents — becomes easy to install. In addition, Intranets themselves are easier to set up and maintain than traditional LANs and WANs.

- "Hard to use." The project-based approach to collaborative work makes document management so easy that the user doesn't even know she's using it.
- "Proprietary." Intranets and the applications that run on them support open, public standards.
- "Too expensive." Because Intranet software resides on servers and require only a standard Web browser to be used, the only per-user pricing model breaks down; the software now becomes highly affordable.

Freed from these limitations, document management at long last can achieve its dream of ubiquity.

Yes, it has to transform itself.

Yes, it has to accept that it becomes a "mere" component of collaborative project software.

Yes, it has to lose some of its document idolatry.

But, having remade itself, it is now ready to become a key contributor to the everyday life of just about everyone with a keyboard and co-worker.

Livelink Intranet

What Is Livelink Intranet?

Livelink Intranet lets your organization leverage the power of the Internet to control and coordinate key business processes of any size or complexity. You get unprecedented support for collaborative efforts that span continents, huge quantities of information and distributed working groups. With just a web browser and a password, your managers and working groups can access comprehensive, integrated tools for workflow, project collaboration, library management, search & access of information. By "putting the web to work," Livelink enables your worldwide organization to work together more effectively and productively than ever before.

Your Organization Can Benefit With Livelink Intranet

Chances are, your organization must support the collaborative efforts of many people across departments, distance and multiple technologies. With Livelink Intranet, you can boost productivity and eliminate the obstacles to working across diverse distributed networks. Managers can control, structure and monitor any number of projects, so strategic business processes stay on track. The Livelink Intranet workflow engine streamlines and automates strategic work processes involving any number of documents and contributors. Universal search and viewing engines remove the barriers to information access, letting you focus on your work instead of cross-platform mechanics. The Livelink Library/ Document Management engine provides centralized control and ensures version integrity for your organization's critical document and information assets.

Functionality Overview

Livelink Intranet lets you facilitate project collaboration and workflow efforts, while also providing information access to authorized users worldwide. The intuitive Livelink Intranet interface is easy-to-use, so you can get productive right away. You access Livelink Intranet directly from your desktop through a standard web browser. The Livelink Intranet suite includes the following powerful engines:

- *Livelink Search* - Offers the industry's most powerful search and indexing tools; including full text indexing of all words, support for document collections of any size and more than 40 different file formats. Search functions include similarity/full phrase/power searching. It also provides multiple format document viewing, automatic summaries of documents, intelligent relevance ranking, document access control and optional crawling software to keep your index comprehensive and up-to-date.
- *Livelink Workflow* - Provides in-box and work package for workflow data and documents; generates easy-to-read, visual workflow status map in real-time; conditional routing based on attributes; serial, parallel and rendezvous workflow paths. It also provides a visual or graphical workflow builder and a complete audit trail.
- *Livelink Library for Document Management* - A robust document management system containing hierarchical structure, access control, custom attributes, drag & drop, , aliases and generations. It also provides document "check out" and "check in"; automatic version control; and lets managers and authorized

users set multi-level permissions and document attributes. Enables document viewing, searching attributes and document
contents.
- *Livelink Project Collaboration* - Virtual team collaboration with
  project components, project team members, project documents,
  project status. This is enabled via project-based workflows and
  libraries; managed discussion database for newsgroup-style
  "conversations"; task assignment and tracking.
- *Livelink Builder* - Visual, object-oriented, cross-platform development environment; supports customization as needed.

Tailored To Meet Your Needs

The basic Livelink Intranet package provides customers with a
choice of either Livelink Search (includes the Netscape Commerce
Server) or the Livelink Library (includes the Livelink Document Management Engine, the Netscape Commerce Server and a database
server). Once you have the basic Livelink Intranet package, you can
add additional Livelink engines - for workflow, project collaboration,
search - to meet your organization's requirements as they evolve. All
basic systems include unlimited Netscape client access.

The Key to Your Corporate Memory

The Situation

The business world is rapidly changing as technology enables organizations to work in new ways and to connect with a vaster audience. More often than not, the exchange of electronic documents is at the heart of these connections. Therefore, the ability of an organization to make sure traveling employees, mobile teams, and business partners can access this information has become especially critical.

In the past 18 months, the increasing use of groupware applications and the Internet has enabled organizations to expand the bounds of the traditional enterprise to include remote sites and mobile users as well as business partners and customers. Consequently, organizations have become increasingly dependent upon document management systems to handle information access and control within the LAN/WAN arena and across the Internet.

If your business is like most, 90% of your critical information is in a variety of electronic forms, spreadsheets, CAD drawings, images, graphics, photos, charts, electronic messages, presentations, electronic forms, and word processing files. Instead of spending countless hours searching through network volumes, directories, and sub-directories for this critical information, smart businesses use electronic document management systems.

The ability to manage and control information among collaborative workgroups, throughout iterative workflows, and across global networks is crucial in gaining an advantage in today's competitive business climate.

Document Management - The Competitive Advantage

Document management is the business-critical application for harnessing an organization's most important asset - its information.

Reprinted with permission from PC DOCS.

For a document management system to provide that competitive edge, it must:

- Protect and leverage your organization's corporate knowledge base
- Preserve existing hardware, software, and network investments
- Easily manage volumes of information on a global basis
- Provide quick and easy access to files and documents by words and phrases, or by attributes like author, project, customer names and account number
- Organize information effectively
- Control access to secure information
- Track multiple revisions of documents and ensure that users have the correct version
- Track all activity on a document for management reporting, cost recovery and allocation purposes

How then do we get this competitive advantage? By selecting the right document management application.

Constructing Your Corporate Memory

DOCS Open is a client-server document management system that offers a secure infrastructure to store, locate and manage your corporate information.

As organizations adopt document management, they need to maintain the freedom to choose the best solution for their enterprise, while maximizing existing hardware and software investments and accommodating future requirements. PC DOCS is committed to an *open* architecture that allows organizations to obtain these benefits.

- <u>Openness</u> - DOCS Open works in virtually any computing environment to manage and control network-based information across a variety of platforms, networks and geographical locations.
- <u>Customizability</u> - Organizations determine how they want to organize their documents, search for information, and present their user interface. DOCS Open's versatility allows it to be tailored to both structured and ad hoc business processes.
- <u>Instant information access</u> - With dramatic speed, DOCS Open searches for information across multiple servers and remote network sites, regardless of the application or database. Users don't need to know where the information exists and don't

need to understand WAN technology.

- <u>Enhanced workgroup collaboration</u> - Version control, the ability to connect mobile users, and document interchange with groupware applications make DOCS Open the most flexible and effective collaborative editing solution for workgroups.
- <u>Security</u> - PC DOCS pioneered network-integrated security. You can secure documents by individual, group, or custom defined attributes to seven access control levels.
- <u>Scalability</u> - Every organization is unique in size and has dynamic needs and requirements. Built for large enterprises, DOCS Open also fits easily into small organizations and workgroups.

DOCS Open provides an electronic library for all files in an enterprise network environment. Through the DOCS Open library you can get rapid access to any document-based information in your organization. These documents comprise the organizations institutional knowledge or corporate memory.

Unlocking Your Corporate Memory

With DOCS Open every document or file has an associated profile stored in a standard SQL database. The profile contains attribute information such as author, document type, date created, as well as other attributes including those defined by the user. This profile information provides the metadata that can then be used to search for documents anywhere in a network environment.

The metadata also provides other information about your documents that is just as valuable as the documents themselves. Just like a card in a library card catalogue can give you important information about a book you may want to checkout, DOCS Open can provide this kind of information electronically including a document abstract or even a preview of the document itself. The metadata essentially unlocks the corporate memory for an entire organization.

To unlock the corporate memory and leverage it within the organization, a document management system must provide some basic functions. DOCS Open provides functions which include:

- Advanced Search & Retrieval
- Version Control
- Automated Check-in/Check-out
- History Log/Audit Trail
- Project Folders
- Complex documents

- Application Integration
- Storage Management
- Customization

Staying true to the product name, DOCS Open provides all these capabilities and more in a truly **open**, **scaleable** and **secure** distributed client/server environment. DOCS Open works with multiple networks including Netware, NT, Banyan and Unix for storing documents and with multiple SQL databases including Microsoft SQL Server, Oracle and Sybase for metadata storage. Security is maintained throughout the entire network and database environment.

Being open means network independence, database independence and protocol independence. This independence is critical for being able to deploy a document management system throughout the global enterprise. This openness is also essential for document management to take hold and provide a real return on your technology investment.

One of the unique aspects of the DOCS Open architecture is its ability to interoperate in multi-network and database environments. DOCS Open can find and management document- based information even in an environment using different networks and databases across a LAN/WAN. DOCS Open can essentially create a homogenous view of a heterogeneous network environment. This allows a user to not have to know anything about the underlying network information infrastructure. They can simply just look for information using natural language queries to find what they are looking for in an instant. They can even search for information via the Internet or on a corporate Intranet. So it does not matter whether you are using Windows NT workstation, Macintosh or an Internet browser you always have access to the corporate memory.

The Keys

In order take advantage of an organizations corporate memory, we must be able to unlock it. The keys to unlock this valuable resource reside in the features and functions of a document management system. Each of these critical keys is outlined here.

Advanced Search & Retrieval: The heart of a document management system is its ability to provide rapid access to document-based information. Of course if searching for information was all you needed then any document manager would do. However, search time is not a luxury many of us can afford.

DOCS Open keeps track of all the documents you have been working on and can retrieve any one or more instantly. Also, DOCS

Open allows you to setup search agents which can dynamically search the entire enterprise for types of documents relevant to you. This search agents not only search the metadata, but also the document contents themselves for specific words and/or phrases.

Version Control: Documents are often a collaborative effort involving several individuals or teams. As these documents are created and routed through their lifecycle they can go through any number of reviews or edit revisions. To manage this process DOCS Open provides built-in version control. This allows you manage all the various changes to any document and be able to compare and consolidate them.

Automated Check-in/Check-out: Society has continued to become more and more mobile. Technology has to mirror this trend in order to be truly useful. You need to be able to take your documents on the road and create new documents when you are in a hotel or on a plane and have them managed the same way as when you are connected to the network. With DOCS Open you have the ability to do just that. You can checkout your documents to your laptop and have complete search & retrieval and revision control while you are out of the office. When you return to the office the DOCS Open replication/synchronization facility re-synchronizes all the document changes to the enterprise network libraries. Dial-in capabilities are also fully supported.

History Log/Audit Trail: DOCS Open has intelligence about all your documents. This intelligence is kept as a part of the metadata indicating everything that happened to all your documents including when and who edited, accessed, viewed or printed them, etc. This information is also available for reporting to analyze the time spent on specific projects.

Project Folders: For further enhanced document creation and collaboration, DOCS Open provides electronic profile folders for grouping documents. These folders can be shared with specific groups and users on the network. Folders can also be nested to give you a hierarchical view of your projects, documents and sub-projects.

Complex documents: While most of the corporate memory is held in word processing files and spreadsheets, there is an increasing amount of valuable information in many other kinds of documents. These types of complex documents include image files, presentations, CAD files, video and many other types of graphics files. DOCS Open is capable of handling the full range of document formats and managing the relationships and links between them.

Application Integration: DOCS Open works right out of the box with all the standard office application suites from Microsoft, Lotus,

Corel and others. DOCS Open also provides powerful tools for custom application integration.

Whenever a user does a file save or a file open DOCS Open is their to capture the information into the corporate memory. To the user DOCS Open becomes a natural extension of how they normally work within all their authoring tools.

<u>Storage Management:</u> As a part of the management of a document's lifecycle, DOCS Open provides the ability to automatically migrate in-active documents to other media including tape and optical subsystems. Unlike traditional Hierarchical Storage Management systems, DOCS Open has knowledge about the documents to know when to migrate them off of magnetic media.

<u>Customization:</u> DOCS Open provides a rich central administration and customization environment. With the DOCS Open tools you can quickly and easily make changes to your save and search profiles without any custom programming. DOCS Open even provides a front-end to your SQL database for creating table and columns on the fly. These capabilities allow you completely customize DOCS Open to your specific environment. These changes can then easily to replicated throughout the enterprise.

DOCS Open also provides a platform for rapid application development. With the DOCS Open object-oriented toolset you can take advantage of all of the document management capabilities in your custom applications. These can be written using C, C++ or any 4GL and can take advantage of our OLE automation support. Their are hundreds of these third-party applications on the market today.

DOCS OPEN

Background

With the release of DOCS Open 2.5, the Enterprise Edition, PC DOCS firmly positioned its DOCS Open product family as the leading source for enterprise-wide document management. DOCS Open 2.5 was built upon an open, distributed client/server architecture which was scalable for enterprise network environments and well-equipped to run in heterogeneous environments.

With DOCS Open 3.0, PC DOCS introduces an extended enterprise architecture which builds upon the foundation established with 2.5 and recognizes the new ways in which our customers are doing business. Specifically, we are focusing on the Internet as a vehicle to reach vast audiences and connect business partners and customers. We have enhanced our mobile offering already the most advanced in the industry and expanded it to include teams of mobile workers. Finally, we have integrated DOCS Open with popular collaboration and communications systems, including Microsoft Exchange and Lotus Notes. This multi-tiered approach will be flexible enough to allow customers to deploy DOCS Open in whatever way is most appropriate to their business needs.

The purpose of this document is to provide a synopsis of the components which are presented in Figure #1 and are the basis of the Release 3.0 architecture.

Figure 1

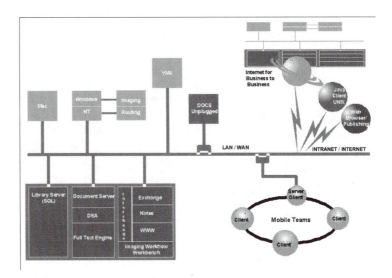

Client/Server Overview

Figure 2

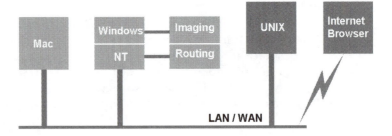

Client Support

DOCS Open has always supported multi-platform environments and this will continue to be the case throughout future releases of the

DOCS Open Release 3.0 (see Figure #2). Clients currently supported include:

- Microsoft Windows 95, Windows NT, Windows 3.X, Windows for Workgroups
- Macintosh System 7 and MacOS
- Support for desktop imaging and document routing

The release 3.0 family will add to that Internet browser support, including Netscape Navigator, Microsoft Explorer and other HTML browsers. PC DOCS will also be adding Unix support in the DOCS Open release 3 family.

Server Based Document Services

The addition of sophisticated server-based processes forms the nucleus of the extensions PC DOCS will be making to the DOCS Open architecture. These new capabilities will be built upon the existing server configuration that has been an integral part of the product since its inception. The net result of these efforts is a modular architecture that offers PC DOCS customers a deployment model for document management that is adaptable to a full range of business requirements.

Library Server and Document Servers

Figure 3

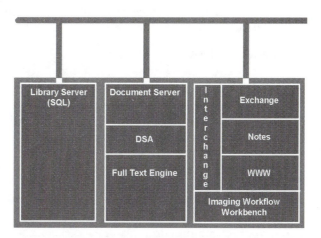

The current DOCS Open 2.5 library - which includes a library server, a document server, and a full-text index server - has been at the heart of the product and its basic configuration will not change. A library server (SQL) consists of a RDBMS running on a server and contains all the profile information or metadata regarding documents in the DOCS Open environment. A document server is a file server which holds the electronic files stored in DOCS Open. Finally, a full-text index server is used for rapid content searches across the enterprise and is typically stored on a file server.

As figure 3 illustrates, new to DOCS Open Release 3.0 are the addition of DSA-security and Verity full-text retrieval capabilities. These processes will be joining our Interchange product family and the Open Imaging/Workflow API.

Document Sentry Agent

The document sentry agent (DSA) is a 32-bit NT-based server process which creates a firewall between users and documents. Residing on the document server, the DSA acts as a sentry in that it grants user access to documents one session at a time. At the completion of a session, all activity performed on the document is recorded in an audit trail owned by the DSA. Because this audit trail is located behind the firewall, it cannot be accessed or changed in any way.

The DSA was designed to meet the needs of users with rigorous security requirements. These include customers in highly regulated environments, such as government agencies or manufacturing sites.

The DSA is a key component of the DOCS Open Release 3.0 security model. Specifically, it is a configurable module which users can apply to those libraries in their organization which contain documents that require DSA-level security. Because we expect many users to only use the DSA in certain parts of their organization, the DSA will be offered as an optional module.

Full-Text Retrieval

Advanced searching capabilities will be a key addition to the DOCS Open Release 3.0 product family. In Release 3.0, we will be using the highly-regarded Verity search engine which can produce the following elements: relevancy ranking, proximity, phrase, sounds like, and fuzzy logic searching capabilities.

In addition to these capabilities, DOCS Open Release 3.0 will also support multiple index servers which scale easily and can accommodate any enterprise's indexing requirements. Finally, PC DOCS recognizes that some of its customers will want to use other vendor's full-text engines and we will support these products via an open API for full text engines, and in some cases vendor specific integration, in the DOCS Open 3.0 product family.

Electronic Publishing

Publishing large volumes of documentation for a wide audience is a time consuming, expensive and labor intensive task for any corporation. While electronic document management and workflow tools can help the workgroup efficiently build documentation, corporations are still inclined to publish paper based information to their readers, thus duplicating the documentation already available electronically. To facilitate electronic publishing within a corporation and beyond to its customers and business partners, PC DOCS has developed the DOCS Interchange product family.

PC DOCS introduced the Interchange product family to enable corporations to publish document-based information electronically, using electronic media such as groupware products and public networks, while still maintaining control and management of the document life cycle within DOCS Open. The Interchange product line adds functionality both at the DOCS server, and at the client of the medium to which documents are being published. The DOCS Open Interchange product family includes: DOCS Interchange for Lotus Notes, DOCS Interchange for Microsoft Exchange and DOCS Interchange for the World Wide Web. In each case, DOCS Open users can publish document content and profiles stored in a DOCS Open Library to: a designated database in Lotus Notes, specified public folders in Microsoft Exchange, or a designated area of a Web server.

DOCS Interchange provides a mechanism for widespread publication of documents via the very specific distribution features of Lotus Notes, Microsoft Exchange and the World Wide Web. The DOCS Interchange product line enables document management capabilities to extend well beyond the bounds of the enterprise.

Imaging and Workflow

Figure 4

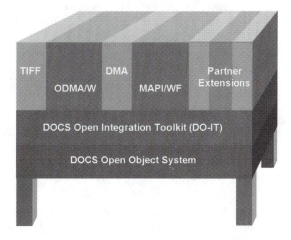

Customers have consistently told us they want the freedom to choose the image and workflow products of their choice to run with

DOCS Open. PC DOCS is committed to integrating best-of-breed imaging and workflow systems with DOCS Open and will be doing so through its Image and Workflow Workbench (I/W Workbench) (see Figure #4). This strategy will ensure that these companion products work together and are the most integrated products in the industry. Today, PC DOCS works with over a dozen partners including Wang Laboratories, Optika Imaging, Action Technologies, Kofax Imaging Systems, Delrina, and Reach Software.

The I/W Workbench extends the DOCS Open architecture to support integration of multiple imaging and workflow vendors. This will take the form of an open API for these two technologies as well as for OLE 2.0 automation objects. This technology approach supports key industry standards, including ODMA and the MAPI Workflow Framework. ODMA is adding workflow extensions supplied by the Workflow Management Coalition while the MAPI Workflow Framework is Microsoft's standard for managing workflow events across different workflow systems. Additionally, PC DOCS is also committed to using the emerging TIFF standards for image viewing as a foundation for its image integration. Where specific capabilities are not addressed by industry standards, PC DOCS and its I/W Workbench partners may develop product and vendor specific integration.

Internet Support

Document management systems have inherently relied upon the underlying network. With the explosion of the Internet as a communications vehicle, an infrastructure is now in place for sharing business-critical information. However, key elements of document management, particularly security are not native to the Internet.

PC DOCS Internet strategy is a multi-product approach that addresses the varying ways corporations use the Internet. With PC DOCS Internet products, businesses can now manage and publish documents within, between and beyond their enterprise.

Internet Strategy

As Figure #5 illustrates, PC DOCS is now building products to take advantage of this infrastructure as document management capabilities move beyond the enterprise. Four business areas form the PC DOCS Internet strategy. These include providing access to a DOCS repository from any Web browser, publishing DOCS Open documents to a Web server, and utilizing encryption technology for business to business document management. Additionally, PC DOCS will implement an interactive, Web based client (using Java, ActiveX) for modular, multi-tiered portable document management.

Figure 5

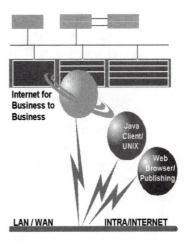

The architecture of this product galaxy is flexible enough to enable corporations to deploy DOCS Open together with the Internet to best meet an organization's unique business requirements beyond the enterprise bounds.

Mobile Support in DOCS Open

Figure 6

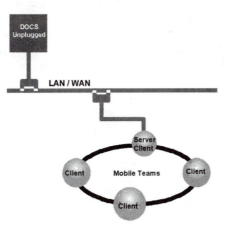

DOCS Unplugged

DOCS Unplugged in DOCS Open Release 3.0 is an extended version of DOCS Mobile 2.5. Besides providing complete document management functionality for mobile workers, DOCS Unplugged will also extend this functionality to desktop users if their network is down or not accessible. As Figure 6 demonstrates, users can now literally "unplug" from the network and continue working without any interruption to the delivery of their document management system. With DOCS Unplugged, seamless access to DOCS Open documents is ensured both on the road and at the desktop.

Mobile Teams

As Figure 6 illustrates, Mobile Teams extends full document management functionality to mobile workgroups who need access to their enterprise's document libraries while working away from the office. In a Mobile Teams configuration, one member of the workgroup is designated as the Mobile Team's client/server and all other members are clients. This server provides library access to the enterprise libraries, thus enabling documents to be accessed as needed and re-synchronized automatically. Mobile Teams is the ideal solution for traveling workgroups whose need for document management does not diminish - and is even likely to intensify - when they are out of the office.

Conclusion

Organizations are rapidly adopting new ways of conducting business. A document management system can assist with conducting the new while *remembering* the old. Leveraging a corporation's memory can really pay dividends when the pace of change is accelerating. The enterprise architecture in DOCS Open recognizes that these changes will have important implications for document management and provides the foundation needed to deploy the configuration most appropriate to each organizations unique needs. DOCS Open supports the already critical role of document management within the enterprise and *beyond*.

17

EDMS Vendor Listing

The following is list of companies that make document repository products. Only the repository vendors are listed as it is the repositories themselves that are heart and sole of any EDMS. This list includes the name, address, phone number and Website address for each company.

As with any technology that is growing as rapidly as EDMS, keeping up is difficult. So to increase the accuracy and usability of this section, we offer a Website at **http://www.goucher.edu/~docman**. This site provides a current and growing list of repository vendors.

The Website has a broader focus covering all the technologies needed for an EDMS, including searching/indexing, workflow, conversion, creation, and viewing/distribution. The site also includes a variety of other document management related information, such as other Websites, conferences, seminars, trade journals and professional associations.

Featured Vendors:

Documentum, Inc.
5671 Gibraltar Drive
Pleasanton, CA 94588
(510) 463-6800
fax (510) 463-6850
http://www.documentum.com

Interleaf, Inc.
62 Forth Ave
Waltham, MA 02154
(617) 290-0710
fax (617) 290-4943
http: //www.ileaf.com

OPENTEXT Corporation
180 Columbus Street, West
Toronto, Ontario N2L 3L3, Canada
(519) 888-7111
fax (519) 888-0677
http://www.opentext.com

PC DOCS, Inc.
25 Burlington Mall Road
Burlington, MA 01803
(800) 933-DOCS
fax (617) 272-3693
http://www.pcdocs.com

EDMS Vendors (Alphabetical):

CabiNet Systems Inc.
900 Corporate Drive
Mahwah, NJ 07430
(201) 512-1040
fax: (201) 512-1650
http://www.cabinet-sys.com

Documentum, Inc
5671 Gibraltar Drive
Pleasanton, CA 94588
(510) 463-6800
fax (510) 463-6850
http://www.documentum.com

Information Dimensions, Inc.
5080 Tuttle Crossing Boulevard
Dublin, OH 43017-3569
(800)-DATA-MGT
fax 614-761-7290
http://www.idi.oclc.org

Intergraph Corporation
One Madison Industrial Park
Huntsville, AL 35894
(205) 730-3896
fax (205) 730-3301
http://www.ingr.com

Interleaf, Inc.
62 Forth Ave
Waltham, MA 02154
(617) 290-0710
fax (617) 290-4943
http: //www.ileaf.com

NOVASOFT Systems, Inc.
8 New England Executive Park
Burlington, Massachusetts 01803
(617) 221-0300
Fax: (617) 221-0465
http://www.novasoft.com

Novell Inc.
1555 N.Technology Way
Orem UT 84057-2399
(801) 222-6000
fax (800) 453-1267
http://www.novell.com

PC DOCS, Inc.
25 Burlington Mall Road
Burlington, MA 01803
(800) 933-DOCS
fax (617) 272-3693
http://www.pcdocs.com

Salix Systems
9345 Byron Street
Schiller Park, Illinois 60176
(847)-678-5600
fax (847) 678-7676
http://www.salix.com

Uniplex Software, Inc.
155 Bovet Road
San Mateo, CA 94402
(415) 577-8789
fax (415) 577-9373
http://www.uniplex.com

Xsoft, a division of Xerox
3400 Hillview Avenue
Palo Alto, CA 94304
(415) 424-0111
http://www.xsoft.com

Open Text Corporation
180 Columbus Street, West
Toronto, Ontario N2L 3L3, Canada
(519) 888-7111
fax (519) 888-0677
http://www.opentext.com

Quality Information Systems, Inc.
10680 West Pico Blvd, Suite 260
Los Angelos, CA 90064
(800) 95DocMgmt
fax (310) 287-1622

Saros Corporation
10900 NE 8th Street
700 Plaza Center
Bellvue, WA 98004
(206) 646-1066
fax (206) 646-0879
http://www.saros.com

World Software Corporation
124 Prospect ST.
Ridgewood NJ -7450
(800) 962-6360
fax (201) 444-9065
www.worldox.com

Xyvision, Inc.
101 Edgewater Drive
Wakefield, MA 01880
(617) 245-4100
fax (617) 246-5308
http://www.xyvision.com

Index

A

Abstract Data Typing 62
Access Control Lists 73
Adobe Acrobat 97, 144
Analysis 170, 179, 203
  alignment 208
  capacity sheet 214
  document profile 211
  environmental profile 213
  organizational profile 208
  process for 207
  user centered 19
  user profiles 209
Annotations
  for review and approval 144, 145
  private and public 162
Architecture 241
Archiving Documents 82

Attributes 60, 64, 167, 253
  custom 65
  multi-value 66
  revision specific 66
  standard 65
Audit History of Document Life Cycle 133

B

Bandwidth 61
Benefits of an EDMS 19
  access to documents 20
  control of documents 21
  distribution of documents 19
  maintenance of documents 20
  production engine 20
  reuse of information 21
  searching for information 20

Bookmarks 163
Business Critical Documents 137
Business Process Reengineering (BPR) 136,
    227

C

Capture—see Imaging
Change Control Plan 237
Check-In 64
Check-Out 69
Collaborative 131
Comments—see Annotations
Common Operating Environments 91
Comparison Matrix 222
Compound Documents 85
Configuration Management 83
Conversion 138
    accuracy 94
    document 92
    graphics 95
    value-adding 92
Coordinator, role of 42
Corporate Knowledge 1, 15
Creating Online Documents 116
    content 118
    design 115
    document sizing 117
    hyperlinks 117
    planning 115
    purpose of document 118
    reader 116
    structure 115
    visual conventions 117
    volume 118
Creation Process 115
Creator, role of 42
Customer Service 30
Customization 241
Customization vs. Configuration 229

D

Databases 37, 48
Delivery—see Distribution
Design 239, 241, 243
    authoring 244
    conversion 244
    custom applications 245
    distribution 245
    high level 242
    indexing 245
    low level 243
    repository 244
    searching 245
    security 245
    workflow 244
Detailed Design Specification 243
Development 239, 246
Distribution 147
    access architecture 157
    adding value 152
    basic architecture 155
    benefits of electronic 150
    costs of 151
    definition of 147
    faster 151
    lists of 148
    paper 148
    print on demand 149
    publishing architecture 156
    repository-viewing architecture 157
    shorter production life-cycles 151
    storage space 151
Document Management—see EDMS
Documents
    critical 39, 211
    definition of 4, 37
    keeping current 198
    lifecycle 45
    non-critical 211
    support 39
Documentum 263

E

EDMS
  definition of 1, 13
  need for 17
  new paradigm 5
Electronic Paper 155, 159
Electronic Performance Support Systems
      (EPSS) 3, 17
  characteristics of 3
  definition of 3
Email 131, 144
Expert Systems 205

F

Feedback Collecting 221, 227
Filenames 67, 237
  as object names 69
  assigned by the system 69
  schemes 67, 68
Filters 94, 244
Flowcharts 242
Focus Group 206
Formats 93
  ASCII 93
  CGM 93
  GIF 93
  HTML 93
  IGES 93
  JPEG 93
  MPEG 93
  PostScript 94
  SGML 93, 119
  TIFF 93
Functional Requirement Specification 184,
      214

G

Gap Analysis 228
Granularity 106, 108, 121
Graphical Workflow 141
Guidelines 247

H

High Level Design 242
History of Document Management 32
  controlling paper 34
  cycles in computing technology 33
  document control 34
  information systems 32
  INTRAnets 35
  networking 35
HTML 119, 161
Hyperlink 162
  as knowledge representation 165
  creating 165
  management of 165

I

Image Processing Software 100
Imaging 47, 92, 97, 100, 244
  capture 92, 98
  clean-up 98
  OCR 48, 98
  scanner 48, 98
Implementation 220, 249, 250
  developers 250
  end users 251
  installation 252
  IS organization 252
  loading documents 252
  planning for 250

prioritization plan 252
rollout 256
Indexing 106
  full-text indexing 96
  inversion of terms 107
  speed 107
  stemming 106
  stopword 106
  workflow 97
Information
  assets 15
  definition 4
  sharing 14
Infrastructure 178, 179, 231, 248
  architecture design 233
  installation 234
  methodology 233
  migration plan 238
  network topology 234
  server 234
  standards 235
  system specifications 234
Integrity of Documents 60
Intellectual Capital 15
Interleaf 96, 149, 165, 278
INTRAnet 23
  conversion for 24
  document management 24
  file grouping 25
  synchronization of files 24
ISO 9000 29

J

Job Aids 255
Job-Task Analysis 209

K

Knowledge 121, 173, 175
  contextual knowledge 122
  domain-specific 122
  structural knowledge 121
Knowledge Acquisition 204
  focus group for 206
  methods in 205
  observation 206
  process mapping in 206

L

Leveraging Information 196
Library Services 63
Lifecycle of Documents 43, 44
Loading Repositories
  attributes 253
  document sets 253
  training 253

M

Maintenance of an EDMS 154
Management of Change 237
Metadata—see Attributes
Methodology 169, 171
  analysis phase 184
  approach 176
  design phase 188
  develop phase 190
  document centered approach 172
  high level overview 178
  implement phase 191
  information sharing 177
  leveraging information 177
  overview 181

pilot 180
prototyping phase 185
user-centered 174

N

Native Format 155
Networking 50
Notes—see Annotations
Notification 138, 166

O

Object Linking and Embedding (OLE) 85
Object Oriented 62
  benefits of object model 63
  inheritance 62
Observation in Knowledge Acquisition 206
Online Documents 155, 160
  content for 153
  custom views 153
  navigation through 153
  organization of 152
  presentation of 153
Online Viewing Features
  annotations 162
  bookmarks 163
  hyperlinking 162
  integration capabilities 163
  outlining/tables of contents 163
  printing 163
  searching 162
  zooming 162
Open Document Management API
  (ODMA) 57, 58
Open Systems 6
Open Text 109, 294
Optical Character Recognition 100
  feature recognition 101

pattern matching 101
validation and verification 102

P

Paper, management of 126
  automated distribution 149
  change pages 149
  controlling 126
  date fields 127
  distribution 148
  print on demand 149
  printing 126, 163
  production of 129
  reduction of 198
  version numbers 127
  watermarks 127
PC DOCS 308
PDF—see Adobe Acrobat
People
  creators 41
People as 40
  consumers 42
  coordinators 42
  producers 42
Performance of System 61
Pharmaceutical 28, 195
Pilot System 180
Planning 179, 194
  choosing an organization 198
  consumption mode 197
  neutral model 197
  project plan 194
  project team 199
  publishing model 196
  standard models 195
Print on Demand 149
Printing—see Paper
Problem Solving 25
Process Mapping 206, 242
Process Safety Management 29

Processing Plant 197
Product Data Management (PDM) 40, 84
Productivity 2
Project Team 199
Prototyping 170, 217
  building 223
  components of 225
  functions of 217
  gap analysis, relation to 228
  process for 218
  scope of 219
  storyboarding, relation to 221
  tool selection 222
  user reviews 226
Publishing 49
PULL Model for Distribution 46
PUSH Model for Distribution 46

Q

Quality Records 133

R

Rapid Application Development (RAD)
  240
Regulatory Compliance 29
Relational Databases (RDBMS) 199
Relationships 84
Replication 62
Repository
  "fat" clients 56
  "thin" clients 56
  architecture 55
  client application 56
  custom interface, building 58
  database component 60
  definition of 55

  file system component 60
  scalability 61
  server application 59
  synchronizing components 61
Resolution of Monitors 148
Retrieval or Searching 111
  boolean 112
  fuzzy word 113
  precision 111
  proximity 112
  ranking algorithms 112
  recall 111
  semantic 112
  synonyms 112
Re-using Existing Materials 198
Risks in EDMS 21
  distribution 21
  information overload 22
  training costs 22
  validity of information 22
Roles 244
Rollout 251, 256
Routes 244

S

Safety
  Regulatory Compliance 208
Scanner 99
  color 99
  flat bed 99
  gray-scale 99
  recognition 99
  resolution 99
  roll feed 99
  sheet-fed 99
Scanning—see Imaging
Searching 105, 110
  interface for 111
  ranking results 112
  retrieval effectiveness 112

types of retrieval 113
Security 71
    access control 72
    controlled access 71
    file system 71
    operating system 71
SGML 119
    definition 120
    DTD 120
    granularity 121
Standards 88, 248
    DMA 88, 223
    ODMA 88, 223
    WFMC 223
Storage Location for Documents 64
Storyboarding 221
Stovepipes 14, 177
Style Guide 236
Styles 123
    configuration files 96
    definition of 123
    HTML 96
    mapping 95
    purpose of 123
    structural knowledge 124
    table of contents 124
Support 257
    channels for 258
    help desk 257
    telephone 257

T

Tables of Contents 163
Team, EDMS Development
    analyst 203
    developer 201
    project manager 200
Templates 125, 236, 244
    boiler plate 125
    definition of 125

headers and footers 125
    styles 125
Testing 246
Time Spent Searching 14
Tool Selection 222
Training 224, 235, 247, 253
    adult learner 255
    analysis for 253
    consumers 256
    coordinators 256
    creators 256
    materials 247
    task based 254
Triggers 142

U

User Centered 19
User Interface 220, 243
    design 243
User Review 224, 226
Users and Groups 74
    Email 76
    maintenance 75
    networking 76

V

Value Add 129, 152
Vaults 64
Vendors 261
    Documentum 263
    Interleaf 278
    listing of 321
    Open Text 294
    PC DOCS 308
Versioning, for Documents
    automatic incrementing 77
    branching 77

control 76
creating a new one 79
diagram 78
drafts 81
linear 77
locking a document 80
major revision 81
minor revisions 81
numbering 76
reconciling different 78
schemes 77
subversions 81
work in progress (WIP) 81
Viewing Technologies 23
Virtual Document 84, 86

sequential 140
structured processes 136
time-driven 141
triggering 136
user interactions 143
versioning 135
Writer Guide 236

W

Waterfall Methodology 169, 181
Web Crawler 109
Webmasters 22, 156, 158
Windows NT 61
Word, Microsoft 165
Workflow 131
    actions 138
    add-on component 134
    ad-hoc 137
    branching 140
    business process reengineering (BPR)
        136
    definition of 131
    Email with 144
    graphical 141
    in-box 143
    integration with repository 133
    ISO 9000 132
    issues in implementation 139
    parallel type 140
    people 138
    relationships 136
    routes, rules, roles 132